GARDENING
THROUGH THE YEAR

GARDENING
THROUGH THE YEAR

A MONTHLY GUIDE TO LOOKING AFTER YOUR GARDEN

Hazel Evans

Macdonald Orbis

Original garden designs and design features created by
Susanna Longley, B.SC. (HORT.)

Original garden designs illustrated by Ross Wardle/Tudor
Arts Studio

Illustrations by Charles Raymond/Artist Partners, Errol
Watson/Garden Studios and Jenny Mitchell/Artist Partners

Copy-editing and additional text by Susan Conder

Text and illustrations authenticated by Kenneth A. Beckett,
gardening writer and consultant

Jacket photographs by Jerry Harper

A *Macdonald Orbis* BOOK

© Orbis Book Publishing Corporation Limited 1985

First published in Great Britain in 1985
by Orbis Book Publishing Corporation Limited

A member of BPCC plc

This edition published in 1987
by Macdonald & Co (Publishers) Ltd
London & Sydney

A member of BPCC plc

British Library Cataloguing in Publication Data

Evans, Hazel   1928
    Gardening through the year
    1. Gardening
    I. Title
    635   SB450.97

    ISBN 0-356-14408-9

Printed and bound in Great Britain by Purnell Book Production Ltd,
Paulton, Bristol

Macdonald & Co (Publishers) Ltd
Greater London House
Hampstead Road
London NW1 7QX

INTRODUCTION

First, a word about this book. It is adaptable to all parts of the United States and adjoining Canada, but in using it you must bear in mind your own specific climate.
For instance, the winter chapters, in particular, apply mostly to the warm areas. Even though in the northern US and southern Canada one may find winter crocus and other early bulbs in bloom in January in warm, sunny pockets, spring really comes with the blooming of the apple trees—in the southwest US, with the blooming of the mesquite, and so on.
North of the latitude of New York City we can rarely dig before April and most outdoor sowing is done in May.
In any case, the gardener's year is very special. Working with plants means that you can't fail to be aware of the passing seasons in all their richness and variety—the first tiny snowdrops, cheerful daffodils heralding spring, the perfume of summer roses, and the blazing colors of the foliage in the fall.
If gardening is to be a pleasure and not a chore, however, careful planning is necessary. In this book, we've set out to show you ways of making gardening simpler and more enjoyable.
Gardening Through the Year is divided into twelve chapters – one for every month – which outline the major tasks to be carried out at that particular time of year. Each chapter has sections on flowers, lawns, roses, fruit and vegetables (including herbs), describing in detail the basic gardening techniques. Attractive step-by-step drawings illustrate the correct procedures and color photographs show you just what's possible with a little forethought and imagination.

Hazel Evans

CONTENTS

CONTENTS

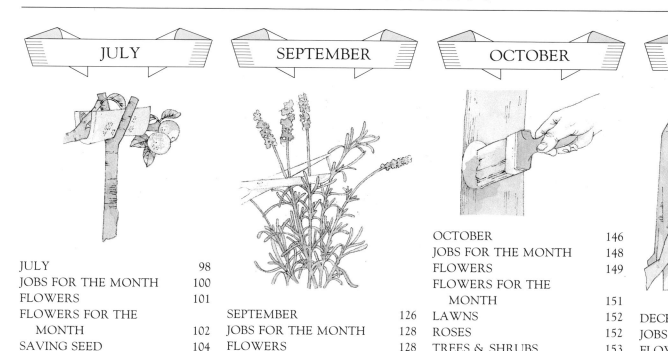
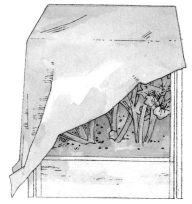

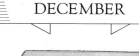

January

January marks the beginning
of a new year, full of promise in the garden. Despite
the low temperatures and short daylight hours, there
is much to do. Where the ground is unfrozen, you
can still plant roses and hardy bare-root deciduous
shrubs and trees. This is the time of year when a
heated greenhouse has great appeal,
especially when the weather is too bad to work
outside. The warmth of a heated frame or
greenhouse or a sunny window indoors enables you
to sow those half-hardy annuals which need a long
growing season. Roots of favorite herbs, lifted and
brought indoors, will provide fresh shoots and
leaves for winter flavor, and the long evenings will
give you plenty of time to browse through the new
seed catalogs.

*Snowfalls in the colder parts of the US and
Canada cloak trees and shrubs with a layer of
sparkling white and turn the garden into a
wintery wonderland*

General
Dig over beds in mild areas
Firm plants after frost heaving
Remove any ice from pools
Order seeds

Flowers
Tidy up herbaceous borders
Plant new lily bulbs where possible
Start off some half-hardy annual
seed indoors

Roses
Plant or heel in new arrivals in
warm regions; bank with soil in
cold ones

Trees and shrubs
Continue to protect plants from
frost and drying winds
Plant trees and shrubs on warm,
dry days where possible

Lawns
Get mower serviced, sharpened
and repaired
Spike compacted lawns in mild
climates

Fruit
Dormant spray tree and bush fruit
Prune fall-fruiting raspberries

Vegetables
Make outdoor sowings of broad
beans and peas in mild areas
Start off some vegetables indoors
Chit potatoes
Force rhubarb, chicory and herbs

For beds that are to be planted in spring, early digging is a good idea, the earlier it is possible the better. This is because the frost acts to break down the soil, and the longer the rough clods of soil are exposed to frost, the easier it will be to get a fine tilth in spring. While you are digging, work in plenty of well-rotted manure or compost to improve texture and richness. Where soils are sticky or frozen you must wait.

If you have planted any trees or shrubs during the winter months, check that they haven't been lifted by frost. Once lifted, they rock in the wind and their roots are slower to get established. Re-firm the plants by pressing down on ·the surrounding soil with your feet.

If the surface of your ornamental pool has frozen solid, and particularly if it contains fish, break the ice with care. If it is very thick, use a little boiling water rather than a hammer, to avoid shock waves which can kill the creatures beneath.

If you have not already done so, order all seeds for the coming season. Failure to do this now may mean they arrive too late for their proper sowing date.

FLOWERS

Tidy up the dead foliage of herbaceous perennials. Cut away any brown or decayed vegetation, as it is a perfect haven for slugs.

If you have sent away for special lilies and they arrive this month, plant them wherever possible. If the bulbs have shrivelled in transit, pack them in damp peat and leave them until they have swelled up. Where planting is not possible, store in a cool place.

STARTING OFF SEEDS INDOORS

Growing your own plants from seed is not only cheap, but very satisfying, and it is often the only way you can grow some of the lesser-known varieties.

Starting off seeds indoors or in a heated greenhouse means that you can cheat the seasons. With the extra warmth you give them, the young plants will be well away by the time they are transplanted outdoors into beds, baskets or window boxes. Just make sure that you have space to keep the growing plants indoors until May and don't be tempted to sow more than you can accommodate.

Only those half-hardy annuals which need a long development period should be sown indoors now: antirrhinums, fibrous-rooted begonias (*B. semperflorens*), carnations, gloxinias, lobelias and sweet peas (if this was not done in the fall). Don't be tempted to sow faster-growing half-hardy annuals now, as they always get too big and sit starving in their boxes long before the weather is warm enough to plant them out. A minimum temperature around 59°F (15°C) is necessary for good germination. If it is not possible to maintain this temperature, sowing should be delayed until next month when the sun's heat will supplement the artificial source.

Though traditionally propagated from cuttings, pelargoniums are great fun to grow from seed sown now at 65–70°F (18–21°C). They grow quickly and during the summer will flower profusely on short, sturdy stems, and at the end of the season you can discard them like half-hardy annuals, without having to go to the trouble of overwintering them.

TYPES OF PROPAGATOR

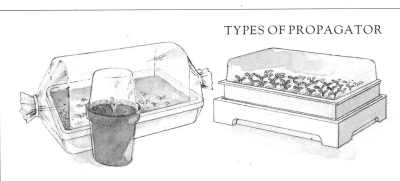

A plastic bag over wire hoops encloses a seed tray; a clear plastic top protects seeds in a pot

A polystyrene honeycomb with clear plastic lid is watered from the reservoir base by a capillary mat

An electrically heated propagator, fitted with separate seed trays, allows control of heat and humidity

SOWING SEEDS INDOORS

1 *Fill the seed tray with a soil mix to about two-thirds of its depth and level it with a block of wood*

2 *Pour the seeds into the palm of one hand and tap gently with the fingers to distribute them evenly*

3 *Sieve a fine, even layer of the mix over the seeds, keeping the sieve low above the tray*

4 *Place a sheet of glass over the tray and keep it covered with paper until the seedlings show*

Equipment and techniques
Seeds need two things to get them started: moisture and warmth, preferably bottom heat of some kind. If you don't have a heated propagator, try using a radiator top with a thick layer of newspaper as insulation to protect the seedlings.

The most dangerous time in a seedling's life is when it is transplanted, but you can minimize the danger by using one of several new products available. Far better than the traditional seed tray is the compartmented plastic tray. A series of individual soil blocks are formed when the soil mix is packed into the compartments. A seed is sown in each one, or several in the case of smaller seeds, and the soil mix watered. As the tiny plants grow, pop out the soil mix cubes, plant the seedlings without disturbing their roots, and re-use the tray for another crop.

There are more sophisticated trays available, complete with water reservoirs, watering mats and clear plastic lids.

Flowers for the month

In mild climates (as the Upper South) winter-flowering bulbs make a brave display if the weather is mild and sunny: *Crocus ancyrensis* (orange-yellow) and *C. imperati* (lilac-purple) can be relied upon, as can snowdrops (*Galanthus elwesii* and *G. nivalis*), winter aconites (*Eranthis hyemalis* and *E. × tubergenii*) and the lovely little rose-purple *Cyclamen coum*. Weather permitting, several shrubs will enliven the winter garden. Those with scented flowers are especially valuable: wintersweet (*Chimonanthus praecox*), winter honeysuckle (*Lonicera fragrantissima* and *L. × purpusii*), *Hamamelis mollis*, *Daphne mezereum*, *Viburnum farreri*, *V. × bodnantense*, *Mahonia japonica* and *M. × 'Charity'*. Showy but lacking scent are winter jasmine (*Jasminum nudiflorum*), laurustinus (*Viburnum tinus*) and *Garrya elliptica* with its long gray catkins and evergreen leaves. Few perennial plants bloom in January but those that do are well worth growing: hellebores (*Helleborus foetidus*, *H. lividus corsicus*) have lime-green flowers, *H. niger* (Christmas rose) has larger white ones. If the winter is a mild one, bergenias and winter heliotrope may even flower, as will the red lungwort (*Pulmonaria rubra*), common primrose and its color forms and hybrids, and winter-blooming garden pansies.

Indoors, many of the plants which arrived as Christmas presents will still be in flower. These include Christmas cactus, cyclamen, poinsettia and azalea. Primulas (*P. obconica*, *P. malacoides*), cinerarias and forced daffodils and hyacinths should also be in bloom.

1 *Helleborus lividus corsicus*

2 *Jasminum nudiflorum*

Another alternative is to use peat discs (Jiffies) which expand to form small, free-standing cylinders when they are soaked in water. You have to be very careful about watering them, though, as peat dries out more fully than soil-based mixtures, and a dried-out seedling is virtually a dead one.

If you are filling trays or plastic or clay pots, a loose, friable mixture is the standard choice, but there are now a number of all-purpose soil mixes available, which can be used for seeds and plants and can be bought in any good garden shop.

Very fine seed should simply be scattered over the surface of the soil mix, then dusted over with sieved soil mix or peat. Mixing the seed with fine sand before sowing is the traditional way of ensuring that it is evenly distributed over the surface.

Hard-coated seeds benefit from soaking first, to speed up germination. They can also have their tough outer coat scratched or chipped to let in the moisture; sweet peas are a prime example. One way of doing this is to line a jar with coarse sandpaper, rough-side inwards, add the seeds, tighten the lid and shake the jar.

Once you have sown the seeds, cover the trays or pots with a lid – glass covered with paper or clear plastic – to keep the soil mix moist and the air humid. When the seeds have germinated, remove the paper covering, if used, as the seedlings will need light as well as warmth and moisture. If the light is coming from one side only, such as a window, turn the trays or pots daily, or the seeds will grow at an angle towards the source of light. Poor light will cause pale, spindly growth.

ROSES

PLANTING A ROSE

Both container-grown and bare-rooted roses can be planted where the weather is mild. Don't do it yet if the ground is waterlogged or frozen, though, as roses detest waterlogged soil. Just damp the roots, wrapping bare-rooted roses in sacking, and keep them in a frost-free shed or garage until the weather improves or heel them in in a box of soil.

For planting, choose a spot with well drained soil, then dig in plenty of rotted garden compost or manure, and a small handful of bonemeal. Give the plants a good soaking, and cut off any damaged roots of bare-rooted specimens with pruners. The roots of containerized roses should be disturbed as little as possible.

Dig the hole at least twice as wide as the container or, if the rose is bare-rooted, wide enough for the roots to be spread out horizontally. Position the rose so that the join of the green stem and the rootstock is just beneath the soil, about 1 in (2.5cm) down; use the soil level mark on the stem as a guide.

Shovel some soil into the hole, then give the plant a gentle shake so the soil settles between the roots and no air pockets remain.

PLANTING A ROSE

1 *Dig a hole large enough to let the plant's roots spread. Remove the wrapping from the rootball*

2 *Settle the roots in the hole and use a cane to check that the base of the plant is at soil level*

3 *Drop planting mixture into the hole and use your hands to work it well into and around the roots*

4 *When the hole is filled, tread the soil around the plant to firm it and then top up the soil level*

Add more soil, firming as you go, checking that the join is still below surface level.

Finally, if it's a bush rose, prune the stems hard, back to three or four buds from the base. Make the cut just above an outward-pointing bud. Cut out any dead, weak or damaged wood at the same time.

TREES & SHRUBS

Continue to protect half-hardy evergreen shrubs and containerized plants in exposed positions from frost and drying winds (see November). Other shrubs, such as camellias and early-flowering rhododendrons, are fairly hardy, but their developing flowers are vulnerable to cold at this time of year. If the shrubs are not too big, surround them with sacking, or newspaper or straw held in place with wire mesh.

On dry, warm days trees and shrubs may often be planted.

LAWNS

January is a good time to take your mower in to be serviced and sharpened and repaired, if necessary, before the big spring rush begins. It should be in good working order before you start the new season's mowing.

Lawns on heavy or compacted soil often tend to get waterlogged at this time of year. When it is possible, spike it with a special hollow-tined fork, if you have one, or a garden fork, at 6–8 in (15–20cm) intervals. Sprinkle a little coarse sand on wet, muddy patches in the lawn's surface and keep it free of fallen leaves or plant debris.

FRUIT

If you haven't already done so, spray dormant tree and bush fruit to kill off any insects and their eggs that may have been overwintering in the bark. Use a proprietary oil wash, diluted according to the manufacturer's instructions. Exclude strawberries from your spraying schedule.

To prune fall-fruiting raspberries, cut back all the canes to just above ground level.

VEGETABLES

SOWING VEGETABLES OUTDOORS

If you did not make a fall sowing of broad beans and peas, and your garden is a sunny sheltered one in the Deep South, sow both now to get an early crop of vegetables (see March).

Space the beans 6in (15cm) apart in rows 2 in (5cm) deep. Make the rows 15 in (37cm) apart. Select any particularly hardy cultivar, good for early sowing. If space is limited, 'The Sutton' is a good dwarf sort.

Be prepared to give the young plants a bit of cloche protection if the weather turns cold.

Even though your garden is sheltered, when you sow peas use a round-seeded cultivar, such as 'Meteor', 'Little Marvel' or 'Feltham First'. Make a shallow trench, the width of a spade and about 1½in (4cm) deep, then put the peas, in two parallel rows, 2 in (5cm) apart, zig-zag fashion. Return the soil to the trench and firm gently. If you are sowing more than one row,

Forcing rhubarb roots under a clay pot (above) and chicons indoors under a black plastic pot (right)

space them at least 18 in (45cm) apart. With peas and broad beans, block-sowing in short, squared-up rows is a good idea.

SOWING INDOORS

In mild climates vegetables can be started off indoors this month: snap beans for forcing, early-maturing cauliflowers and onions. Lettuce sown now will provide a late spring crop.

CHITTING POTATOES

Place the potatoes in a box with the eyes pointing upwards

At planting time, pick those that have grown short, sturdy shoots

CHITTING POTATOES

Where winter is short get early potatoes under way, by 'chitting' or sprouting them in a cool, light place. They will then be well advanced when you plant them outdoors in spring. Choose potatoes the size of a hen's egg, though larger potatoes can be cut in half and both halves sprouted. Place the seed potatoes in the hollows of empty egg boxes, 'eye' upwards. And if you do divide large potatoes, make sure each piece has an 'eye', as the sprouts develop from the 'eyes'. If you have more potatoes than egg boxes, simply place the potatoes upright in a single layer in a shallow box, again in a cool (but frost-free), light place.

FORCING VEGETABLES

Continue to force rhubarb for winter eating. It needs a rich soil if it is to give you a regular crop. Cover the crowns with soil or leaves and a large upturned box or bucket in your hotbed. Indoors, chicory can be forced, too. Plant the roots vertically in moist peat or compost in boxes or pots. Cover the roots with 1 in (2.5cm) peat or compost and encase the pot in a black garbage bag to exclude all the light. You need a minimum temperature of 50°F (10°C) but in a month's time you will be rewarded with delicious fat and creamy white chicons.

HERBS

To enjoy out-of-season herbs in warmer areas, dig up a small piece of mint, thyme or marjoram root, bring it indoors and pot it up in a warm place. Fresh shoots will soon appear as the plant adjusts.

PLANNING A GARDEN

This is a good time of year to plan a new garden or take a fresh look at an existing one. Whichever the case, and whatever the size of the garden, take your time. It is far better, and you will be much happier with the results, if you first assess various factors before springing into action.

What are your garden's strong and weak points? With the trees leafless now, and most of the herbaceous plants out of sight, you can see the bare 'bones' of your garden, unsoftened by summer foliage.

The aspect of your garden—which way it faces in relation to the sun—is very important. Aspect determines what time of day your garden gets the sun, where the sun reaches, and for how long each day. If you have a choice of where to build a patio, site it where the afternoon sun reaches, all else being equal.

Though it would be nice if all gardens faced south or west, and made the most of the all-too-shy early sunshine, this isn't the case. Those with shady gardens needn't despair; with a little bit of thought, planning and careful plant selection (see Shade-tolerant plants, page 71) a shady garden can be every bit as lush as a sunny one and even more intriguing.

Closely related to aspect is exposure, another very important factor. Wherever the prevalent wind is a southwesterly one, it means that gardens facing southwest, though blessed with sun, have wind to contend with. But the most bitter, cutting winter wind tends to come from the north.

If your garden is a windy one, then you may need to think about windbreaks, in the form of fencing or wind-tolerant shrubs and trees. Remember, though, that what you gain in shelter you may lose in light, if your windbreak is a tall one.

Privacy is every bit as valuable as shelter, and you may want to put in screening from your neighbors, especially around a sitting-out area. You may also want to screen unsightly utility items.

Take a good look at the levels in your garden. A garden that slopes towards the house can be a problem in heavy rain. Frost flows like water, so the lowest bit of your garden, especially if it is surrounded by hedging or fencing, is liable to be a frost pocket, cold and uncomfortable for plants and people alike.

A little knowledge about your soil type goes a long way, too. It's well worth the trouble of buying a soil-testing kit from your local nursery and finding out which type of soil you have—sand, clay, chalk or loam, or a combination (see Glossary).

What sort of garden do you want?
What you want to use your garden for is every bit as important as the physical structure of the garden itself, when it comes to thinking about garden design.

For some people, the garden is a sitting-out place, and for others, something to be viewed from the house, rather than actively used. More often, though, gardens serve several purposes, and we hope that the variety of gardens we have included in this book will cover most needs.

Getting down to it
If you've just moved house, it is tempting to have a real bash at the garden, totally redesigning it in one fell swoop. Try to resist the impulse, and live with your garden for a year, or at least a growing season, just to get the feel of it.

You'll be surprised at the number of flowers that appear, as one month follows another. Where you actually end up wanting a sitting-out area may be completely different from where you first thought. A tree which seemed to have no purpose at all might, when in leaf, prove to be invaluable as a shield from the neighbors' gaze. And the route that you or the children naturally take from one bit of the garden to another, or from the back door to the vegetable plot, might not be the same right-angled path you originally had in mind.

By all means brighten up a new garden and clear it out; no garden has room for couch grass or bits of old bed springs. Use annuals to give you a fast and fabulous first-season display. Try at least a few of the less common sorts to add distinction to the display: spider flower (*Cleome*), African daisy (*Arctotis*), bartonia (*Mentzelia*), *Browallia*, *Leptosiphon* and *Rhodanthe* are all recommended.

If there are shrubs that you can't resist buying, keep them in large tubs for the first season. When you decide where they are to go, they will move happily to their permanent position.

Making a plan
Once you know roughly what you want to do, draw up your garden on graph paper, making a note of the scale at the bottom. Mark north on as well, to remind you which bits of the garden are shady.

Mark out the paths, beds and borders, and special areas for sitting out, play equipment and so on. Cut out circles to represent existing trees and shrubs, seen from above—judge the diameter by eye. Cut circles to represent the trees and shrubs you are planting; a good catalog will give you their eventual diameters. Remember, though, that the final size of a tree may take fifty years to reach, so count on infill planting in the meantime.

You may find it useful to plan an elevation of one or more sides, to give you an idea of relative heights: the principal plants, fences and, indeed, the house itself.

Once you are happy with the project on paper, try it out on site, using string or rope to mark out the beds and paths.

Try to decide first of all what type of garden you are aiming for – who will use it? what will it be used for? how much time will you want to spend on maintenance? Take a good look at the existing features and plants and decide which ones you want to retain or highlight and which ones you want to screen or remove altogether. Make a list of the new plants and features you're planning to introduce and work out their approximate dimensions and positions. It's a good idea at this stage to use a black and white photograph to help you visualize the projected changes. Make an overlay from tracing paper and roughly sketch out your ideas. This will make it much easier to draw up a detailed aerial plan on graph paper, complete with accurate measurements.

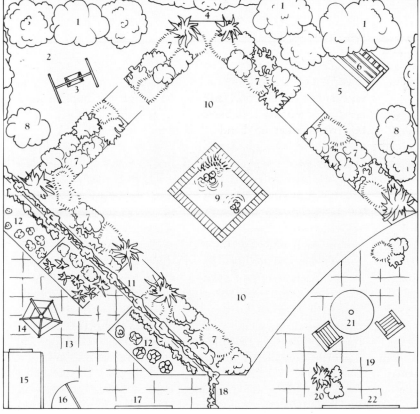

1 Existing trees and shrubs
2 Play area with rough grass
3 Swing
4 Access for lawnmower
5 Rough grass planted with bulbs
6 Bench
7 Flowers and small shrubs
8 Large shrubs
9 Ornamental pond
10 Lawn
11 Pergola covered with roses
12 Vegetables and herb plot
13 Paved utility area
14 Clothes line
15 Shed
16 Back door to kitchen
17 Kitchen window
18 Screen with access between utility and sitting areas
19 Paved sitting area
20 Tubs of plants
21 Garden furniture
22 Sliding door to house

THE FAMILY GARDEN

A small family garden has got to work hard for its living. It must cater to the often conflicting and changing needs of adults, children and sometimes pets too. In addition space may be needed for bicycle storage, hanging out the laundry and possibly growing some home produce.

But gardens are essentially places of enjoyment, and whether this means peace and relaxation for parents or the freedom to be boisterous for their children, a well-thought-out garden can provide the best of both worlds.

This garden has been divided into three main areas: a paved patio, a sedentary area, and a place for more active pursuits. The patio provides somewhere to sit when the grass is damp as well as a practical place for outdoor eating. The sunken sandpit is clearly visible from both the kitchen window and the decorative lawn, so that very young children can play in safety. Since the pit is set into the paving, spilled sand can easily be swept back into it. Make sure you have a tight-fitting cover for it, to keep out leaves, neighborhood cats and rain. When toddlers have grown out of building sand castles this pit will easily convert into a small flower bed for herbs, shrubs or colorful bedding plants. Alternatively it would make an attractive small water garden, a feature to be avoided with very small

1	*Hedera helix hibernica*	20	*Potentilla fruticosa*	39	*Arundinaria nitida*
2	Fan-trained gooseberry bush	21	*Yucca glauca*	40	*Mahonia japonica*
3	Apple tree	22	*Senecio greyi*	41	*Rosa rugosa*
4	Fan-trained red currant	23	*Erica tetralix* 'Alba Mollis'	42	*Hypericum calycinum*
5	*Parthenocissus tricuspidata*	24	*Hebe pinguifolia* 'Pagei'	43	*Lonicera nitida*
6	*Cotoneaster horizontalis*	25	*Wisteria sinensis*	a	6 ft (2m) brick wall
7	*Juniperus × media*	26	*Pelargoniums*	b	semi-detached sheds
8	*Cotoneaster conspicuus*	27	*Santolina chamaecyparissus*	c	optional fence to protect fruits
9	*Berberis thunbergii*	28	*Rosmarinus officinalis*	d	coarse grass lawn
10	*Prunus lusitanica*	29	*Yucca filamentosa*	e	swing
11	*Clematis montana rubens*	30	*Tamarix pentandra*	f	6 ft (2m) lapped fencing
12	*Bergenia crassifolia*	31	*Clematis montana*	g	rustic gate
13	*Iris pallida*	32	*Cotinus coggygria*	h	fine lawn
14	*Viburnum davidii*	33	*Artemisia arborescens*	i	10 in (25cm) brick wall
15	*Lavandula angustifolia*	34	*Hebe × 'Bowles Hybrid'*	j	garden table and chairs
16	*Syringa vulgaris*	35	*Viburnum tinus*	k	paved patio
17	*Salvia officinalis*	36	*Philadelphus × lemoinei*	l	french window
18	*Ruta graveolens*	37	*Choisya ternata*	m	soil-filled pillars
19	*Rosa rubrifolia*	38	*Ceanothus × burkwoodii*	n	sand pit

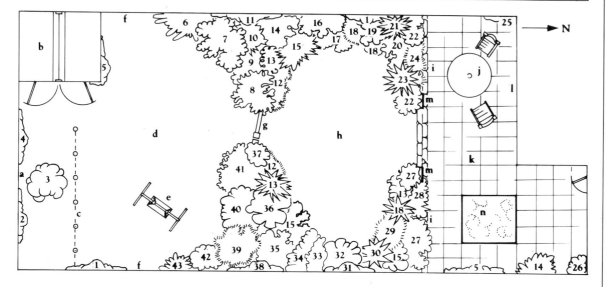

children as even shallow water can be dangerous. This is also the ideal area to hang a retractable clothes line, or insert a removable rotary dryer.

The sedentary area is planted with shrubs which require little in the way of maintenance from busy parents, and yet at the same time, being mainly flowering evergreens, provide an attractive outlook throughout the year. There is a bias towards mauve and yellow flowers and gray foliage since a one- or two-colored planting scheme is more restful than a multicolored one.

The children's play area at the bottom is physically separated from the rest of the garden by a small gate and a hedge of highly resilient shrubs. These afford privacy and also deaden sound. Even the lawn is made up of especially tough grasses which should survive the roughest games. A well-anchored swing, which can also function as goal posts or a tent frame, is sited on the lawn in case of tumbles. A large shed, such as the one here, can be partitioned inside to provide space for the storage of garden tools, bicycles and so forth on one side, while the other half can act as a small playroom. Very strong, mature fruit trees can act as climbing frames as well as providing useful produce.

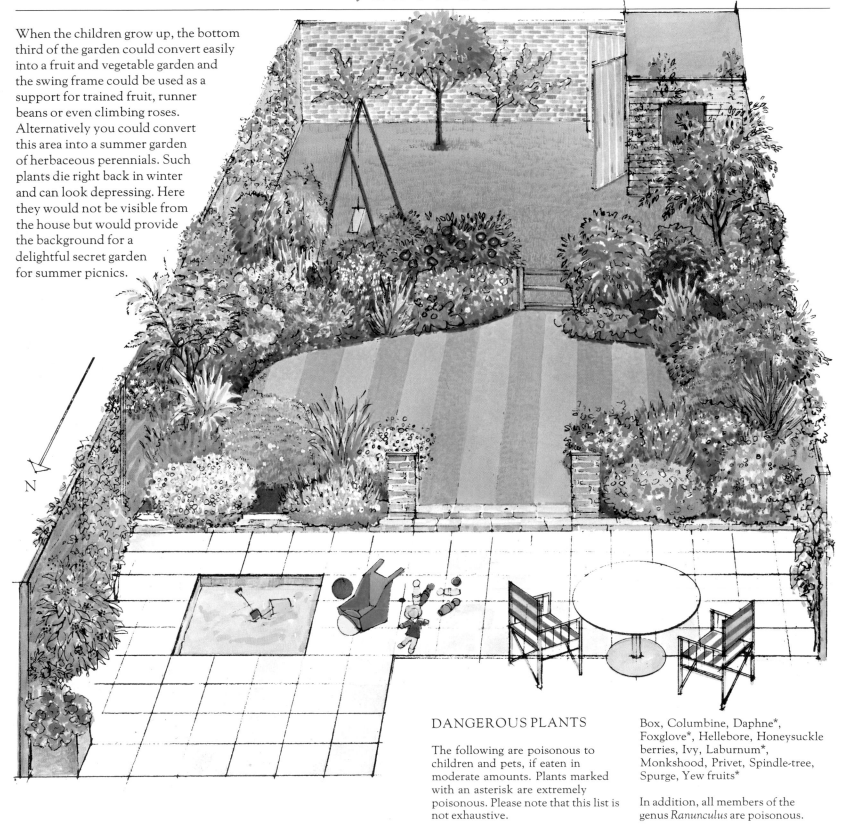

When the children grow up, the bottom third of the garden could convert easily into a fruit and vegetable garden and the swing frame could be used as a support for trained fruit, runner beans or even climbing roses. Alternatively you could convert this area into a summer garden of herbaceous perennials. Such plants die right back in winter and can look depressing. Here they would not be visible from the house but would provide the background for a delightful secret garden for summer picnics.

N

DANGEROUS PLANTS

The following are poisonous to children and pets, if eaten in moderate amounts. Plants marked with an asterisk are extremely poisonous. Please note that this list is not exhaustive.

Box, Columbine, Daphne*, Foxglove*, Hellebore, Honeysuckle berries, Ivy, Laburnum*, Monkshood, Privet, Spindle-tree, Spurge, Yew fruits*

In addition, all members of the genus *Ranunculus* are poisonous.

February

February comes, and with the lengthening days, the first small signs of spring may appear. Though the weather may be cold, wet and even freezing, the sweet violet joins the snowdrop and colorful crocus in some gardens. Sap will soon be rising, and some shrubs and climbers need pruning if they are to flower their best later on. Hedges can be planted now, to give the garden a green frame, and vegetables sown outdoors, for a late spring and summer harvest where the weather permits.

However bleak the garden may
seem in the early months of the year,
flowers like these creamy-white crocuses (left)
can be brought on indoors, to provide a bright
splash of color on a sunny window-sill

Jobs for the month

General
Continue digging over the ground where possible
Tackle annual weeds
Warm up the ground with cloches for sowing
Store indoors or heel in newly arrived plants in bad weather

Flowers
Sow the slower-growing summer bedding plants under glass
Plant outdoor annual seeds, weather permitting
Start off winter-stored dormant plants
Bring in bulbs for forcing
Take chrysanthemum cuttings
Plant lilies and anemones
Divide Christmas roses after blooming

Roses
Prune large-flowered and cluster-flowered roses

Trees and shrubs
Continue planting ornamental trees and deciduous shrubs, where

weather permits
Plant a hedge, if possible
Prune late-flowering climbers and shrubs

Lawns
Treat moss on established lawns
Prepare bald patches for sowing
Mow where lawns are growing
Disperse worm casts

Fruit
Protect blossoms of early flowering varieties from frost
Plant new fruit trees and bushes, weather permitting
Prune some soft fruits
Continue spraying fruit trees and soft fruits; commence feeding in warm climates
Bring on early strawberries under glass

Vegetables
Continue sowing under glass
Prick out mature seedlings
Make outdoor sowings of early crops
Plant shallots where possible

If you have dug over the ground earlier in the season, now is the time to begin breaking it down to a fine tilth; the frost will have done most of the work for you. Try to finish any digging still left to do now, if you live in a warm climate.

Prevent next season's crop of annual weeds with a pre-emergence weedkiller, based on an approved ingredient. If you have some spare cloches, use them to warm the ground for seed sowing later.

Continue firming any plants lifted by frost (see January) and trim established hedges.

HEELING IN

With the growth of garden centers and the popularity of container-grown plants, the old winter practice of heeling in is not often done. It is worth knowing how, though, for the odd occasion when it would be useful. You might have received several fruit trees or roses, for example, which arrive bare-rooted, and you know it will be some time before you can plant them properly. Select a sheltered

HEELING IN

Space the plants quite closely along the sloping side of the trench and cover them with soil

spot and dig a trench, one side vertical and the other at a 45° angle. Lay the plants on the sloping side, first removing any plastic or other wrapping from the roots. Spread the roots out along the bottom of the trench, water if the soil is dry, then fill the trench with soil, firming it lightly.

FLOWERS

Late February is a good time for sowing summer bedding plants from seed, either in a greenhouse or in a propagator indoors, provided you have somewhere to grow them on until it is warm enough to plant them out.

Tender abutilons, which are usually grown in a greenhouse or indoors, can be used as tall 'dot plants' among summer bedding, and come easily from seed.

Cannas are another 'dot plant' for summer bedding, a little old-fashioned, perhaps, but striking nonetheless, with their bright flowers and broad leaves. Soak the seeds in water overnight, to soften the hard coating. Cannas need quite a high temperature, 75°F (24°C), to germinate.

It's time to sow busy Lizzies (*Impatiens holstii*, *I. sultanii*), to plant out in hanging baskets and window boxes later on. They also make very good bedding plants, given a reasonably moist soil, and will do well in light shade.

Don't forget the old favorites: carnations and pinks (*Dianthus*) and the sweetly scented tobacco plant (*Nicotiana*). Antirrhinums and the butterfly flower (*Schizanthus*) can be sown now, and ten-week stocks.

There are a couple of annual climbers to sow: the cup-and-saucer vine (*Cobaea scandens*) has purple, bell-shaped flowers right through the summer, and the Chilean glory flower (*Eccremocarpus*) will give a fine display of bright orange flowers. The latter is really a perennial, and sometimes survives even a coldish winter if grown against a warm wall.

Primula seed is so fine that sowing it outdoors is a risky business. Start the seed off in trays. For greenhouse primulas, keep the temperature at about 60°F (16°C); outdoor types can be left in a lightly shaded cold frame or greenhouse. In both cases, cover the trays with a pane of glass, or enclose them in plastic and water from below.

WINTER-STORED DORMANT PLANTS

Start off dahlia tubers this month, indoors or in the greenhouse, to provide shoots for cuttings. Any tubers that have rotted in storage should be discarded, and shrivelled ones soaked overnight in tepid water to plump them out a bit. Then plant the tubers shallowly in a 6 in (15cm) deep tray of moist peat, so the tops of the tubers are just covered. Once the new shoots appear, give them plenty of light.

Cut back overwintering geraniums, both zonal and ivy-leaved, and start to give them a bit more water, and more heat, if you can.

BULBS

You can still bring in potted bulbs from outside to flower early, and forced bulbs that have finished flowering can be set aside for putting out later. They include hyacinths, daffodils and tulips.

The transition from indoors to the garden and vice versa should be a gradual one (in both directions); use a gently-heated greenhouse or a well-lit, frost-free shed to acclimatize the bulbs to the change in temperature.

CHRYSANTHEMUMS

Indoor chrysanthemums can easily be propagated now from cuttings. Choose healthy young shoots barely 2 in (5cm) long which are growing near the base of the plant. Cut them cleanly with a sharp knife or razor blade. Take off the lowest pairs of leaves and trim the base just below the joint to which the leaves were attached. Dip the cuttings in hormone rooting powder, then plant 1½ in (4cm) apart around the rim of a pot filled with two parts peat to one part sharp sand. Just about half the cutting should be buried in the soil. Enclose the pots in large, clear plastic bags to conserve moisture until they have rooted.

PLANTING OUTDOORS

Continue planting lilies (in pots, if it is necessary to hold them indoors—see January). Sharp drainage and good loamy soil with plenty of leaf-mold dug in is essential. Plant stem-rooting lilies—the tiger lily, for instance—8 in (20cm) deep, all others 6 in (15cm) deep.

Both St Brigid and de Caen anemones can be planted this month for a good show in summer; plant them 5 in (13cm) apart and 2–3 in (5–8cm) deep.

Towards the end of the month, or when Christmas roses have finished flowering, large, long-established clumps can be lifted and divided. Choose a fine day; lift

Flowers for the month

Several bulbous plants are at their best this month where the weather is mild. Especially fine are the blue *Iris histrioides major* and the yellow *I. danfordiae* which bloom just above the soil. Spring snowflake (*Leucojum vernum*) follows on the snowdrop theme, sometimes with two flowers per stem. Several squills start early, too, the best being *Scilla tubergeniana* (blue-veined white) and *S. bifolia* (blue). Among the crocuses are the yellow to orange *C. aureus*, *C. balansae* and *C. chrysanthus*. Lavender to blue crocuses include the indispensable *C. tomasinianus* and *C. sieberi*.

Look out, too, for the sweet violet (*V. odorata*), a sign of early spring, and lungwort (*Pulmonaria*), with its white-spotted leaves and clear blue flowers.

The lenten rose (*Helleborus orientalis*) will be showing its creamy white or pink-tinted flowers, and, on a larger scale, winter-flowering shrubs come into their own. Among shrubs, *Hamamelis japonica* in yellow and reddish shades and the yellow stars of cornelian cherry (*Cornus mas*) are particularly noticeable in season. Evergreen foliage and early flowers are found in the various kinds of *Sarcococca*, *Arbutus*, *Daphne odora*, *Mahonia japonica*, M. × 'Charity' and *Pieris*, and camellias where they grow.

This need never be a 'dead' time in the garden if you plant wisely and carefully.

1 *Crocus tomasinianus* 'Ruby Giant'
2 *Iris danfordiae* 3 *Pieris*

the plants carefully, teasing the roots apart with your fingers. Old tough clumps may need the aid of a knife. Plant them 18 in (45cm) apart in a moist, partially shady spot. For really good blooms, they need shelter from the morning sun and wind. Water them if the soil is dry, until they are established.

ROSES

Where the weather is mild, the end of the month may be the time to tackle large-flowered and cluster-flowered roses–these are the new names officially given to Hybrid tea and Floribunda roses respectively. Cut away any dead, diseased or frost-damaged wood, cutting back until healthy green (not brown) wood is reached.

The final example is the correct cut to make when pruning roses

Then cut out thin, twiggy wood and crossing branches. With large-flowered roses, cut back the remaining healthy shoots to remove half, or a little more than half, of their length. Cluster-flowered roses benefit from slightly lighter pruning, with a third to a half of the length removed. With cluster-flowered roses, you should also cut out, almost to ground level, a bit of the very old wood each year, to get the finest displays. In each case, make the cut at a 45° angle $\frac{1}{4}$ in (6mm) above an outward-pointing bud, for a well shaped bush. (See also page 143.)

PRUNING CLUSTER-FLOWERED ROSES

Cut away dead wood, crowded or crossing stems and any weak or diseased growth

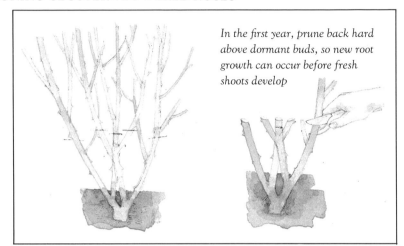

In the first year, prune back hard above dormant buds, so new root growth can occur before fresh shoots develop

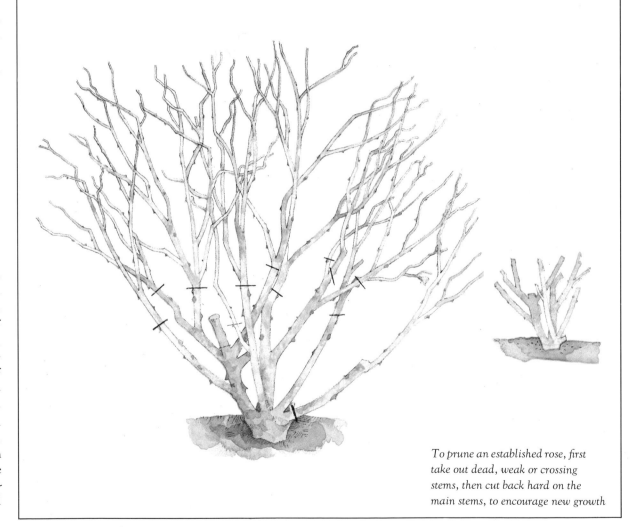

To prune an established rose, first take out dead, weak or crossing stems, then cut back hard on the main stems, to encourage new growth

TREES & SHRUBS

If conditions are favorable you can plant ornamental trees and deciduous shrubs. Established hedges should be cleared of decaying matter which might harbor pests. It is also a good time to plant a hedge, if digging is possible.

PLANTING A HEDGE

A mild spell in the South is a good time to plant a hedge, and will leave you less busy in March, when the spring rush begins. The one exception is broad-leaved evergreen hedges, made from plants such as holly and eleagnus, especially if they are bare-rooted. Though the method is the same, leave them until later, when the soil and the air are a bit warmer, and there is enough moisture about to keep the leaves from drying out before the roots have become fully established.

Hedges can vary in height from dwarf lavender hedges of 1 ft (30cm), to those of yew or hornbeam, which can be grown as high as it is practical to trim. Whatever plants you choose, make sure they are sturdy specimens, well furnished with growth at the base, rather than taller, spindly ones.

A week or two before planting, prepare the site carefully—your hedge will hopefully be there for some time. Clear the ground of perennial weeds because it will be almost impossible to get at them afterwards.

Dig the strip where the hedge is to go, at least half as wide again as the planting width. Turn the soil over to loosen it, so the plants' roots can penetrate. At the same time, dig in plenty of well-rotted compost or manure. Let the ground settle, then just before planting, sprinkle on a good general fertilizer, fork it into the soil, and firm by treading it.

Use a garden line, as for sowing seeds in drills, to keep the hedge straight. Soak bare-rooted plants, first pruning off any roots that are broken or damaged. Container-grown plants should also be

Attractive and functional – this hedge of Rosa mundi forms a *dense boundary with the tumbling effect so charming in old roses*

watered thoroughly. Don't disturb the root ball, except to gently tease out any roots growing in a spiral at the bottom.

Dig a hole and position the first plant at the correct depth, spreading the roots well out if it is bare-rooted. The soil level when firmed should match the soil level mark on the stem. Space out the second and following plants at the correct distance (use a home-made rule to save time), and firm each one with your feet before planting the next. Water thoroughly, and keep the plants watered if the ground is at all dry over the next few weeks.

There are all sorts of exciting alternatives to the ubiquitous privet. Quite apart from its functional use as a screen or wind break, a hedge can provide pleasure in the form of flowers, berries or colorful foliage. *Cotoneaster simonsii* has white flowers in summer, followed by bright scarlet berries, while snowberry has long-lasting white berries right through the fall and into winter. Escallonia makes a lovely seaside hedge, as do less hardy hebes; both have attractive evergreen foliage and a wealth of flowers.

If you've got the room for it, a big beech hedge will add character to any garden. Though not evergreen, the coppery brown leaves clothe the branches all winter, until replaced by the fresh pale green leaves in spring.

The rugosa roses make strong-growing, if prickly, hedging and certainly keep intruders out. Try mixing several varieties: 'Sarah van Fleet', with its lilac-pink blooms, and the rich, crimson-purple of 'Roseraie de l'Hay'.

For a compact, low-growing hedge, you could opt for fragrance and pink lavender, or one of its dwarf, compact forms. Rosemary also makes a lovely scented hedge.

PLANTING A HEDGE

1 *Use a garden line to mark the position of the hedge and dig a trench to the required length*

2 *Put in the first plant, firming the soil around it. Repeat this procedure, spacing plants evenly*

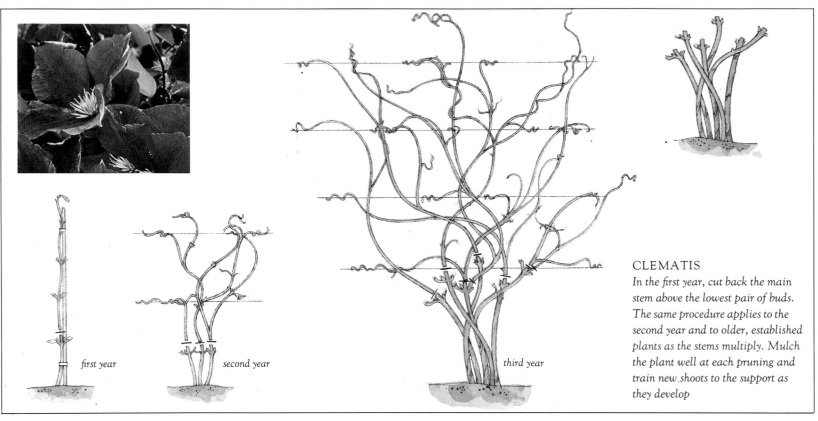

CLEMATIS

In the first year, cut back the main stem above the lowest pair of buds. The same procedure applies to the second year and to older, established plants as the stems multiply. Mulch the plant well at each pruning and train new shoots to the support as they develop

first year

second year

third year

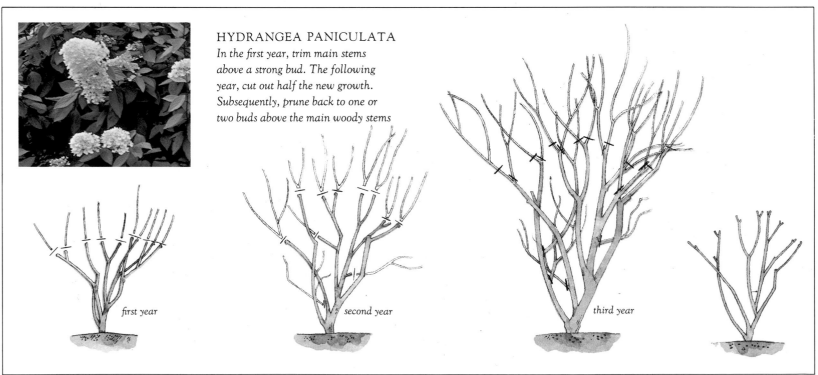

HYDRANGEA PANICULATA

In the first year, trim main stems above a strong bud. The following year, cut out half the new growth. Subsequently, prune back to one or two buds above the main woody stems

first year

second year

third year

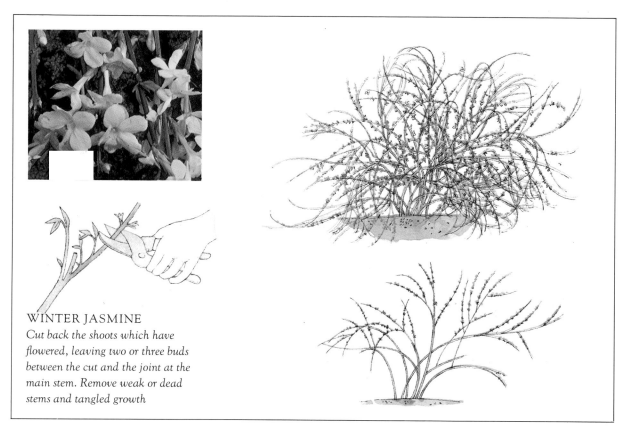

WINTER JASMINE

Cut back the shoots which have flowered, leaving two or three buds between the cut and the joint at the main stem. Remove weak or dead stems and tangled growth

HONEYSUCKLE

Remove dead, diseased and tangled stems from the climbing sorts and cut away laterals. Cut back the oldest main stems close to the base. Make sure the remaining branches are securely tied to the support

WINTER PRUNING

Late winter is the time to prune *Clematis* 'Jackmanii' and other late-flowering clematis. Cut them back hard, to 1 ft (30cm) from the ground. If you want to keep a larger framework of stems, in order to produce a larger display of flowers, you should leave the main framework of stems and cut the side-shoots back to one pair of buds from the stem.

Buddleia, *Spiraea japonica*, tamarisk and hydrangea (*Hydrangea paniculata*) should be pruned too. The woody growth made last year should be cut back hard to one or two buds from the old wood. If the plant is young, leave some of the strong new growth to build up the plant's framework.

Once the winter-flowering jasmine has finished its display, prune back the flowered shoots by about half, thinning out any overcrowded ones at the same time. Cut back the summer-pruned extension shoots of wisteria to two or three buds to build up extensive flowering spurs.

With overgrown climbing honeysuckle, pruning is more drastic. Cut one or two of the main stems back to ground level, then remove any remaining dead or diseased wood. It may be necessary to detach the branches completely from the support, to unravel twining growth and cut the stems cleanly. When the pruning is completed, arrange the branches on the support and tie them in place. You may prefer the look of honeysuckle if it is rambling and quite bushy, so prune only when it becomes too large or very unkempt. Types which flower on new growth will benefit from careful pruning.

LAWNS

Treat affected lawns with a proprietary moss killer, if the weather is settled, first raking up the worst patches with a spring-tooth rake. If the moss is caused by drainage problems or poor soil, you might want to consider longer-term correction (see Improving your soil, page 176).

If you are planning to re-turf or sow bald patches this spring, weed them and fork them over to break up the soil.

An established lawn that has become thatchy, with dead or decaying vegetation at the base of the grass, should be scarified, ideally with a powered machine. Work the ground, first in one direction and then at right angles.

In mild regions some lawns may need an occasional mow in winter, to keep them neat and to prevent deterioration.

Worm casts should be regularly dispersed from lawns wherever they appear.

FRUIT

Protect the blossoms of early-flowering trees from frost with heaters; hand-pollinate if necessary.

Any new fruit trees or bush fruits which have arrived bare-rooted should be planted without delay, or stored or heeled in.

Prune any standard and half-standard plums, gages, damsons and figs, fan-trained cherries, peaches and nectarines, and apricots (see pages 171–2).

Continue spraying fruit trees and soft fruits and commence feeding in warm climates.

STRAWBERRIES

For early strawberries in the warm states, cloche a few young plants. Weed the bed first and scatter some slug pellets along the plants to be on the safe side. Remember, too, that you have to provide access for pollinating insects, if you are not pollinating the flowers by hand. Leave the ends of the cloches open, or space them slightly apart during the day.

Strawberries started in pots outdoors can be brought indoors to a cool greenhouse and gently brought on. Once signs of growth are visible, give them a little more water and raise the temperature gradually to 50–60°F (10–16°C), to encourage early flowers and fruit.

There is a new cultivar of strawberry, 'Sweetheart', which is grown from seed like an annual, to bear fruit in the late summer. Start them off indoors now in seed trays or, better still, small peat pots filled with moist soil mix. Scatter the minute seed over the surface of the mixture, then cover with just a dusting of finely sieved soil. Keep the trays in a warm, sunny spot – a temperature of 60°F (16°C) should suffice.

If sown in trays, the seedlings may need pricking out or thinning when they are large enough to handle. As the young plants grow, pot them up singly and then plant out, 1 ft (30cm) apart, when all danger of frost is over.

VEGETABLES

Chit seed potatoes if you did not do so in January in warm areas.

UNDER GLASS

Continue starting off vegetables indoors or in a greenhouse if you have the space to do so, and can provide a temperature of at least 60°F (16°C). Heated propagators make economical sense if you don't want to heat your greenhouse to this temperature. But you need to think about where to keep the young seedlings once they are too big for the propagator. One solution is to gradually harden them off in the propagator before transferring them to the cooler, greenhouse conditions. Their growth rate will slow down temporarily, but will quickly pick up again as the natural (sun heat) temperature rises.

Eggplants, peppers and tomatoes can be sown now in containers filled with moist seed mixture. Scatter the seed evenly on the surface and just cover with the merest dusting of finely sieved mixture. Eggplants can take up to three weeks to germinate – tomatoes and peppers are quicker, and the seedlings should be visible at the end of two weeks or so.

If you made an earlier sowing of tomato seeds last month, those in seed trays may need pricking out. Wait until the seedlings show the beginnings of a pair of true leaves between the pair of seed leaves. Discard any seedlings with uneven or very ragged leaves – they will not crop well. For this reason, it's a good idea to sow a few more tomato seeds than you really need.

CLOCHES FOR STRAWBERRIES

A plastic cloche over hoops can be adjusted to the required length

Clear corrugated plastic sheeting is held in place with aluminum frames

'Glasshouse' cloches are protected at each end by a sheet of glass

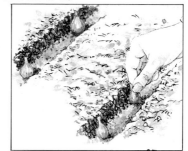

Push the bulbs into the soil, to about two-thirds of their depth

Alternatively, plant in shallow drills and cover all but the tips

Keep the greenhouse bench orderly, with pots and seed trays labelled

Transfer the seedlings, with as much soil mix around the roots as you can manage, into 3 in (8cm) pots filled with potting mixture. Water in with a fine-rosed watering can, and keep in a lightly shaded place for a few days while the plants get adjusted to their new surroundings.

Sowings may also be made under glass of lettuce, carrots, and quick-maturing beets for cropping under glass.

PRICKING OUT

Some of the seedlings sown last month may be ready for pricking out. Do it before they get too big, or their roots will get entangled and you won't be able to separate them without damage. As soon as the seedlings are large enough to handle, usually when the seed leaves and one true leaf have formed, use a pencil or metal dibber to lift them out, with as much of each root intact as possible. Then ease them into pots or deep seed trays, spaced 2 in (5cm)

PRICKING OUT SEEDLINGS

1 Lift the seedling from the tray by one leaf, easing up the roots with a flat plant label or dibber

2 Use a dibber to make evenly-spaced holes in a fresh tray of potting soil and insert each seedling

apart in each direction. The pots or trays should contain good quality potting mixture, and it helps if you make the little planting holes before lifting out the seedlings. After pricking out, water lightly and leave in a shaded spot for a day or two, until the seedlings become established.

OUTDOOR SOWINGS IN WARM AREAS

Towards the end of the month, if the soil is in good condition, you can start sowing hardy vegetables outdoors, as well as making additional sowings of broad beans and peas for successional crops. Jerusalem artichoke is a good vegetable to plant now—this relative of the sunflower is as tough as can be and doesn't mind the poorest soil—in fact, once established, you may have some difficulty getting rid of it. Plant the tubers 15 in (37cm) apart, about 4 in (10cm) deep, but remember that the plants grow enormously tall and may overshadow other vegetables. On the other hand, they make good windbreaks for the edge of a vegetable patch, and can always be planted in a rough bit of ground in an unwanted corner. Plant at least 3 ft (1m) away from the nearest row of other vegetables.

Parsnips can be sown outdoors now to get a head start. Sow them sparingly, though, as they will need thinning to at least 6 in (15cm) apart, and there is no point in wasting seed. And if the weather is extremely kind, you might try making early sowings of salad onions and hardy cultivars of lettuce—which are surprisingly cold-resistant—and radishes.

If your soil is warm and well drained, you can start to plant shallots for harvesting in the fall. Shallots are especially useful in cooking, as they have a milder taste than onions, and are often called for in French recipes. Each bulb will produce a cluster of bulbs. Prepare the ground first, making sure the soil has a fine tilth and firming it down. Cut off the dried remains of old leaves, and push the bulbs firmly into the soil, leaving the top third of each one exposed. Space the shallots 9 in (23cm) apart, in rows 1 ft (30cm) apart. An alternative method is to set the bulbs in shallow drills, and then cover all but the tips with soil. Frost and birds can loosen the newly planted bulbs, so check them from time to time.

March

With the arrival of March,
spring begins in the South, and so does the amount
of time spent working in and enjoying the garden.
Brighter, longer days produce blooms even in severe
weather. Bird watchers may benefit from fixing
nesting boxes to the north sides of trees, out of the
reach of cats. There is still time to buy and plant a
climber to liven up a wall, and put in trees and
shrubs as a long-term investment for the garden.
In the North most gardening is still
restricted to indoors.

*Bursting through the dead leaves
and twigs left over from the previous fall,
purple-blue spikes of Iris reticulata (left)
mix with the softer shades of
spring crocuses*

Jobs for the month

General

Begin control of perennial weeds and continue tackling annual weeds where possible

Protect plants from slugs and birds

Finish digging and fertilizing beds to be sown or planted soon

Give more ventilation to plants under glass

Flowers

Choose new herbaceous plants and lift and divide established ones

Sow half-hardy annuals and alpines under glass and pinch out seedlings from previous sowings

Take cuttings of fuchsias, pelargoniums and dahlias under glass

Plant cold-resistant gladiolus and montbretia corms

Trees and shrubs

Continue pruning late-flowering climbers and deciduous shrubs

Plant evergreens and conifers, and ornamental trees and shrubs

Continue protecting delicate shrubs from late frosts

Plant new climbers and check supports for existing ones

Fruit

Complete planting of new trees and bushes including gooseberries where permitted

Continue spraying against pests

Plant strawberries outside

Plant raspberries, summer- or fall-fruiting

Lawns

Rake and brush over lawns

Begin mowing established lawns

Trim edges

Apply fertilizer evenly

Sow new lawns

Vegetables

Sow seed outdoors, tender in the Deep South, hardy in the Upper South

Plant horseradish

Plant out potatoes chitted indoors

Divide rhubarb and chives

Make a raised bed to force crops

As well as encouraging growth in plants, warm March days bring out pests, weeds and diseases so be on your guard. Continue control of annual weeds (see page 20) and tackle any perennial weeds.

Newly planted herbaceous perennials and emerging seedlings are particularly susceptible to slugs and snails, especially in the Pacific Northwest. Scatter slug pellets containing metaldehyde or another approved material around vulnerable plants.

Birds, too, become annoying now, pecking at buds of fruit trees and bushes, newly planted brassicas and vegetable seedlings. Fruit cages and cloches offer the most effective protection; temporary netting and black cotton thread, zig-zagged across plants, can also help.

If you have time, finish digging over beds to be planted.

The temperature inside a greenhouse, cloche or frame can rise very quickly on a warm, sunny March day, so be prepared to give plenty of ventilation. Sudden changes of temperature can lead to weak, drawn plants, vulnerable to damping off.

FLOWERS

Visit your local garden center or nursery now, to stock up with herbaceous plants, while there is still a good selection. Established perennials that have been growing for three years or more will need lifting and dividing, so they continue to flower well. Use a spade or fork to dig up the clumps, keeping as much soil on the roots as possible. Pull each clump apart into several sections with your hands or – in the case of tough-rooted plants – two hand forks placed back-to-back and then levered apart. With very thick or fibrous roots, you may need to slice through them with a sharp spade. The sections taken from round the edge of the clump are the best ones to use, rather than the older, central portion. Remove any weeds and dead leaves or other debris from the new plants before planting them where they are to grow. Check established plants, too, to clear out weeds and decayed leaves or stems, before new growth starts fully.

DIVIDING PERENNIALS

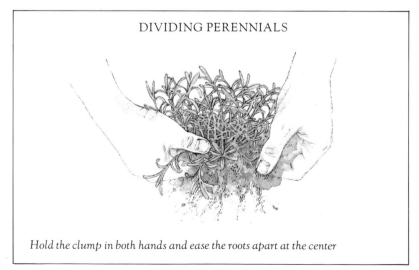

Hold the clump in both hands and ease the roots apart at the center

Flowers for the month

March brings the golden yellow bells of forsythia, echoed by the yellow of the first daffodils in warm areas (cold ones having to wait until next month). Species tulips, too, put in an appearance—look for *Tulipa tarda*, pure white with a bright yellow center. *Helleborus orientalis* hybrids put on a fine display, and primroses sown from seed a year ago or planted out in the fall, should be flowering.

Most *Camellia japonica*s flower now in the areas they can be grown, joining forsythia in a spring display. And the charming *Magnolia stellata* shows its starry white blooms on bare branches; the form 'Rosea' has pink flowers. Some rhododendrons flower earlier, but March starts their season if sheltered, in mild areas. *R. leucaspis* (white) and *R. intricatum* (lilac-blue) are under

$3\frac{1}{4}$ ft (1m) tall; *R. lutescens* (yellow) and *R. thomsonii* (crimson) are twice as tall. *Viburnum × burkwoodii*, with its pale-pink, waxy flowers, may be filling the garden with scent and, in a sheltered spot, corylopsis (*C. pauciflora*) will give you showers of golden, cowslip-scented flowers.

Some of the early flowering cherries may be out, given mild

weather, also almond (*Prunus dulcis*) and perhaps peach (*P. persica*).

The evergreen *Clematis armandii* also flowers, to liven a dull wall, and heathers, especially *Erica carnea* and its many named forms, add their color to the scene.

There may be much to see in the garden this month as it begins to come alive and signal the arrival of spring and warmer weather.

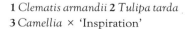

1 *Clematis armandii* 2 *Tulipa tarda* 3 *Camellia* × 'Inspiration'

4 *Magnolia stellata* 5 *Narcissus* 'Dutch Master'

HARDY ANNUALS TO SOW NOW

The following can be sown outdoors this month in the Deep South and California, with additional sowings in April for lasting displays.

Alyssum (*Lobularia*) This useful, wide-spreading annual grows 3–6 in (7.5–15cm) high, and flowers from spring through September. 'Snowdrift' is a good dwarf form for edging. A sunny position and well drained soil are necessary.

California poppy (*Eschscholzia*) Single or double, poppy-like flowers are produced from June to August. 'Mission Bells' will give a colorful mixture of 9 in (23cm) high flowers; 'Monarch Art Shades' produces 15 in (37cm) high flowers, good for borders or picking. Sow in full sun and not too rich soil; a fall sowing gives flowers the following spring, even in the North.

Candytuft (*Iberis*) An easy-to-grow annual, candytuft varies in height from 8 in (20cm) to 1 ft (30cm) and ranges in color from white through pink, deep carmine and purple. 'Dwarf Fairy Mixed' and the taller-growing 'Red Flash' are good forms. Provide full sun and a not-too-rich soil for flowers from May to September; a fall sowing may give flowers the following spring.

Clarkia Another easy-going annual, clarkia has spikes of pink, scarlet, mauve or white flowers 18 in–2 ft (45–60cm) tall, produced from July to September. Seeds of mixed and single-colored flowers are available; 'Enchantress' is a particularly nice salmon-pink form. Full sun and not too rich soil are best.

Convolvulus With morning-glory flowers, convolvulus grows 15 in (37cm) high and flowers from June through September. 'Royal Ensign' is a good deep-blue form, while 'Cherry Crimson' has deep crimson flowers. Any reasonable soil and full sun give best results.

Cornflower (*Centaurea*) This lovely cottage-garden annual ranges in height from 1 ft (30cm) to 3 ft (1m); the shorter-growing ones, such as 'Polka Dot Mixed' are superb for bedding. 'Blue Diadem' is a tall-growing form for the back of the border. Flowering from June to September, cornflowers stand light shade, and seeds can be sown in the fall for overwintering.

Chrysanthemum These sun-loving annuals can be had in a wide color range, and in dwarf forms, 6 in (15cm) high, as well as good-sized border plants, 2 ft (60cm) in height. Try the multi-colored 'Monarch Court Jesters', or yellow 'Golden Gem'. Any reasonable soil will suffice; tall forms may need support.

Lobularia maritima 'Little Dorrit'

Convolvulus tricolor 'Royal Ensign'

Eschscholzia californica

Centaurea cyanus 'Polka Dot'

Clarkia unguiculata

Chrysanthemum (Pompon)

Godetia Flowering from June through September, godetias range in height from 1 ft (30cm) to 2 ft (60cm). 'Dwarf Mixed' will give a good selection of colors: white, pink, lilac and rosy red. Godetias prefer a not-too-rich soil and plenty of sun; sow in September for spring flowers in mild areas.

Gypsophila A mass of pretty, tiny, pink or white flowers, 15–18 in (37–45cm) high, is produced from June through September. Full sun and a neutral or limey soil give best results. 'Covent Garden' is a good white form; 'Rosea' has bright rose flowers.

Love-in-a-mist (*Nigella*) Well known for its blue flowers, feathery leaves and attractive seed pods, love-in-a-mist grows 15–18 in (37–45cm) high and flowers from May through September. It can tolerate light shade and fall sowings; it is a rampant self-seeder.

Mallow (*Lavatera*) A border plant growing 2–3 ft (60cm–1m) tall, mallow flowers from July through September and likes sun and poor soil. Most forms are pink, but 'Splendens Alba' is a beautiful white form. Mallow can often be sown in September and overwintered.

Nasturtium (*Tropaeolum*) This popular annual prefers poor, dry soil and can cope with a little shade. Bushy forms, growing 10–15 in (20–37cm) high, and larger, semi-trailing forms are available. 'Tom Thumb' is a good dwarf form, and 'Gleam Strain' produces a wide range of colors on semi-trailing plants. Nasturtiums flower from July through fall.

Poppy (*Papaver*) These brightly colored flowers can be had ranging in height from 12 in (30cm) to 3 ft (1m) or more. Single and double 'Shirley' poppies are particularly popular, as is the 'Paeony-flowered Mixed' strain, with huge double flowers. Poppies bloom from June through September, and prefer sun and well drained soil.

Pot marigold (*Calendula*) These cheerful, cottage-garden annuals grow 1–2 ft (30–60cm) high and are extremely tolerant of poor soil and a bit of light shade. Flowers are produced from June through October, and it is hardy and a well known self-seeder.

Sunflower (*Helianthus*) A giant among annuals, sunflowers can reach 10 ft (3m) in height, though the form 'Dwarf Sungold' is only 2 ft (60cm) high. Sow in a sunny position, and provide staking for the tall-growing forms. It flowers from July through September.

Viper's bugloss (*Echium*) An old-fashioned annual needing sun and a dryish soil, viper's bugloss comes in white, pink, blue and purple forms, ranging in height from 1 ft (30cm) to 3 ft (1m). It flowers best in full sun, and will bloom from July through September.

Gypsophila paniculata 'Bristol Fairy'

Lavatera olbia 'Rosea'

Nigella damascena

Papaver rhoeas 'Shirley'

Echium lycopsis

UNDER GLASS

Sow now the quicker-growing half-hardy annuals indoors or under glass, to plant out later or to grow in pots for a greenhouse display, eg arctotis, African and French marigolds, cosmos, and verbena. Provide a temperature of 60°F (16°C). Try sowing a few hardy alpines now – campanula and saxifrage, for example – to brighten up the garden later. Alpines need less heat to germinate, and do well in a cold frame.

TAKING CUTTINGS

Begin taking cuttings from fuchsias and geraniums–the latter are technically pelargoniums. Choose strong young shoots; 2 in (5cm) is quite long enough for fuchsias, while geraniums can be a bit longer, say 3 in (7.5cm). Cut them off with a sharp knife immediately below a leaf joint, or node, remove the lower leaves and dip the bottom of the shoot in hormone rooting powder.

Put the cuttings round the edge of a pot filled with potting mixture or a mixture of sand and peat–a 5 in (12.5cm) pot will hold five cuttings. Water lightly and cover the fuchsias with clear plastic bags and keep in a lightly shaded place. The geraniums do not need the humidity of a plastic covering and are better without it. Remove flower buds that form while the cuttings are rooting.

Dahlia tubers that were started off in damp peat last month should be sprouting now; begin taking cuttings once the new shoots are 2½–3 in (6–7.5cm) long. Sever the shoots just above the tuber and trim the base to just below a node. Remove the lower leaves, dip in hormone rooting powder, then treat as for fuchsias but provide a temperature of 60°F (16°C) to encourage rapid rooting.

CORMS

Start planting out gladiolus corms. For a change, provided the soil is frost-free and not too wet, try planting the delicate Primulinus hybrids, such as 'Rosy Maid' or 'Salmon Star'. Gladioli look best planted in clumps, rather than in rows. Set the smaller-growing ones 3 in (7.5cm) apart, but if you are growing them for cutting, space them 6 in (15cm) apart. Where the soil is heavy or hangs wet, set each corm on a 'cushion' of sharp sand, for good drainage, in holes 4 in (10cm) deep. For planting in groups, dig one large hole, and set the corms in place, then backfill with soil. For a long-lasting display, plant in succession, every three weeks or so.

Montbretia (*Crocosmia*) can be planted out now. In cold areas start the corms off in trays of moist peat; once the new shoots appear, plant them out, spaced 4 in (10cm) apart. Full sun and well drained soil produce the best display of flowers in summer and the fall. Once planted they can be left *in situ* in all but the coldest states. Several cultivars are now easily obtained in bright and soft shades of pink, orange and red and they make an attractive display.

TAKING PELARGONIUM CUTTINGS

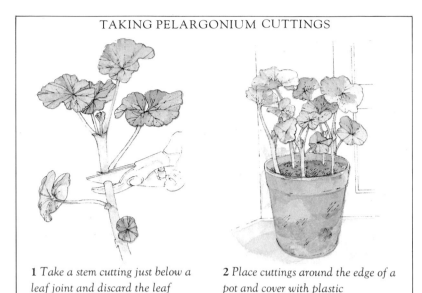

1 *Take a stem cutting just below a leaf joint and discard the leaf*

2 *Place cuttings around the edge of a pot and cover with plastic*

TAKING DAHLIA CUTTINGS UNDER GLASS

1 *From a tuber starting new growth, cut off a shoot above the base*

2 *With a sharp garden knife, trim the shoot below a leaf joint*

3 *Dip the stem in rooting powder and place cuttings in fresh soil mix*

4 *Keep moist in an unheated propagator in the greenhouse*

SWEET PEAS

In Mid-Atlantic states sow sweet peas now, 9 in (23cm) apart. Taller-growing forms should be given stakes at the same time; the popular, low-growing bushy forms, such as 'Bijou' and 'Colour Carpet' don't need staking.

Sweet peas sown last month will need pinching out, because much better flowers are produced on the side growths, or laterals, than on the main stem. Pinch out the growing tips when the young plants are about 4 in (10cm) high.

TREES & SHRUBS

March is a busy month for shrub growers. Continue pruning late-flowering climbers and shrubs which flower on last year's shoots (see February). Plant evergreens and conifers as well as the more delicate gray- or silver-leaved shrubs such as lavender, rosemary, santolina and artemisia. Begin mulching and continue protecting delicate shrubs from late frosts. Check existing supports for established climbers and tie in new growth. Use soft plastic or twine, tied in a figure-of-eight pattern, to allow the young shoots room to expand. Plant new climbers to brighten up a wall or fence, but first provide some support.

SUPPORTS FOR CLIMBERS

You will need to provide support of some kind for those climbers which are not self-clinging, and even those need some initial support. Wooden trellises are the traditional choice; treat them beforehand with a non-toxic wood preservative to prevent rotting.

Fix the trellis about 1 in (2.5cm) or more from the wall, by nailing small wooden blocks to the wall at intervals and fixing the trellis to the blocks. That way, climbers have room to twine round the trellis, though some, such as roses, will still need tying in. Keep the bottom of the trellis clear of the soil, or it will tend to rot.

Rigid, plastic-coated mesh is an alternative choice, but watch the weight of your climbers—they can be amazingly heavy when fully grown, especially when in leaf.

For annual climbers, light-weight mesh can be stretched over a batten frame and fixed in place. If you are growing the annuals against a wooden fence, fix the mesh to the fence with a domestic staple gun. This method also works well for fixing garden twine to a fence.

A more permanent method of support is to screw eyes or metal pegs in a wall. These have holes through which galvanized wire is threaded. The wires are usually spaced 12–18 in (30–45cm) apart horizontally, if necessary with vertical crosswires to help support the climber.

PLANTING A CLIMBER

Prepare the soil and fix any supports in place before planting.

If you are planting against a wall, as opposed to a trellis or fence, clear any rubble or bricks away from the base. It is worth remembering that old walls containing lime mortar tend to make the nearby soil limy—perfect for clematis, but not so good for lime-haters. Check that your planting position is not too near drains or dry wells, as the climber's roots could eventually become trouble-some. A narrow border between a wall and pavement or patio is likely to have a very confined root run, so choose a shallow-rooting climber.

Dry soil can be a problem near walls; the plants are shielded to some extent from the rain, and if there are projecting eaves or guttering above, then even less water reaches the plants. Dig plenty of organic matter into the soil, to make it more moisture retentive. A mixture of moist peat and bonemeal can be substituted, if necessary.

Make the planting hole large enough to accommodate the plant's roots comfortably, especially in the case of bare-rooted plants. And keep it well away from the wall – 6 in–1 ft (15–30cm) is ideal – that way the plant will get the benefit of shelter without the problem of bone-dry soil. Plant the climber as described above. Tie the cane to the wall support, angling it firmly away from any nearby downpipes at the same time. Climbers, such as wisteria, produce thick, woody stems which can get behind and sometimes damage pipes and gutters, if they are allowed to grow unchecked.

Keep the newly planted climber weed-free and make sure it is well watered during the first growing season.

PLANTING AND SUPPORTING CLIMBERS

Plant a climber well clear of the wall, so roots can find moisture

Provide wires for a plant that clings naturally with tendrils

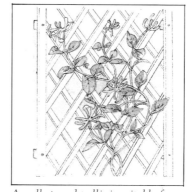

A well-spaced trellis is suitable for plants with twining growth

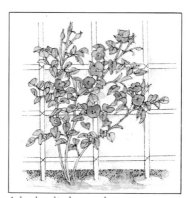

A bushy climber, such as a rose, must be tied to a trellis or fence

CHOOSING A TREE

A tree is one of the most worthwhile investments you can make in your garden, so it's very important to choose the right one, particularly if your garden is small. Trees cast shade while in leaf and have a root spread equal to the spread of the crown above, so the area under its crown can be dry as well as shady, with the tree roots robbing the soil of its nourishment.

A good catalog will give you the approximate eventual heights and spreads of garden trees. Try to find out, too, the rate of growth of a particular tree, as growth rates can vary enormously. Choose a tree that has something to offer when it's not in flower–perhaps a lovely habit of growth, attractive fall foliage or winter bark color. Lastly, make sure your garden soil is suitable for the tree

A well-placed tree with fresh, bright foliage is an excellent focal point in a broad flowerbed

you have in mind (see Soil types, Glossary).

Go for a specimen with a good, all-round shape and evenly distributed branches rather than height alone. With bare-rooted trees, try to pick one with a good-sized rootball still intact. Check that the tree's roots are evenly distributed and without fine white roots growing from the tips, this being a sign that the tree has been out of the ground and in a storage bin for far too long. If the tree is in leaf, it is too late to plant it without risk.

Container-grown trees are less risky, but there are still things to look for. Trees in weed-covered or split containers are likely to have been neglected, and trees with thick roots growing through the container are likely to have been containerized for far too long.

PLANTING A TREE

Container-grown trees can be planted at any time of the year, as long as the soil is not frozen or waterlogged. It is safest to settle them in, though, while growth is dormant. In practice, this means between October and the end of March, and for open-grown trees, planting during the dormant season is absolutely necessary.

Evergreen trees have slightly different requirements, as they are never dormant in the way a deciduous tree is. Early spring or September/October planting suits them best. The soil and air should be warm and slightly moist then, and there is less chance of the tree becoming dehydrated before its roots get established.

Bare-rooted trees should be planted in the manner illustrated on this page, but container-grown trees, and trees such as conifers,

PLANTING A TREE

1 *Soak the roots and trim away any that are broken or too long*

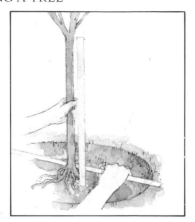

2 *Position the tree with the graft bulge 2 in (5cm) above soil level*

3 *Cover the roots with soil and tie the tree to the stake*

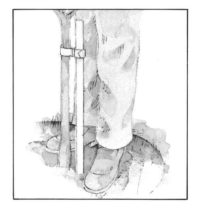

4 *Tread the soil around the base to firm it and apply a mulch*

which are often sold root-balled, with their fine roots and soil wrapped in sacking, are planted slightly differently. Dig a hole slightly deeper, and twice as wide, as the container or root ball. Fork over the bottom of the hole and incorporate well rotted manure or garden compost into the soil. You can substitute a mixture of bone meal and damp peat for the compost or manure, if necessary. Put the stake in position.

Soak the roots thoroughly in water, then carefully remove the container or sacking. If the container doesn't come away easily, cut it with shears down both sides and slide the plant out. Do not disturb the roots of container-grown or root-balled trees, though any roots wrapped round the inside of the container should be gently teased out. Position the tree in the hole and return the topsoil, or mixture of topsoil and compost, firming as you go. Fix the tree to the stake as before, and keep well watered and weeded for the first growing season, after which it should have become very firmly established.

FRUIT

Complete planting of any new trees or bushes that have been heeled in as soon as weather permits. Firm newly planted ones that have been lifted by frost. Spray apples, cherries, peaches, pears and plums against pests (see illustration for correct stage).

STRAWBERRIES

Late summer or early fall planting is often advocated for strawberries, but you can start new beds now. Select an open, sunny site, and make sure it has been deeply dug and well manured. Space the plants 18 in (45cm) apart, in rows 2 ft (60cm) apart. Check that you haven't covered the growing points of the crowns with soil. Keep well watered and weeded, and, ideally, pick off all or most of the flowers for the first season, to give the plants a chance to get established.

Continue to bring into the greenhouse strawberries grown in pots, to bring them on. Don't forget to ventilate those grown under cloches, especially on sunny days.

RASPBERRIES

Raspberries may also be planted now, or left until the fall. It is easier to plant raspberries in trenches than in individual holes, as they are spaced relatively close together, with 18 in (45cm) between plants. Select a sunny, sheltered site. This is especially important for summer-fruiting raspberries, because they flower earlier than fall-fruiting ones, and the flowers can be ruined by

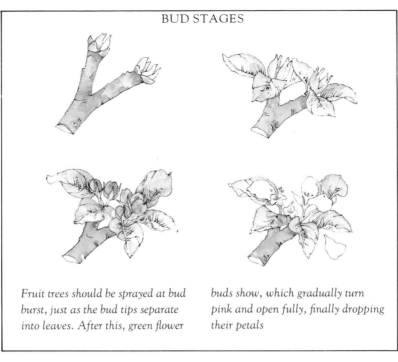

BUD STAGES

Fruit trees should be sprayed at bud burst, just as the bud tips separate into leaves. After this, green flower

buds show, which gradually turn pink and open fully, finally dropping their petals

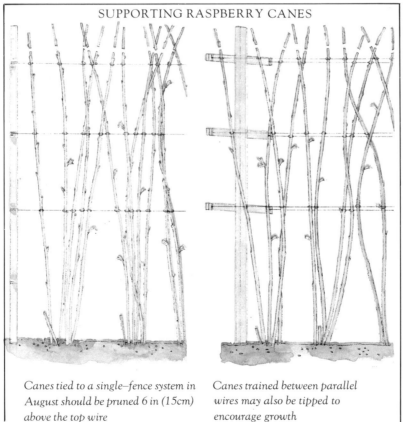

SUPPORTING RASPBERRY CANES

Canes tied to a single-fence system in August should be pruned 6 in (15cm) above the top wire

Canes trained between parallel wires may also be tipped to encourage growth

late frosts. Dig the trench the width of your spade and 4 in (10cm) deep, then set in the canes, making sure that the roots are well spread out. Cover with soil and firm with your foot before moving on to the next. Cut the canes back to 9 in (23cm) above ground. Good annual pruning and training is essential to get a good crop.

GOOSEBERRIES

Gooseberries need a moisture-retentive, rich soil containing plenty of potash if they are to do well. Gooseberries, though, will give good crops in light shade as well as sun. Buy two or three year-old plants and space them 5 ft (1.5m) apart. Gooseberries may be grown like little trees, on short trunks, so before planting, remove any growth buds or suckers on the roots or trunk. After planting, cut the main shoots back by half, and remove any weak, dead or diseased wood completely. It may seem drastic, but really it is the only way to ensure a strong, healthy and good-cropping plant. Gooseberries and currants are forbidden in white pine country.

CURRANTS

Blackcurrants, red currants and white currants can be planted out now, 5 ft (1.5m) apart. Set blackcurrants into the ground 2 in (5cm) below the soil mark on the shoots. This encourages strong shoots, which will form a framework. After planting, cut back the shoots to three or four buds above the ground.

Red currants and white currants are grown like gooseberries, on small trunks, and should be planted and pruned in the same way.

LAWNS

The lawn will need your full attention now, particularly if you weren't able to give it any attention during the winter. Rake it vigorously, first in one direction and then another, to get rid of any dead leaves and moss that may have accumulated (see February). Brush over the raked lawn to scatter any worm casts, using a stiff yard or similar broom to do so. This will bring the blades of grass upright, at right angles to the blades of the mower.

With growth just starting, the blades should be set fairly high; 2½ in (6.5cm) is about right. Later, when the weather is hot, you can raise the blades.

Rolling the grass at this time of the year has its pros and cons. Its advocates say it levels out any areas of turf that may have been lifted by sharp frost. Against this, on heavy or very wet soils, rolling can do more harm than good, compacting the soil. This leads to a hard, caked layer which cracks

when dried out in summer, and favors the growth of broad-leaved weeds. An alternative is to top-dress any hollows with good soil, a little at a time, as this will eventually even out the levels without compaction. On balance, if you use a reel mower, it is best to leave rolling until a bit later in the season.

Now is a good time to trim the edge of a lawn where it meets a flower bed, using a sharp, half-moon edging tool for the purpose. Stand on a plank placed alongside the edge of the lawn and, if the edge is straight, use the plank as a guide when you cut. From then on, you can usually keep the edges of a lawn tidy using a mechanical edger or shears, but an occasional vertical trim will be necessary as the grass slowly encroaches into the bed.

If you haven't done so already, give the lawn a feeding with a special complete lawn fertilizer which contains a high proportion of nitrogen—nitrate of soda is a common source. This will give you a good green sward which will be strong enough to withstand

drought later on. Feed the lawn on a warm day after there has been a spell of rain and the soil is moist, but the grass dry. If more rain is forecast, this is ideal.

Make sure you distribute the fertilizer evenly—mechanical distributors are available—or you may end up with scorched and patchy growth. Some fertilizers have a special colorant in them so you can see where they have been applied.

If you have dug over an area to be turfed or seeded this spring (see page 167), now is the time to finish the soil preparation. Choose a day when the soil is fairly dry; working on a waterlogged soil is a hopeless task. Break up the rough clods of soil and remove any rubbish, stones and perennial weeds. Rake the surface to a fairly even tilth, apply a complete fertilizer then rake again.

A healthy lawn lends a vibrant atmosphere to the whole garden, showing off neat flowerbeds and surrounding foliage to advantage. Lawns must receive regular attention, however, if they are to remain attractive

BRUSHING AND RAKING A LAWN

Clear away worm casts and dead leaves by brushing with a broom

Use a garden rake with narrow tines to lift compacted debris

FERTILIZING A LAWN

Follow straight garden lines when laying fertilizer from a hopper

CHOOSING A MOWER

The choice of lawn mower depends on several factors: how much grass you have, how much energy you have, the shape and level of the lawn, and what kind of finish you want. An initial decision should be made between hand, gasoline and electric mowers. Hand mowers require the most muscle, but are usually the least expensive. They are also easy to store and the sensible choice for the small, flat garden. Gasoline mowers can be tricky to start–though some are available with electric starting systems–and heavy to operate. Electrically-powered mowers are much safer than they used to be but they do have trailing cables that can sometimes get in the way.

Rotary mower
A mower of this type runs on wheels with a single blade rotating horizontally under a protective cover, like a helicopter propeller slashing its way through the grass. It is traditionally used for the average lawn where a close-cut finish is not absolutely necessary.

Hover mower
This mower cuts in the same way as a rotary mower but has no wheels and glides over the surface of the lawn on a cushion of air. Fast and mobile, this mower is not only easier to use than other mowers, but it can be used on steeper slopes. With both rotary and hover mowers, wear stout shoes and collect any sticks and stones that may be lying on the lawn before you start. Newer models may have plastic blades.

Reel-type mower
Reel mowers work by a series of blades rotating in a clockwise manner, cutting the grass as they roll along. The action of the blade often automatically throws the cut grass into the collecting box. They may be hand-propelled in their most simple form, or powered by gasoline or electric engines. The roller attachment gives the 'stripe' to lawns.

The orbital mower
This works in a similar way to the rotary mower but has a revolutionary new safety factor: it has a polymer cutter instead of the conventional metal blade. This is strong enough to cut grass but dramatically reduces the risk of cable cutting or injury to limbs. Faced with anything tougher than grass, it simply snaps off and can then be replaced by another disposable blade.

Trimmer
This machine cuts grass in places which are normally inaccessible to mowers, such as around posts, trees and walls. It has a nylon filament which rotates horizontally at sufficient speed to cut even the thickest grass.

hand-propelled
reel mower

gasoline hover mower

gasoline rotary mower

electrically-driven orbital mower

weed trimmer

SOWING A LAWN

Sowing a lawn should take place in early spring or fall, while sod may be laid almost any time. However, starting off grass from seed is by far the cheapest way to make a lawn, and it's not as difficult as you might think. Another advantage over buying turf is that you can choose exactly the mix of grasses you need for your particular lawn. A lawn that has to stand up to hard wear needs a goodly proportion of tough grass in it, whereas one that is simply going to be admired and walked on only a little, can be made up entirely of the fine grasses. Unless you get your lawn preparation and care right, the mixture of grasses you start off with may be very different from that with which you finish. In most lawns, there is a constant battle between the coarser grasses and the finer ones, which tend to get taken over. The type and fertility of soil, the frequency of mowing and how heavily you mow, and the amount of water and sun available all affect the growth rates of various grass seeds. Seed companies have worked on the problem

and developed proprietary lawn mixes, each suited to a particular situation. In the South, Bermuda and southern grasses are used.

How much grass seed will you need?

The amount of seed you need is easy to calculate. Measure the length and width of your lawn to get the number of square yards (meters). Allow $1\frac{1}{4}$–2 oz per sq yd (35–60g per sq m), the higher figure if birds or weather conditions are likely to be a problem, or if you are using a heavy-duty mix.

Preparation

As with making a new flower bed, the rough digging, removal of perennial weeds, stones and twigs, and the addition of organic fertilizer should all be done two to three months in advance of sowing. This is to allow the soil to settle down, the manure or compost to become well and truly incorporated into the soil, and any remaining weeds to declare themselves.

Any major problems with levels should be corrected during rough digging, and final levels checked when you are working the soil

surface to a fine tilth, a week to ten days before sowing. The best way to do this is to take a piece of level wood or plank 7 ft (2.25 meters) long, a spirit level and some wooden stakes, each with a clear mark or notch at the same distance from the top. Drive in one stake so that either the top or the mark is at the final level you want to achieve. Hammer in the other stakes to form a circle around the first one so that each one is no more than 6 ft (2 meters) away from the next one. Place one end of the plank on the central stake and the other end on each stake top in turn and use the spirit level placed on the plank to adjust the level of the outside stakes. Continue until all the pegs lie in the same horizontal plane over the area to be seeded. If there are serious bumps or hollows, add or remove soil until it reaches the top of the peg or the mark.

Firm the ground before removing the stakes, by treading it over systematically. Then give it a dressing of lawn fertilizer–there are several specially formulated ones available–according to the manufacturer's instructions. Rake in the fertilizer, working first in

one direction and then at right angles to it, removing any stones, twigs or newly emerging weeds as you proceed.

Sowing the seed

When you sow the seed, choose a day with little or no wind and make sure the soil is not too wet. Give a final raking of the surface, if necessary. To get really even germination, the soil particles on the surface should be no larger than a grain of wheat.

If the area to be sown is very large, it may be worth using a seed sower–try to hire or borrow one. Otherwise, divide the lawn into one-yard (one-meter) squares, using bamboo canes or string for the purpose. Weigh the seed and divide it according to the number of squares to be sown. Sow half the seed for each square in one direction, the remaining half at right angles to it, for even coverage.

After sowing, lightly rake the surface, first in one direction and then in another. 'Lightly' is the operative word here–covering the seed too deeply will reduce germination. Alternatively, you can roll

---

PREPARING THE GROUND FOR A LAWN

1 *Check the level of the ground by hammering in marked pegs*

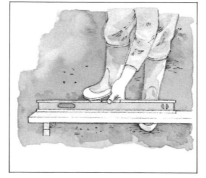

2 *With a board and spirit level, adjust all pegs to the same height*

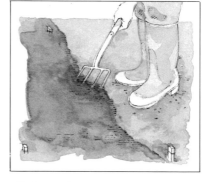

3 *Fork over the soil to level it with the marks on the pegs*

4 *Take out the pegs and tread the ground lightly to firm it*

SOWING LAWN SEED

1 *Rake the ground and mark a grid with string. Scatter the seed*

2 *Rake lightly, working across the direction of the first raking*

3 *Protect the seed from birds with black thread tied between pegs*

the seed in, again very lightly, to embed it in the soil. A few proprietary lawn mixes are treated with bird repellent–pigeons are particularly troublesome with newly sown lawns–or you can zig-zag black cotton on sticks a few inches above the soil surface.

A newly sown lawn must never be allowed to dry out, but make sure you use a fine spray for watering, so you don't disturb the distribution of the seed or even flood out the seedlings. Germination can take anything from a week to three weeks, or more, depending largely on the weather and the mixture of seed sown.

Once the grass is about 1½ in (4cm) high, brush the lawn very gently with a broom, to scatter any worm casts. Great care is needed, and the whole operation is best postponed if the soil is at all wet. After sweeping, roll the lawn lightly with the roller of a reel mower.

When the grass is 3 in (7cm) give it its first mowing. Make sure the mower blades are sharp and at their highest setting–all you want to do is to take the tips off the grass to encourage it to grow more thickly.

No matter how meticulous your preparation, weeds are bound to show up sooner or later. The annual and less persistent perennial weeds should be killed off by regular mowing, and perennials can be hand-weeded if the lawn is not too large. When you pull out the weed, try not to disturb the grass nearby, and smooth the surface over afterwards, if necessary. A kitchen fork is a useful tool for weeding on this scale. Special lawn weed-killers will harm young grass, but can be used successfully once the lawn is a year old.

A WILD-FLOWER LAWN

If you have a relatively large patch of garden that is going to be looked at rather than heavily cultivated, or a good-sized area that is an awkward shape to mow, why not try sowing a wild-flower meadow? A sunny or lightly shaded spot is best–dark, heavy shade is unsuitable, as is a tiny piece of ground, which would only end up looking weedy.

You can buy a special wild-flower and grass mixture, containing all sorts of native field flowers. Before you sow, make sure that the site is as well weeded and prepared as a conventional lawn, or you will have unwelcome visitors in the form of perennial weeds which could smother the flowers.

Shake the seed packet well, to mix the seeds thoroughly before sowing. With a very large area, it helps to mix the seed with 20% damp sand before sowing, for even distribution.

Cultivation could not be simpler–let the lawn grow until the wild flowers have finished, then give it a light cut, first with a scythette (or old-fashioned scythe if you can use one) then with a mower, the blade set at its highest.

Naturalized bulbs are decorative in a wild-flower lawn

Having made your new lawn, remember that it is basically a bed of thousands of tiny plants, and will need regular care just as other plants do. Aerate the ground from time to time, using a garden fork or special aerating tool (see page 12). It also needs scarifying to remove dead vegetation from the base of the blades of grass once the lawn is established. There is a special tool available, but an ordinary garden rake, used with care, will do the job. Collecting grass cuttings after mowing, rather than leaving them on the ground, will also help prevent the formation of thatch, as compacted, dead vegetation is called. Lawns need feeding and watering (according to season), treatment for the removal of moss and weeds, and possibly of moles and worms. You might need to take remedial action in the case of any bald patches that develop. It is very unlikely, though, that you will be faced with all of these problems, and as long as you look after your lawn reasonably, it will reward you with a lovely green carpet to set off the flowers and shrubs in your garden.

VEGETABLES

With the warmer weather and increased light, many more vegetables can be got under way.

UNDER GLASS

Either in a heated greenhouse or indoors, continue sowing tomatoes, eggplants and peppers, as well as snap beans for forcing. Start sowing melon, cucumber, celery and celeriac.

SOWING OUTDOORS

In climates like Maryland and Virginia start carrots, parsley, turnips, cabbage, Brussels sprouts, summer cauliflower, early peas, summer spinach, lettuce and radishes. You can still sow broad beans, leeks, onions, parsnips, seakale and kohlrabi outside without protection.

VEGETABLES TO PLANT

There is still time to plant out Jerusalem artichokes and shallots (see February), as well as garlic and spring cabbage. Fall-sown onions will need planting out now, too. Space them 6 in (15cm) apart. You can also plant rhubarb; give it a rich soil, heavily manured beforehand, and plenty of room.

HERBS

Herbs can be put in this month. Mint can be planted now. Indoors in the North sow basil, chervil, thyme, sage and marjoram. Farther south sow borage, chives and dill outdoors in a sheltered spot, handy for the kitchen.

METHODS OF SOWING

To make seeds easier to handle, they are sold encased in cardboard tabs which fall away as the plants grow. Pelleted seeds are coated to increase the size and are sold in a plastic dispenser

For fluid sowing, seed is first germinated in a tray lined with damp kitchen paper, kept warm and moist. When germinated, the seeds are mixed with one part wallpaper paste to two parts water. To sow, pour the mixture into a plastic bag, tie it and snip one corner. Squeeze out the paste evenly into a prepared drill

SOWING VEGETABLES

Make sure that the soil is well broken down, finely raked and with a firm surface. It is usual to run the rows from north to south, so all the plants get some direct sunlight during the day. Mark out the rows by drawing a length of garden twine as taut as possible between two wooden pegs knocked into the ground at either end of the row. Use the edge of a hoe, drawn along the twine, to make a narrow V-shaped channel for the seed.

To avoid wasting seed and to minimize the effect of damping off disease in growing seedlings, sow thinly. Seed firms now supply some varieties of fine seed in forms which greatly reduce the need to thin them later. Some glue seed to individual pieces of card, like book matches, which can be torn off individually and pushed into the ground as far as the marked depth. Others are coated to form a pellet which is easy to dispense. Then there is fluid sowing where the germinated seed is suspended in paste (not containing a fungicide) which you squeeze into the appropriate place.

PLANTING HORSERADISH

You can put in horseradish now, for lifting from later summer onwards. If it is not to over-run the space allotted to it, horseradish is best planted in a small raised bed on its own. Sink strips of corrugated iron, rigid plastic or even roof-

SOWING SEEDS OUT OF DOORS

1 *Make a drill, drawing the corner of a hoe against a garden line*

2 *Sow seeds or seed pellets by hand, finely along the drill*

3 *Rake the soil lightly to fill in the drill, covering the seeds*

Broadcast sowing *Rake the whole area and scatter seed finely*

PLANTING HORSERADISH

Make a raised bed with strips of corrugated iron or plastic sunk in the soil. Space roots evenly so the plants are not crowded

ing part-way into the soil all the way round the bed, to keep the roots from spreading. The strips should be a good 2 ft (60cm) deep, and the bed mounded up with extra soil.

Buy the thong-like roots from a garden center, beg some from a fellow gardener, or even lift some from the wild—its dock-like leaves can often be seen along road edges and on waste ground. Plant single thongs, 9–12 in (23–30cm) long, vertically, spaced 1 ft (30cm) apart, then cover with 3 in (7.5cm) of soil. Aside from keeping weeds down and watering in very dry weather, they are trouble-free plants—the only problem you are likely to have is in getting rid of them, because each little bit of root broken off will form a new plant. It is an extremely hardy perennial and any roots left over winter will give you a good crop the following year. Make sure, therefore, that you contain this vigorous vegetable.

PLANTING OUT POTATOES

Early potatoes which were chitted indoors can be planted out (see January) in the latter half of the month in mild areas, if the soil isn't too cold or wet. The sprouts should be about 1½ in (3cm) long. If necessary, rub out the weaker ones to leave two or three sprouts per tuber.

There are several ways of planting potatoes. You can dig a trench 6 in (15cm) deep, then place the tubers in it, sprout-upwards, at 10 in (25cm) intervals, and cover carefully with soil. A refinement, but one worth making, is to dig the trench slightly deeper, then place a layer of well rotted garden compost or manure sprinkled with proprietary potato fertilizer in the bottom, and proceed as before. Always replace the soil gently, so you don't damage the sprouts.

Another method is to plant the tubers individually, using a trowel to make the holes. You can also try placing the tubers on the soil surface, then drawing up soil from either side over them, using a hoe.

Be prepared with newly planted potatoes to give them some pro-

Potatoes planted in pots need fertilizer as well as water. Put in a top dressing of rich soil as the plants develop

tection against frost once shoots appear—it won't necessarily kill them, but it can blacken the leaves and delay cropping. Cloches are ideal for this, otherwise, if frost is forecast, cover the plants temporarily with weighted-down news-

paper, leaves or straw. You can also start earthing them up immediately after planting, to give extra protection to the shoots. Draw soil up over the filled-in trench from either side, using a hoe.

If you have some sprouted potatoes left over after planting, and some room in your greenhouse, try growing potatoes in pots. Half-fill 8 in (20cm) pots with good soil mix, put one tuber in each pot, then top up with soil as the plants grow. Water regularly and give liquid fertilizer every two weeks. When the potatoes are ready, simply tip the pot, slide the plant out, take off one or two potatoes, then return the plant to its pot for further cropping.

POTATO CULTIVARS

Check with your garden center or seed merchant to find out the best potatoes to grow in your particular area, but the following are generally considered to be first-class varieties. One bushel of seed potatoes will produce just over five bushels of potatoes.

Early:
'Cherokee'
'Cobbler'
'Norland'
'Norgold Russet'

Mid-season:
'Chifferva'
'Grand Falls'
'Kennebec'
'Pennchip'

Late:
'Katahdin'
'Menominee'
'Ontario'
'Russet Burbank'
'Saranac'

PLANTING OUT POTATOES

Plant potatoes in a 6 in (15cm) trench, sprouting ends up

Alternatively, make an individual hole for each tuber with a trowel

DIVIDING CHIVES

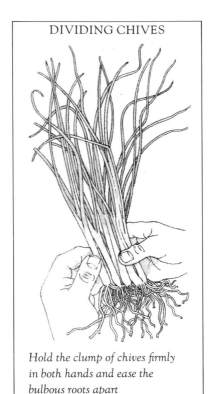

Hold the clump of chives firmly in both hands and ease the bulbous roots apart

DIVIDING CHIVES

Established clumps of chives can be divided now or in September. Simply dig up the plants, tease the roots apart, and replant in smaller clumps, spaced 10 in (25cm) apart. Alternatively, use two small hand forks, placed back-to-back, inserted into the clump to divide the plants.

DIVIDING RHUBARB

Old clumps of rhubarb which have become too big can be tackled now, with a spade and plenty of muscle. Dig out the roots, which are tough and fang-like, then cut them into several pieces with the edge of the spade. Make sure that each piece has at least one fat bud on it, then plant the severed roots 3 ft (1m) apart.

THE INTENSIVE BED METHOD

With today's smaller gardens there is a definite trend towards growing vegetables, particularly salad crops, more intensively. This is achieved by broadcast sowing or spacing evenly apart in all directions rather than in rows. Because the plants are spaced that much closer together, weeds are soon smothered. The soil around the plants does not get compacted from constant walking up and down rows, and the roots can range freely.

The beds are usually 3–4 ft (1–1.2m) wide—the determining factor is how far you can reach comfortably from the surrounding paths—and as long as you like. Before planting prepare the soil by double digging to loosen the subsoil, incorporating well-rotted compost or manure. Creating a 'raised bed' by removing topsoil from the paths and using it to build up the growing area will improve drainage. Once the bed has been dug and manured, it will only need minimal forking over for the next three or four years, and doses of appropriate quick-acting fertilizers from time to time.

The use of a pre-emergence weed-killer, approved and sold by your local dealer, will cut down the initial weeding to a minimum, but make sure you follow the manufacturer's instructions.

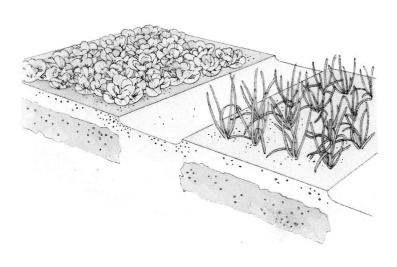

In well-prepared beds for salad and vegetable crops, the subsoil is loosened, drainage improved and compost or fertilizer added. You can work the small beds comfortably from the paths without treading the topsoil. The close-growing crops are extremely healthy (below)

UNUSUAL VEGETABLES

Globe artichoke This attractive, gray-leaved perennial can be planted in a flower bed or vegetable patch; its somewhat thistle-like but spineless young flower buds are eaten. Start from suckers planted 3 ft (1m) apart in April. Remove flower buds that form the first season, thereafter remove the central terminal bud to encourage side buds. Serve cooked, with vinaigrette dressing.

Pumpkin An easy-to-grow plant, pumpkins can produce huge gourds – 'Connecticut Field' is a prize-winner cultivar. Start seeds off in pots indoors in March, then plant out 3 ft (1m) apart in late May. Keep well watered and pinch out the growing tips when five leaves have formed. Use in soups and pies, or bake and serve as a vegetable.

Seakale This is a perennial vegetable grown for its delicately flavored, blanched shoots. Cut the thong-like roots into 6 in (15cm) pieces, making an angled cut at the bottom. Space 2 ft (60cm) apart, with the tops just below the ground, in late March or April. If thongs are difficult to obtain, sow seed *in situ* in groups of two or three, the same distance apart. Thin to one healthy seedling when the plants are 3 in (7.5cm) high. Cover the mature plants with flower pots the following winter to blanch. Cook and serve like celery.

Snow pea Sugar peas produce tender pods that are eaten whole; 'Sugar Daddy' is a good version. Sow in March as for peas, and push twigs into the soil to support the plants. Keep well watered and harvest when young. Cook whole and serve with mint and butter.

Salsify Often called the oyster plant because of its taste, salsify makes a delicious winter root vegetable. Sow $\frac{1}{2}$ in (15mm) deep in April or early May, then thin to 9 in (23cm) apart. Harvest the roots in the fall in your area. Peel and boil, with lemon juice added to the water to keep the roots white.

Kohlrabi This unusual-looking vegetable is related to the cabbage and produces a thick, globe-like stem. Begin sowing now, in rich, moist soil, and continue sowing at two-week intervals for a good supply.

Thin the seedlings to 6 in (15cm) apart. Harvest when no bigger than a tennis ball and serve raw, grated in salads, or boiled and served with butter.

French sorrel This hardy perennial plant is grown for its pleasantly acid, spinach-like leaves. Sow seeds in April and thin to 9 in (23cm) apart. Remove any flowerheads that form, to ensure a good production of tender leaves. Use them raw, or cooked and puréed.

Swiss chard Sometimes called seakale beet, Swiss chard has a delicious, spinach-like flavor. There is a very pretty form available with bright red stems and leaves. Sow outdoors in mid-spring, then thin to 9 in (23cm) apart. Pick the leaves with stalks attached, and cook like spinach

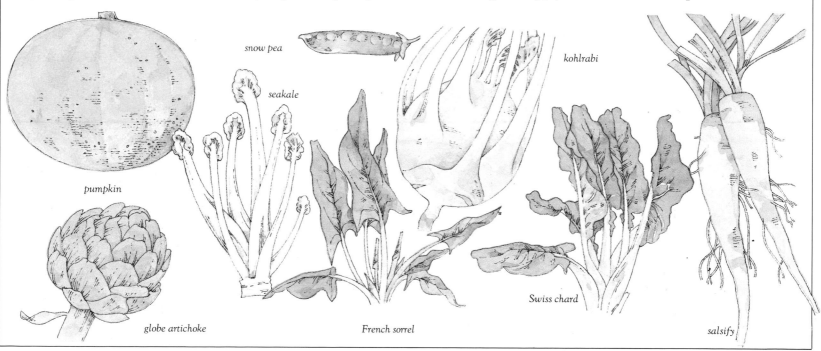

pumpkin

snow pea

seakale

kohlrabi

globe artichoke

French sorrel

Swiss chard

salsify

April

The days grow longer and warmer now,
and this is a busy month in the garden for plants
and gardeners alike. Though April is traditionally
a month when showers can be expected, be prepared
for dry, windy spells, and wary of frost in the North
and parts of Canada which can still be
troublesome. Despite the unpredictable weather,
many of the most colorful flowers are in bloom,
with bulbs putting on a fine display and fruit trees
covered in blossom in the milder states, such as the
Middle Atlantic and parts of the Northwest.

Quite at home in a shadier
part of the garden, the bright blue
flowers of Omphalodes cappadocica (left)
peep out from a secluded corner
of the shrubbery

Jobs
for the month

General
Weed and hoe under hedges and in beds and borders everywhere

Flowers
Finish planting and dividing herbaceous perennials
Start feeding established perennials
Continue taking cuttings of bedding plants
Sow hardy annuals in the North
Thin seedlings sown in March
Sow freesia seed under glass for flowering in late fall
Plant out violas, pansies, sweet peas and antirrhinums
Harden off rooted dahlia cuttings in the Upper South
Repot container grown plants
Plant alpines
Deadhead early bulbs

Roses
Spray against aphids
Mulch and feed rose beds

Trees and shrubs
Mulch and water newly planted shrubs and trees
Propagate shrubs by layering
Prune spring flowering and gray-leaved shrubs
Plant evergreens in all areas

Fruit
Plant strawberries
Disbud young strawberries and everbearing sorts where budded

Protect peach and apricot blossom from frost and thin fruitlets as they form in the North and Mid-West
Remove and burn grease-bands from fruit trees
Spray as necessary against pests and diseases
Mulch and water fruit trees and bushes
Sow melons indoors in cold climates

Lawns
Increase mowing and apply fertilizer in all areas

Vegetables
Make sowings under glass of cucumbers, pumpkins and sweetcorn; also salsify in the coldest areas, French sorrel and Swiss chard (see page 45)
Start or continue sowing Brussels sprouts and cauliflower, maincrop carrots, second early and maincrop peas, beets, red and summer cabbage, leeks and turnips in the North, Mid-West and Northwest
In warm areas make a first sowing of shell beans towards the end of April
Prepare trenches for celery
Plant out globe artichoke suckers (see page 45)
Plant second early and maincrop potatoes and earth up early potatoes
Make an asparagus bed

April is a busy time for sowing seeds, starting new plants and dividing old stock. Make way for the acceleration of new growth by taking out weeds and tidying the ground in flowerbeds and borders, under hedges and around shrubs.

Pay special attention to the lawn, if you have not already done so. Mow the grass more frequently, on dry days. Give a spring feeding. There is still time to sow a lawn, if you have not yet done so in the North and Northwest US.

FLOWERS

Plants are putting on new growth quite visibly now, so if you have any perennials to lift and divide, or new ones to plant, do so as early in April as possible—if you leave it they will take that much longer to settle in. Start feeding established perennials.

Continue taking cuttings of fuchsias and geraniums, for late-flowering display. Towards the end of April, begin hardening off those that were taken in March and have formed roots.

SOWING HARDY ANNUALS

Start sowing hardy annuals in the Northern US (see pages 32–3), in nursery beds or where they are to flower. Sow thinly and save some seed to make additional sowings in May for a long-lasting display. For an informal, cottage-garden effect, sow the seed broadcast, in rough, overlapping semi-circles, rather than in military-style rows. Annuals sown in nursery beds last month should be thinned, if necessary, to leave 2 in (5cm) between the seedlings. Overcrowded seedlings are vulnerable to damping off, and never flower well. Start to harden off annuals sown under glass earlier in the year.

Freesias may also be sown now, under glass, for flowering in late fall and early winter. Half-hardy herbaceous perennials—such as delphiniums and lupins—may be sown either in cold frames or in open, prepared beds.

April is a busy and colorful month, with spring flowers, such as these primroses and Anemone blanda, appearing in profusion

SUPPORTING SWEET PEAS

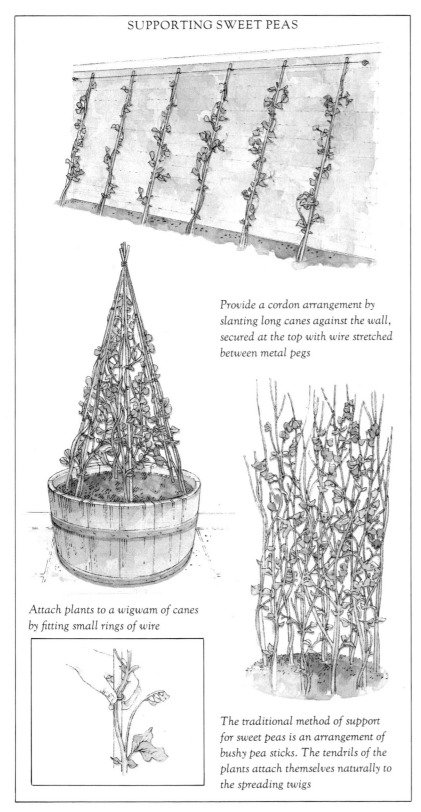

Provide a cordon arrangement by slanting long canes against the wall, secured at the top with wire stretched between metal pegs

Attach plants to a wigwam of canes by fitting small rings of wire

The traditional method of support for sweet peas is an arrangement of bushy pea sticks. The tendrils of the plants attach themselves naturally to the spreading twigs

PLANTING SWEET PEAS

To get the best display of flowers from sweet peas grown outdoors, plant them out as early as possible and provide canes or pea sticks for the taller growing varieties. Sweet peas root deeply and need plenty of nourishment. Plant them in rich soil in a sunny, sheltered position.

Grow them cordon-style to encourage large blooms for cutting. Choose the strongest shoot on each plant and tie it to the support. Nip off side tendrils and shoots as they form to concentrate growth in the main stem.

When space is short in outdoor beds, or for a patio or balcony, grow sweet peas in a tub, trained on canes placed in a circle and tied to a tent shape at the top. If you prefer the rambling, natural growth, which means smaller but quite plentiful flowers, let them climb freely on bushy pea sticks.

VIOLAS AND PANSIES

Violas and pansies can be planted out now, either ones bought from a garden center or your own seedlings, even in the coldest areas. Light shade is appreciated, and watering at the first sign of dry weather. Antirrhinums, sown January or February or propagated from cuttings last fall, can also be planted out, provided they've had a bit of hardening off first. If anything, err on the side of caution—it would be a shame to lose these carefully nurtured plants to a late severe night frost.

DAHLIAS AND CHRYSANTHEMUMS

Dahlia cuttings, once rooted, should be hardened off from late April in the North. Use a cold frame or find a sunny, sheltered spot outdoors. Leave the plants there during the day, but bring them in at night, when temperatures drop.

Continue taking cuttings of chrysanthemums, and pinch out the growing point when the rooted cutting is about 6 in (15cm) high. This encourages the young plant to produce side shoots, which in turn will produce flowers, rather than expending all its energy in producing a single, tall stem.

REMOVING SUPERFLUOUS GROWTH

Remove young tendrils and side shoots from sweet peas

Pinch off young flower stems that bear fewer than four buds

REPOTTING

1 *Crock the new pot and remove the plant from its original pot*

2 *Loosen soil around the roots and remove any pieces of crocking*

3 *Hold the plant in place in the new pot and add fresh soil*

4 *Fill the pot to ½ in (1cm) below the rim and firm the soil*

Check any container grown plants that may need potting on into larger containers. Those that have reached their full size may need re-potting into fresh soil mix. This will also apply to any garden plants grown in containers. For potting on, choose a pot with a diameter about 1 in (2.5cm) larger than the previous one—if the pot is much bigger, then the plant's roots do not penetrate all the soil mix, leading to sour soil mix and root rot. Plastic pots need crocking for drainage, as clay pots do. For the latter, place broken bits of flower pot, convex-side up, over the drainage hole. Cover the crocks with a layer of good-quality, loam or peat-based pot soil. Carefully knock the plant to be repotted out of its old pot, and remove any crocks that may be caught in the tangle of growing roots.

Place it centrally in the new pot, then slowly pour your soil round the sides until the pot is full. Tap the pot once or twice to allow your soil to settle, firm lightly then top up, leaving room for watering. Water with tepid water and put the plant in a lightly shaded spot for a day or two. This is a good wet-weather chore, and quite pleasant to do in the evenings. The plants will be grateful for this pot change, and will reward you with fresh foliage and flowers in due course, once they are accustomed to their new home.

Pot-grown alpines can be planted now. Remove the plant from its pot and place it in a hole large enough to take the roots comfortably. Work the soil firmly around the roots with your fingers or a

Container grown plants add to the display of flowers in a small garden or enliven a stone patio

trowel handle, then place a layer of chippings around and under the plant—these help keep weeds down and keep the roots cool in warm weather. At the same time, check that established alpines have not been lifted by frost. This can happen in the first year after planting, so be on the lookout.

As the flowers of the larger, early-spring bulbs fade, remove the flower heads, to stop them expending energy in setting seed. This isn't really practicable, or necessary, with many of the smaller bulbs—scilla and grape hyacinth, for instance—and they can be left to seed themselves quite happily. It takes at least a couple of years for the self-sown, naturalized seedlings to reach flowering size, but in time they will form sheets of color in early spring.

ROSES

Keep an eye on your roses now, as they break into leaf and new shoots appear. Sadly, the rising temperatures that encourage this growth are also encouraging to aphids. You may need to spray with systemic insecticide to ward off pest attacks.

Roses need a good deal of food and water. Weeds use up some of these supplies so take them out or apply weedkiller if necessary. From their second year onwards, roses can be mulched to provide extra nutrients. Mulches keep moisture in the soil and reduce annual weed seedlings.

Apply a 2 in (5cm) layer of well-rotted animal or vegetable manure over the rose bed, but leave a small ring of bare soil around the base of each plant. Compost can also be used, or garden peat.

Flowers for the month

In the North and Northwest US especially, it is the smaller flowers which attract attention in April, with rockery plants like alyssum and aubrieta coming into bloom. Cascades of color – pink, white, yellow and purple – transform walls, edgings and alpine gardens. The mossy saxifrages (S. × 'Peter Pan' and S. × 'Pixie') add their clear pink and red flowers to the scene.

Look out for the tiny purple alpine pansy (*Viola calcarata*) and the little yellow alpine violet (*V. biflora*). Lily-of-the-valley will be making its appearance in sheltered, lightly shaded spots, and filling the air with its heavenly scent. Many bulbs are still providing splendid color, notably hyacinths and grape hyacinths (*Muscari armeniacum*), together with early single and double tulips. And the little snake's head fritillary (*Fritillaria meleagris*) nods its chequered, bell-shaped flowers in meadows as well as gardens now. Its even more resplendent cousin, the crown imperial (*F. imperialis*), is also in flower, with its clusters of tulip-shaped flowers in brilliant yellow, orange or red.

Bergenias will be showing off their white, pink or deep-rose flowers, carried well above their large leathery leaves. The wallflowers planted in the fall, *Chieranthus chieri* and *C. allionii*, will be coming into flower, together with the forget-me-not.

In the shrub department, brooms (*Cytisus* × *kewensis, C. praecox*) will be at their finest, looking like fountains of pale, golden yellow. Tiny yellow – and orange – flowers hang from the arching stems of the many berberis in bloom.

Magnolia × *soulangeana* displays its elegant flowers on leafless branches in April, and Japanese cherries brighten up many a northern and mid-western suburban garden.

1 *Alyssum saxatile* 'Citrinum' **2** *Fritillaria meleagris* **3** Forget-me-not **4** *Bergenia purpurescens* 'Ballawley' **5** Crab apple *(Malus × eleyi)* **6** *Berberis darwinii* **7** *Magnolia × soulangeana*

TREES & SHRUBS

April can be deceptively cruel to newly planted trees and shrubs. Though its reputation is that of a rainy month, there are often long, dry periods which, combined with winds, dry out both evergreen and tender, young deciduous leaves. Use the hose or watering can regularly, and keep a special eye on shrubs and climbers planted near walls. Mulching with well-rotted compost, manure or even grass cuttings will help retain soil moisture, as well as keep weeds down and eventually add nutrients to the soil when they decompose.

LAYERING

It's a good time, now, to propagate shrubs everywhere by layering—it is slow, but so little trouble is involved after the initial five minutes or so, that it is well worth the wait. Rhododendrons, azaleas, magnolias, figs and laurels are good subjects—any shrub, in fact, that has branches low enough to touch the ground and supple enough to bend. Select one such branch, of fairly new growth, and make a nick on the underside, using a sharp knife, where it touches the ground. Replace heavy soil directly below the stem with a mixture of peat, loam and sand. Scoop out some of the mixture and peg down the nicked section with wire. Bend up the stem and support the growing tip above the ground with a cane. Cover the pegged section with soil. Water it immediately and then from time to time—make a note of where it is, or you may forget it entirely if your garden is a large one. In the fall, give a gentle tug to see if it has rooted—magnolias may take two years or more – and if it has, sever the branch from the parent plant with pruners. Next spring, move it to its final position.

PRUNING

Pruning is an ongoing activity—even in the month of April. Tackle the gray-leaved and other dwarf evergreen shrubs grown mainly for their foliage, eg lavender and cotton lavender (*Santolina*). Wait until the danger of really cold weather is over, then trim them back to encourage fresh, bushy growth from the base, and keep them from becoming leggy and bare.

The butterfly bush (*Buddleia*) should be pruned back by about two-thirds in mild areas to encourage strong erect stems, and to the ground in cold ones.

Hardy fuchsias may be coming into bud, and dead branches will declare themselves. Prune these out completely, and also remove any weak or crowded wood. Cut the remaining healthy wood back by about a third.

Lastly, cut wood from spring-flowering shrubs in California and the South. Take out dead wood and cut back a few old, heavy stems almost to ground level. As blooms fade on younger, flowering stems, cut just above a point where new growth is emerging. Prune selectively or flowering may be inhibited in the following year. Trim some stems lightly, cut back others more radically.

PRUNING SANTOLINA

A fully grown plant will become untidily shaped and straggly

Prune hard, right back to the young shoots clustered at the base

LAYERING

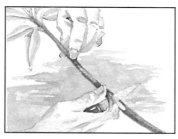

1 *Trim the leaves from a strong shoot and nick the underside*

2 *Make a hollow in the soil and peg down the nicked stem section*

3 *Cover the stem with soil and provide support for the leafy tip*

4 *When the stem has rooted securely, sever it from the parent plant*

Careful pruning of fuchsias is rewarded later with strong new growth and plentiful flowers

PRUNING FORSYTHIA

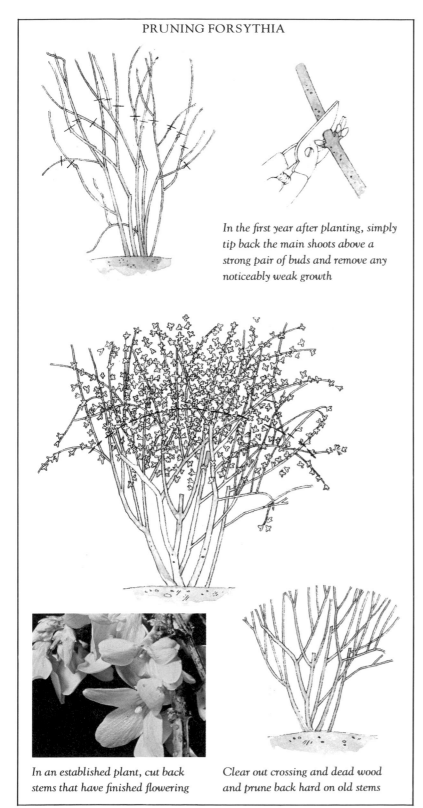

In the first year after planting, simply tip back the main shoots above a strong pair of buds and remove any noticeably weak growth

In an established plant, cut back stems that have finished flowering

Clear out crossing and dead wood and prune back hard on old stems

EVERGREENS IN THE GARDEN

Evergreen trees and shrubs play an important part in the framework of a garden, giving color and cover all year round. Besides hiding unsightly objects or views, they can offer shelter to more delicate plants, screening them from prevailing winds.

The range of shapes and sizes available is huge, from the tall, slim, Lawson cypress to yucca, with its striking, sword-like leaves and the dwarf, ground-hugging prostrate junipers. And the choice of color is equally wide. Holly, for instance, can be had with gold- or silver-variegated leaves; and others, such as cryptomeria, change color with the advent of cold weather, becoming a rich, deep bronze.

Many evergreens have beautiful flowers, too. Camellias and rhododendrons spring to mind at once, but there are others, such as escallonia and pieris, which put on first-class floral displays. Berries are an additional bonus from evergreens—just think of holly, cotoneaster and others.

Site your evergreens carefully—remember that some of them are slightly tender and may need shelter. Keep in mind their ultimate height and spread, and give them plenty of room to grow, using quick-growing filler plants if they seem a bit lost at first.

Now is the best time to plant evergreens, especially open-grown ones, so they can establish themselves before the hot, dry days of summer. However, in areas prone to spring droughts the fall is the best time of year. Whenever you plant evergreens, make sure you give their roots plenty of room,

When planting close to a wall or fence, allow room for the eventual spread of both roots and foliage

If the evergreen needs support, insert a stake in the appropriate position as you replace the soil

and water them copiously for the first growing season if rainfall is light or non-existent. Spray their foliage with water from time to time, too, to keep them from drying out. In strong, drying winds, it is sensible to erect some temporary screening on the windward side as a further precaution. Use woven wooden screening or burlap held up by posts driven into the ground.

EVERGREENS

Aucuba This shrub will grow in almost any situation as far north as Long Island. One form, *A. japonica* 'Crotonifolia', has leaves heavily marked with golden yellow. Bright red berries are produced by female plants only if there is a male near by.

Box (*Buxus*) Box is a very useful evergreen if you want a slow-growing one for the Upper South. It is also one of the plants used for topiary. Though attractive in its glossy, dark-green form, there are variegated forms as well. Try *B. sempervirens* 'Argentea', with gray and cream markings, or *B. s.* 'Aureovariegata', splashed with creamy yellow.

Camellia One of the popular evergreens for the South and the West Coast, camellia is noted for its large, exotic-looking flowers, through winter and spring. It is more lime tolerant than rhododendrons, but will not stand really limy soils. It is excellent for container growing. It dislikes an east-facing site – frosty nights and early morning sun damage it.

Cedar (*Cedrus*) Not all cedars are huge – *C. libani* 'Nana' is a lovely dwarf form, perfect for a rockery. *C. atlantica* 'Glauca Pendula' is a scaled-down, weeping version of its grand cousin, just right for growing in small areas.

Cotoneaster A hard-working group of plants – there are some deciduous cotoneasters as well – evergreen cotoneasters range from fair-sized trees, such as *C.* 'Cornubia', to creeping, ground-hugging shrubs, such as *C. congestus*. Known for their brilliant red fruit in the fall, cotoneasters also put on a pretty spring display, with white or pale pink flowers.

Cypress (*Cupressus*) The true cypress is not as easy to grow as its relative, the false cypress (*Chamaecyparis*). It dislikes being transplanted, so avoid bare-rooted trees, and young plants are particularly vulnerable to damage in exposed positions. In a sheltered, sunny garden, try the miniature *C. macrocarpa* 'Pygmaea', with tiny, scale-like leaves, or the medium-sized *C. glabra* 'Pyramidalis', a conical tree with gray-blue foliage.

Daisy bush (*Olearia*) This attractive evergreen has silvery white undersides to its leaves and scented, daisy-like flowers in summer. *O.* × *haastii* is the hardiest version, particularly good for town gardens and hedging in California.

Elaeagnus A fast-growing shrub, especially tolerant of exposed sites, hardy to 10°F (−12°C). Flowers are tiny but very fragrant. Try *E. pungens* 'Maculata', which has yellow variegated leaves, or *E.* × *ebbingei*, which has large leaves with silvery undersides.

Escallonia Particularly good for growing by the sea, escallonias will thrive inland in a sunny, sheltered spot. The glossy leaves, aromatic in some forms, and the tubular flowers are delicate in appearance. The flowers, which range from white to pale pink, rose-red and crimson, give their best displays late summer on in the Deep South and California.

Eucalyptus Some of the many species of Australian gum tree will grow quite happily in sunny California. Choose *E. gunnii*, one of the hardiest. Its juvenile leaves are round and deep silver-blue. The adult leaves are sickle-shaped and grayish green. Plant small, pot-grown specimens in spring and protect them from cold winds.

Eucryphia Less well known than it should be, eucryphia needs moist loam and a sheltered spot to thrive. It is suitable for the Gulf Coast and California. Both the deciduous and evergreen species have pure white flowers towards the end of summer. Young plants are slow to flower. One of the most striking kinds is *E.* × *nymansensis* 'Nymansay', a small or medium-sized tree, with flowers up to $2\frac{1}{2}$ in (6cm) across.

Euonymus Two evergreen species, *E. fortunei* and *E. japonicus*, make up the vast majority of euonymus available at garden centers. The former is a ground-hugging, trailing plant which will change

Camellia japonica 'C.M. Wilson'

Eucalyptus gunnii

Eucryphia × *nymansensis*

Euonymus fortunei radicans

Ilex × altaclarensis

Cryptomeria japonica

to a self-clinging climber if grown near a wall. Named forms include *E. f. radicans* 'Variegatus' with leaves variegated white, gray and pink, and *E. f.* 'Coloratus', whose leaves turn a striking shade of purple during winter. *E. f. radicans* 'Silver Queen' is a small compact shrub with cream variegated leaves. *E. japonicus* makes a good-sized shrub. *E. j.* 'Ovatus Aureus' has leaves edged in creamy yellow, and *E. j.* 'Macrophyllus Albus' has wide, white margins round the leaves. Euonymus are very shade tolerant and happy in the coldest states.

False cypress (*Chamaecyparis*) The false cypress has become one of the most useful conifers in the garden. Lawson cypress (*C. lawsoniana*) is a traditional hedging plant, but named forms range from the tiny *C. l.* 'Pygmaea Argentea', a white-variegated conifer for a rockery, to *C.l.* 'Lutea', a columnar tree with yellow-tinted foliage. *C. obtusa* 'Crippsii' is another choice golden-foliaged specimen tree, smaller and more conical in form. All false cypresses need good, moisture-retentive loam to thrive, but they are surprisingly tolerant of soil conditions and cold hardy.

Hebe This huge range of evergreens varies enormously in size, form, color and hardiness, and you could easily fill a small garden with a selection of hebes without any repetition. Hebes like well drained soil and a sunny spot, and are particularly suited to West Coast conditions. Try *H. pinguefolia* 'Pageii', a mat-forming, gray-leaved form. *H.* 'Midsummer Beauty' is much larger-growing, with lavender flowers and showy, red under-sides to its leaves. *H. salicifolia* 'Spender's Seedling' is a lovely, free-flowering small shrub. The summer-borne flowers are fragrant.

Holly (*Ilex*) Hardy to Boston, holly comes in many attractive color combinations. They are usually labelled as male or female, so for the best display of berries, select a female clone and provide a male holly to fertilize the flowers. *I. aquifolium* 'Amber' has large, bronze-yellow berries and *I. a.* 'Bacciflava', bright yellow berries. The leaves of *I. × altaclarensis* 'Golden King' are edged in yellow. Despite its name, it is actually a female form. There is a lovely weeping holly, *I. a.* 'Argenteo-marginata Pendula'.

Japanese cedar (*Cryptomeria*) A very unusual conifer in that the foliage of many forms turns deep russet in winter, Japanese cedar can be had in a range of shapes and sizes. *C. japonica* 'Elegans' makes a small tree, while *C. j.* 'Vilmoriniana' is a slow-growing dwarf bush which is suitable for a rock garden.

Juniper (*Juniperus*) The common juniper (*J. communis*) is well known, with its prickly, gray-green foliage and dark, bloom-covered fruit. There are dwarf and prostrate versions, too, popular in miniature and rock gardens. Try *J. c.* 'Depressa Aurea', a wide-spreading, dwarf form with golden foliage in spring.

Laurel (*Prunus laurocerasus*) A tough, useful evergreen for screening or shelter, hardy to 10°F (−12°C), that copes with deep shade and poor soil. There is a creamy white variegated form, *P. l.* 'Variegata', and *P. l.* 'Zabeliana' is low-growing with horizontal branches. The narrow, willowy leaves are more delicate than those of the common laurel.

Magnolia The most famous evergreen magnolia (*M. grandiflora*) merits a place in any garden that can accommodate it. If you can provide sun, shelter and rich, well drained soil, it can be grown in the open to form a free-standing tree, often as far north as Philadelphia. *M. g.* 'Exmouth' is best, and its large, scented flowers are produced while the plant is quite young.

Mexican orange blossom (*Choisya*) An attractive flowering shrub with glossy, dark-green leaves, suitable for Southern California. Sun or light shade are equally suitable if a bit of shelter is provided. Pretty, scented white flowers appear in early summer, and on and off through the year.

Pieris Pieris likes moisture retentive, acid soil, shelter and light shade and is very hardy. If happy, it will reward you with masses of white flowers, similar to lily-of-the-valley, in April and May. Some forms such as *P. formosa forrestii*, have pretty, bright red young leaf shoots in spring. *P. japonica* 'Variegata' has green leaves streaked with creamy white, pink-tinted in spring.

Pittosporum tenuifolium This delicate evergreen, much used by florists, needs a mild, sheltered spot in the South to do well. It is available in many named forms. Try *P. t.* 'Garnetii', with variegated green, white and pink leaves, or *P. t.* 'Purpureum' with dark, bronze-purple leaves. The almost black flowers are quite inconspicuous, but scented.

Rhododendron One of the most popular evergreen shrubs, there are literally hundreds of species and cultivars. Free-draining, acid soil, shelter and light shade are the basic requirements. Some are immensely hardy, while others need greenhouse treatment; some grow to tree size, others are dwarf, slow-growing and suitable for tubs or large pots. Before buying a rhododendron, read a good catalog, so you can choose sensibly for the space and color scheme you envisage.

Silver fir (*Abies*) Ranging from the giant Caucasian fir (*A. nordmaniana*), up to 200 ft (60m) high, to the tiny *A. concolor* 'Compacta', which barely reaches 3 ft (1m) high, silver firs give year-round color and interest. *A. koreana*, with purple cones in the fall and white undersides to the foliage, is good for a small garden. They all grow best on moisture-retentive loams, and most are hardy.

Spruce (*Picea*) The most famous of these is the Norway spruce (*P. abies*), but there are others. None needs shelter but they do need good, moisture-retentive loam. Try *P. pungens* 'Koster', a lovely blue spruce, typically conical in shape, but small enough to fit into most gardens.

Strawberry tree (*Arbutus unedo*) Besides glossy, evergreen leaves, the strawberry tree offers a deep brown, shredding bark, lily-of-the-valley-like flowers and strawberry-like fruit in late fall. The fruits are edible, but tasteless. With age, the trunk may become gnarled, and makes an attractive feature. It is suited to the Deep South and the West Coast.

Viburnum These include deciduous, semi-evergreen and evergreen shrubs. One of the most beautiful of the semi-evergreens is *V. × burkwoodii*; its sweetly scented, white flowers, pink in bud, can begin opening in April and are carried into May. The fully evergreen *V. davidii* is much lower growing, and plants are often grouped to make effective ground cover and also to ensure a good crop of bright blue berries in the fall. *V. tinus* (or *laurustinus*) makes a large, tolerant shrub, hardy to 10°F (−12°C). Its white flowers are not particularly showy, but very cheering in winter, when so little else is in bloom.

Yew (*Taxus*) The traditional English yew (*T. baccata*) forms very dense foliage, and is often used for hedging. The seeds inside the bright-red berries are poisonous, and yew should not be planted where animals or young children have access. The golden Irish yew, *T. b.* 'Fastigiata Aureo-marginata' forms a large, columnar tree with attractive golden-edged foliage.

Yucca One of the most exotic-looking of all the evergreens, yucca adds an instant, tropical look to any garden. It is hardy and forms huge clumps of sword-like leaves and produces tall spikes of bell-shaped flowers in hot summers. *Y. filamentosa*'s flowers are white; *Y. gloriosa*'s are cream, sometimes red-tinted in bud. *Y. gloriosa* eventually forms a thick stem and can reach a height of 10 ft (3m). There is a pretty variegated form with creamy yellow stripes at the margins of the leaves. Another type, *Y. recurvifolia*, has softer leaves with a central yellow stripe. Grow in well-drained soil, in a sunny spot.

Abies koreana

Picea pungens 'Globosa'

Arbutus unedo

Rhododendron 'Lady Rosebery'

FRUIT

You can plant strawberries in the North, but pinch out the flower buds for their first season. Do this with the everbearing varieties now, but for a different reason. If you let them flower now, then they will crop at exactly the same time as the main strawberry season, but if you delay their flowering for a few weeks, then they will pick up where the main crop ends, giving you luscious berries well into fall. 'Ozark Beauty' and 'Old Gem' are good everbearers. 'Baron Solemacher' strawberries, sown earlier this year, should be coming along nicely under glass, for planting out next month and cropping towards the end of summer. After the end of their season, you simply discard the plants and start another batch from seed.

If you are lucky enough to have peaches or apricots in your garden, remember to provide their delicate flowers with protection from frost. If possible, cover them at night with fine nets hung from battens. Lift the nets during the day, for the benefit of pollinating insects.

Towards the end of the month, if the weather has been mild, you can start thinning the young fruitlets, as the trees produce many more than they can sensibly cope with. Thinning should take place over several weeks, starting when fruitlets are the size of large peas and stopping when they are about as large as walnuts. Also, these trees have a natural fruit fall a little later on, and if you thin over-zealously to start with, you may end up with a smaller crop than you anticipated. First remove any misshapen fruitlets and those growing towards the wall, then remove one fruit from each pair. With apricots, which have a very heavy natural fruit-fall, light, even cautious, thinning pays off.

Now is the time to remove and burn any grease-bands you put on your fruit trees last fall. Various pests—such as woolly aphid and a few others—will have been trapped in the sticky band while making their way up the trunks to lay eggs.

Insects will be very much on the move now. Check your blackcurrants for any sign of big bud, caused by the blackcurrant gall mite. The mites live in the closed buds, causing them to swell up unnaturally, and damaging the baby leaves at the same time. Pick off and burn swollen buds, and spray the bushes with a good miticide (see page 184). Spray again towards the end of the month. Some varieties are especially sensitive to lime sulphur, and can't be sprayed with it—check with your country agent if you are unsure.

Various kinds of aphids, too,

THINNING FRUIT

Thinning should begin when fruitlets are the size of large peas

will be pitting their wits against yours in the fruit garden by the end of the month, so keep an especially close watch and be prepared to spray as necessary. Do not use insecticides when flowers are open, or you will kill pollinating insects along with pests, with an inevitable lack of fruit. Check apples for woolly aphid, and plums for leaf-curling plum aphid (see page 184).

On the disease front, gooseberries should be given a once-over for any sign of American gooseberry mildew—it shows up as powdery white growth on the stems, especially new growth. Badly infected wood should be cut out and the bush sprayed (see page 184) once before the flowers open, again when the fruits have set and, lastly, about two weeks later. If your apples and pears have suffered from scab in previous years, spray them now (see page 184).

Mulching fruit in April is always a good idea, provided the ground is not bone dry when you do it. Use well-rotted manure or garden compost and spread it liberally round all fruit trees and bushes. Watering in dry weather is a must, especially for newly planted fruit trees and bushes.

If you want to try your hand at growing melons, sow them now. Sow the seeds individually in 3 in (7.5cm) pots, and provide a temperature of not less than 65°F (18°C)—actually the warmer the better (75–80°F/24–26°C is optimum), and a warmish radiator is a good idea if you don't have a heated propagator. Germination is usually quite quick, so check the pots regularly and once the seedlings appear, move them to a light and sunny spot, and keep well watered.

Big bud on blackcurrant bushes is caused by a mite infestation

Inspect new growth on apple trees for clinging white woolly aphids

These gooseberries show the typical white, powdery effect of mildew

VEGETABLES

To get a steady supply of vegetables right through the summer and well into the fall, continue successional sowing. If you haven't already done so, now is the time to sow any cucumbers and pumpkins under glass. You can sow seeds of sweetcorn now, but use peat pots which can be planted straight into the ground, as sweetcorn is notoriously difficult to transplant. Shell and snap beans, along with celeriac, will get a head start if sown in the same way.

Second early and maincrop potatoes should go in this month, except in the northern states. They tend to produce heavier crops, and so need wider spacing than earlies (see March). Leave at least 1 ft (30cm) between the seed potatoes, and 3 ft (1m) between rows. Check on the early potatoes now, as the new shoots will almost certainly be showing in mild areas and they will need earthing up.

Red and summer cabbage may also be planted now, and trenches prepared for celery. Towards the latter half of April make successional sowings of peas, but switch to second early or maincrop peas – 'Drought-Proof' and 'Dwarf Telephone' are good second earlies; 'Alderman' and 'Show Perfection' are safe maincrop choices.

Maincrop carrots should be sown now, too, but switch to the intermediate or long-rooted cultivars. If you have the space, make one or two more sowings of the early, stump-rooted sort to give you tender carrots in summer, some time before the maincrop ones are ready.

Combine fast-growing lettuce with slow Brussels sprouts

This is also the month to sow spinach and seakale beet, beet, broccoli and cauliflower.

INTER-CROPPING

When planning your vegetable patch, try a bit of inter-cropping, to make the most of the space you have. The idea is to sow fast-growing vegetables next to, or even mixed in with, slow-growing ones. A typical example of this partnership is the combination of parsnips and lettuce – the latter is up and away long before the former. Parsnip, like most root vegetables, doesn't take kindly to transplanting, so it is sown well-spaced out, where it is to grow. Filling the space in between with lettuce couldn't be simpler, and it keeps the weeding down to a minimum at the same time.

Brussels sprouts are relatively slow growing, and lettuce, radishes, spring onions or stump-rooted carrots will grow happily between the rows. You can mix and match vegetable partnerships endlessly, according to your own taste in vegetables and the space you have to play with. Keep in mind, though, that with some of the taller-growing crops, such as peas and tomatoes, you will need to select shade-tolerant partners. Spinach is ideal in this respect, and thrives in the shade of runner beans, broad beans or peas. Shaded and lightly watered, the spinach is less likely to bolt. Brassicas, such as winter cabbage or turnips, can be partnered with peas or beans, and a new asparagus bed is an ideal spot where you can find some space for quick-growing salad crops.

One more thing to keep in mind when inter-cropping is that you will still need access to the vegetables, to weed, water and hoe between them, and also to harvest them. If you get carried away with inter-cropping, and pack the plants too close together, you may find yourself walking on one crop while looking after the other. No matter how shade-tolerant a crop is, it will still need plenty of air circulating round it – plants packed too tightly together are an open invitation to pests and diseases, such as fungal infections.

The best yield will come from tomato plants properly watered, fed and supported at all stages

PLANTING TOMATOES

Tomatoes sown in a heated greenhouse are now ready for transplanting. Transfer to greenhouse soil, plant up in 9 in (23cm) pots or growing-bags; or use rings, (bottomless pots on pebbles, where seasons are too short, as in Upper Canada or Alaska.

GROWING TOMATOES IN CONTAINERS

For greenhouse cultivation, plant tomatoes in ring containers on a *pebble base, in individual pots, or evenly spaced in growing-bags*

SUPPORTING TOMATOES IN THE GREENHOUSE

1 Plant so the top of the rootball is level with the soil surface

2 Knot soft string around the stem and attach to a taut wire above

3 Tie the stem to a tall cane and tie in new growth as it occurs

The plants should be 6–9 in (15–23cm) tall, with first flower buds just opening. Space them 18 in (45cm) apart and water before and after planting. Keep them moist and apply a liquid feed regularly.

Tomato plants need support. Indoors or out, tie them loosely to canes. Otherwise, tie a soft string under the first truss and attach it to a wire running horizontally above the plants. Twist the stems gently around the string as they grow.

GROWING-BAG CROPS

Growing-bags are the perfect solution if you don't have as much open ground in your garden as you would like—and they are certainly indispensable to towns where perhaps a patio or balcony is all the 'garden' you have. Even if you are blessed with a good-sized garden, there are occasions when growing-bags are still to be preferred. Their special, peat-based soil mix is free from all the pests, diseases and weed seeds that so often plague normal garden soil. In addition, it has been specially manufactured to give the right balance of miner-als, nutrients and trace elements needed by plants if they are to thrive and crop well.

If you shop around, you may very possibly find them, even though they are not yet commonly sold in the US or Canada. It is sometimes cheaper to buy your soil mix in the form of growing-bags rather than in the usual sacks. As well as the usual size, about 3 × 1 ft (1m × 30cm), you can buy half-size bags, too – ideal for windowsills. With this smaller size, you have to be careful about watering–they can quickly dry out on the one hand, or get water-logged on the other, if you get your timing or quantities wrong.

The one thing growing-bags can't accommodate is deep-rooting plants–root crops, for instance. Tomatoes are fine, though, and seem to be a favorite growing-bag crop, likewise runner beans and shell beans. If you are feeling more adventurous, try any of the *Curcubit* family: cucumbers, marrows, even melons, especially if your growing-bag is in a greenhouse. On an equally exotic note, eggplants and green peppers are ideal growing-bag plants, especially if you select one of the forms specifically developed for container growing. Some produce masses of small peppers, about 3 in (7cm) long, pretty to look at and delicious to eat. 'Black Prince' is a good eggplant to select for container growing, as it has been especially bred for compactness.

You can make your growing-bag work even harder by underplanting tall-growing subjects with low-growing ones—lettuce, perhaps, parsley, or radishes. Alpine strawberries have such nice leaves and cheerful flowers that it is worth growing them for those reasons alone—the exquisitely fragrant berries are a gourmet's delight.

Let's face it—the bags themselves are not all that attractive, and there is a great temptation to shove them into a shaded, out-of-the-way spot. The bright colors selected by the various manufacturers to draw your eye to them at the garden center are just what you don't want as a focal point in your garden. Do not despair, though, as there are ways round the problem. Firstly, put the bag in the best position for the plant you intend to grow—usually this means full sun, and shelter as well. Healthy plants give more pleasure to the eye than sadly struggling ones. Next, disguise the bag. You can edge it with a double row of bricks, then scatter a thin layer of shredded bark, peat or pebbles over the surface. Suitable lengths of log propped round the bag will do the trick, too, and if the plants' growth eventually hides the edges, better still.

DISGUISING GROWING-BAGS

Stack a double row of bricks or logs around the bag, enclosing it tightly,

and scatter pebbles over the top to disguise the surface

Growing-bags can be placed on a balcony or similar confined space

Some importers even sell attachments for growing-bags, including a trellis-like framework to which climbing plants can be attached. Some growing-bags come with a built-in reservoir which you top up with water, and you can also buy special drip-feed equipment, to do the watering for you. On the whole, the larger growing-bags dry out less quickly than other containers, but it is a good idea to check them regularly, especially if you are growing tomatoes.

Try improvising, too. If, for example, the growing-bag is against a wall, then increase the light available to the plants by fixing a sheet of heavyweight aluminum foil behind – but not touching – the plants.

At the end of the growing season, there is no reason to discard the soil mix. Cut the bag open and, if you have a proper garden, use as a mulch or dig the soil mix into your soil to improve its texture. If you haven't a garden, use the contents, mixed with a soil-based mixture, for potting up plants.

GROWING ASPARAGUS

Although asparagus is looked upon as a luxury vegetable, it is surprisingly easy to grow if you have the space, and the time and patience to wait until the plants are ready to harvest. Unlike most other vegetables, it is a perennial and so needs a bed to itself, though you can sneak in some salad crops between the young asparagus crowns for the first year. If you do have bit of open, sheltered garden with well drained soil, why not treat yourself?

An area 6 ft (2m) square will take a dozen plants – enough to feed two – and if you plant two-year-old plants, you need only wait one year before you can start cutting the spears. Ideally, you should prepare the bed in the fall for planting in the following spring. Dig over the bed and incorporate plenty of well rotted garden compost or leaf mold, or a mixture of peat and bonemeal, and leave the surface rough over winter.

When you are ready to plant in spring, dig out three trenches, each the width of a spade and evenly spaced apart in the bed. Make the trenches 9 in (23cm) deep, and fork over the bottom to loosen the soil. Check for perennial weeds and remove every last trace of them, or they will grow in among the asparagus roots and will plague you for life. Next, replace some of the soil in the bottom of each trench, to make a slightly domed center, about 3 in (7.5cm) high. Keep the asparagus crowns well wrapped up while you prepare the trenches, so they don't dry out.

Place the spider-like crowns at 18 in (45cm) intervals along each trench, with the crowns on the domed center and the roots spread out over the curved sides. Cover with 3 in (7.5cm) of soil, and top it up gradually through the summer, as the young plants grow. By the end of the growing season, the trenches should be completely filled in. Water generously during the first growing season. They make very pretty, fern-like growth – the bit that is eaten is actually the tip of the young growing shoot – which should be left until it turns yellow and starts to die down in the fall. In windy sites it may need the support of bamboo canes, but be careful not to damage the crowns or underground shoots when you push them into the soil. Cut it back to 1 in (2.5cm) above the ground, and mulch with some well rotted compost – asparagus really does need a fertile soil.

Next spring, give the asparagus bed a good dose of fertilizer, such as a mixture of fish, blood and bonemeal, to encourage growth, and in early summer you should be able to harvest a spear from each plant. Leave the rest for the young plant to continue building up its strength – greed now will result in poor crops later. To get long, white stems, earth the plants up, in the same way as potatoes are earthed up: draw up the soil from either side of the trench, in late spring. Cut the spears cleanly with a sharp knife about 4 in (10cm) below the surface – you can buy special asparagus knives for the purpose. At the end of the season, gently scrape away the earthed-up soil.

It takes a good four years for a newly planted asparagus bed to start cropping heavily, and cropping is confined to six weeks a year, but this delicious vegetable is worth waiting for.

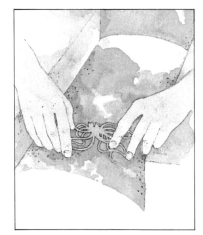

Plant crowns in a trench and let the radiating roots spread out

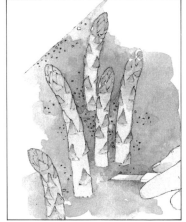

When harvesting, push a sharp knife under the soil to cut spears

UNUSUAL CROPS

Chinese cabbage (*Brassica cernua*) Sold as 'Pe-tsai', this vegetable is equally delicious cooked or served raw in salads. It is rather like a cos lettuce in appearance, with a pale green heart. Chinese cabbage does not transplant at all well, so sow it in June, where it is to grow, and thin the seedlings to 1 ft (30cm) apart. Keep well watered in dry weather and harvest from August onwards.

Endive (*Cichorium endivia*) This attractive, half-hardy annual has finely curled leaves, and makes a good late-fall and early-winter substitute for lettuce–it is considered a delicacy in Italy and France. Sow 'Moss Curled' from April to July for fall harvesting, 'Batavian Green' from July to September for winter crops. Blanch by covering with a pot or tying up the outer leaves to remove the bitter taste.

Corn salad or Lamb's lettuce (*Valerianella locusta*) This has smooth, ovoid leaves which are delicious at any time of the year but especially in winter salads. Sow in succession as for endive, and make sure you choose a sunny, sheltered spot for fall sowing. It is pretty enough to grow in pots, but don't let it flower, or the leaves will coarsen, and the plant will die. You can harvest lamb's lettuce either by pulling up the whole plant, like harvesting round lettuce, or picking a few leaves from each plant, so they continue to produce tender, young leaves over a longer season.

Land cress (*Barbarea praecox*) True watercress is difficult to please–it needs wet ground to thrive–but land cress, or American cress, as it is sometimes called, will give you the same peppery taste without any of the trouble. Successional sowings starting early provide summer crops, and a fall sowing will be ready where winters are late. A lightly shaded spot is best and provide water if the soil is at all dry.

Radicchio Devilishly expensive in the shops, if you can find it at all, this is a salad vegetable well worth growing. The sharp-tasting, dark-red leaves are veined with white, and just one or two leaves added to a mixed salad will make it special. Grow it as you would lettuce, sowing it successionally from May onwards. Because it is perennial, radicchio can be left over winter–given a bit of protection–to crop again in the spring. Radicchio, sometimes known as red chicory, can also be blanched.

Winter radish (*Raphanus sativus*) Quite unlike the ordinary radish to look at, winter radish grows to a great size and can weigh 18 oz (500g) or more. 'China Rose' is the red-skinned form; 'Black Spanish' is the black-skinned alternative. Both have crisp, white flesh. Sow in July and again in August, and thin to 6 in (15cm) apart. They can remain in the ground until you need them in winter, but be prepared to give them a bit of protection in very hard weather. Slice or grate them in salads, or lightly cook them.

Dandelion (*Taraxacum officinale*) One of the most notorious garden weeds can, in another guise, pep up salads with their sharp-tasting leaves. Give dandelion a try if you have an odd corner in your garden–just make sure the seed heads don't form. Sow in April or May, and pick the leaves any time of year. To give a milder taste, blanch them like endive by tying the leaves tightly together, or earth the lower leaves up, like celery, for the same results. However you choose to eat them, eat them young, as they get bitter with age.

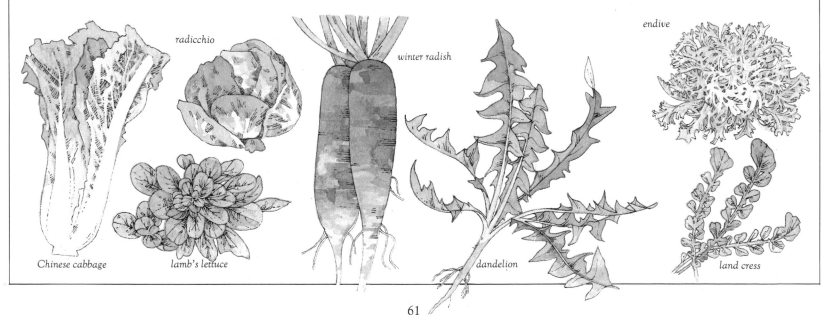

radicchio

winter radish

endive

Chinese cabbage

lamb's lettuce

dandelion

land cress

May

The garden is alive with growth
and flowering now, and lilacs, rhododendrons and
azaleas are at their finest. Summer seems just
around the corner—but night temperatures can still
dip to freezing, so be wary of planting out half-
hardy bedding plants and vegetables too soon.
Lengthening evenings make working in the garden a
pleasure, and the first crops are almost ready, but
keep a look out for the first surge of garden pests.

A dazzling mass of blooms
covers a Kurume hybrid azalea (left).
These evergreen hybrids are more tender than
deciduous azaleas and need protection from
cold winds and early-morning sunshine

Jobs for the month

General
Plan and plant a flower border
Deal with weeds among flowers,
vegetables and fruits and in the
lawn
Attend to container-grown plants

Flowers
Support herbaceous perennials in
windy sites
Continue sowing annuals
Harden off fuchsias and
pelargoniums to be planted
outside; pot on those to be kept in
containers
Plant out hardy perennials and
alpines grown from seed
Trim alpines after flowering and
propagate by division
Place lilies grown in pots outdoors
Harden off bedding plants
Plant out dahlias in late May and
chrysanthemums in early May in
sheltered gardens
Lift and heel in spring bulbs
Begin planting hanging baskets and
tubs

Lawns
Increase mowing and deal with
remaining weeds

Roses
Remove suckers and spray against
insect pests

Trees and shrubs
Remove faded flowers from
rhododendrons, lilacs, camellias,
azaleas and pieris
Begin planting tender shrubs
Clip hedges and begin training
topiary plants

Fruit
Remove suckers and thin
raspberry canes
Mulch strawberries and protect
from slugs and frosts
Bark-ring non-flowering apple and
pear trees
Start to thin gooseberries and
established plums and cherries
Plant out melons
Train grape vines

Vegetables
Continue sowing vegetables in
succession, including winter
cabbage, carrots, turnips, lettuce,
spinach, rutabagas, salad
cucumbers, zucchinis, pumpkins,
squash and marrow
Sow chicory, Chinese cabbage,
radicchio (see page 61) and
sweetcorn
Sow basil, marjoram and
edible pod peas outdoors
Plant out self-blanching celery
Harden off eggplants, peppers and
tomatoes
Continue earthing up potatoes
Pinch out the growing tips of
broad beans
Fix supports for runner beans and
shell beans, and sow or plant
out
Provide supports for peas
Thin vegetable seedlings sown
earlier in spring, including carrots,
onions and leeks
Feed tomatoes and pinch out
unwanted side shoots

Plants of all sorts will be making a big effort in your garden now, both those you cherish and the weeds, which are quick to take advantage of the warm weather. There is no substitute for hand weeding newly emerging flower and vegetable seedlings, though you can hoe between the rows in seed beds. Herbaceous and mixed beds will need your attention, too. Once the perennials, annuals and bedding plants are full size, they will smother any weeds that appear beneath their foliage, but it is a bit early in the season to rely on that alone.

While there is plenty of work to do in flower and vegetable beds, it's a good time to attend to container-grown plants, which will soon form a flourishing outdoor display now that summer is on the way.

Herbaceous veronicas grow easily in well-drained soil and a sunny and open position

FLOWERS

As the weather becomes warmer and drier, take more note of your plants' needs. Water seedlings and water and liquid-feed established plants as necessary.

STAKING HERBACEOUS PERENNIALS

Herbaceous perennials will be putting on rapid growth now. Tall-growing ones, such as delphiniums, or those with very heavy flower heads will need staking. 'Does not need staking' is often a selling point with many of the new, dwarf forms of old favorites, developed by plant breeders. These scaled-down plants carry huge flowers but tend to lack the gracefulness of their taller-growing cousins.

Three or four bamboo stakes per plant will give strong support—as the young plants grow, take strong twine from cane to cane and criss-cross it through the center. There are other ingenious plastic and metal devices, including a metal ring on three legs. The plants grow up through the center.

Plastic mesh netting can be stretched horizontally between four bamboo stakes. As the plants grow you can add a second layer of netting for extra support. An old-fashioned, but economic and very sensible solution is to use twiggy brushwood or pea sticks, pushed vertically into the ground around the plant. Be careful not to harm young growing shoots, and if you slant the brushwood slightly outwards from the center, the plants will follow the lead, letting in plenty of light and air.

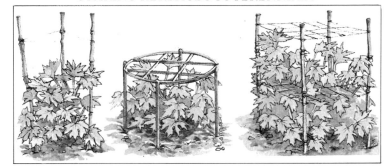

STAKING HERBACEOUS PERENNIALS

Let the young plants grow into the support – heavy canes and twine, a wire plant support, or wire mesh stretched between four canes

HARDY AND HALF-HARDY ANNUALS

You can still sow hardy annuals, to flower in late summer. Half-hardy annuals can be sown now, too, but outdoors give them shelter under cloches. Many annuals can be transplanted to tubs, window boxes or hanging baskets (see page 68).

Cuttings of pelargoniums and fuchsias taken in spring can be moved into larger pots and hardened off now, for planting out towards the end of the month. Half-hardy annuals grown from seed or bought ready-grown in trays should be hardened off as well. If you are using a cold frame, give the plants as much fresh air as possible. Take the cover, or 'lights', off during the day, and return them at night when the temperature drops. Cherry pie, or heliotrope, and old-fashioned cannas are particularly frost-tender, so keep them under cover for an extra week or two.

ALPINES

Any hardy perennials or alpines sown from seed early in spring can

Potted lilies can now be moved outside. Place in a sunny, sheltered spot and keep well watered

be planted out now, but they are unlikely to flower this year, so keep them in a nursery bed. Alpines that flowered last month can do with a trim, to tidy up their appearance. Cut back hard, as it really is a case of having to be cruel to be kind. They will put on rapid new growth and some will even reward you with a second, late-summer crop of flowers. You can make more alpines now, by dividing them into several small plants. Use two kitchen forks, placed back-to-back, to gently tease the roots apart.

LILIES

Lilies grown in pots can be moved out towards the end of the month to light up the garden with their good looks. Give them a sunny, sheltered spot and remember to keep them well watered.

UNDER GLASS

Harden off bedding plants and do not plant out until all danger of frost is over.

HEELING IN BULBS

Daffodils, tulips and hyacinths may well be past their best now, but still taking up valuable space in the garden. You may want to get on with bedding out summer plants, or sowing another batch of hardy annuals, and the bulbs need moving. If their leaves are still green, it means that the plant is producing and storing food for next year, which will in turn provide the energy for flower production. They will need heeling in until the goodness in the leaves and flower stem has found its way back into the bulb.

Select an out-of-the-way spot, preferably sunny. Dig a V-shaped trench, about 6 in (15cm) deep. Lift the bulbs carefully, retaining the fine white roots, and snap off the spent flower head. Place the bulbs in the bottom of the trench, with their leaves and stems pointed upwards. Replace the soil and firm it, taking care not to crush the stems. A scattering of slug pellets is a good idea.

Once the foliage has died down–or if it has already died down when you come to lift the bulbs from their flowering positions–they can be lifted and stored indoors until the fall. Clean them carefully, rubbing off any soil still sticking to them, and store in a single layer in a dry, cool place.

Finally, always resist the temptation to snip off the green leaves, in the interest of tidiness, once the flowers are over. This weakens the plant so much that the following year's flowers are jeopardized.

BIENNIALS TO GROW FROM SEED

Though it seems a long time away, from now until July you can start off biennials from seed for next spring's display. With most biennials, the sooner you sow, the better, to get good-sized, strong plants by the time the fall cold sets in. After that, no more growing is done, and all the energy goes into flower production. Two exceptions to the rule are Brompton stock and pansies which, if sown now, will flower prematurely and weakly, in the fall, and give you nothing next spring.

Because they take so long to reach flowering, compared to annuals, if you can, start them off in a nursery bed and move them next fall to their final positions. Alternatively, try one of the annual Sweet Williams on the market— sow in spring for summer flowering and cut out the wait.

LIFTING BULBS

1 Dig deeply to lift the plants, to avoid damaging roots or bulbs

2 Put them into a V-shaped trench and cover the bulbs with soil

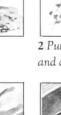

3 Lift the heeled bulbs and clean off soil and dead skin

4 Store the bulbs until the fall, in a box, kept cool and dry

BIENNIALS

Canterbury bell (*Campanula medium*) A tough biennial up to 3 ft (1m) high, Canterbury bell comes in pink, white or blue forms. 'Calycanthema' can be had in single or double forms.

Double daisy (*Bellis perennis*) Though classified as perennial, double daisies give the strongest displays when treated as biennials, replaced by fresh stock once flowering is over. Most grow to 6 in (15cm), but there are dwarf forms, 4 in (10cm) high. Colors range from white through pink, rose and deep crimson.

Forget-me-not (*Myosotis*) An old-fashioned and most charming flower, heights range from 6–15 in (15–37cm) and colors from the typical bright-blue to deep ultramarine and rose-pink. Forget-me-nots, if happy where they are, will self-seed in every nook and cranny.

Honesty (*Lunaria*) Better known for its silvery, oval, paper-thin seed heads, honesty has pretty purple flowers from April onwards. 'Variegata' has white-splashed leaves and pale flowers. Quite happy in shade, honesty self-seeds and will establish itself permanently.

Iceland poppy (*Papaver nudicaule*) This is a short-lived perennial often listed as a biennial in seed catalogs. 'Champagne Bubbles' is a good

F_1 hybrid, 2 ft (60cm) tall, in a wide range of pastel colors. For a dwarf form, try 'Garden Gnome Mixed', 1 ft (30cm) high, with white, yellow, orange and red flowers.

Polyanthus (*Primula*) A perennial giving the best display when treated as a biennial, polyanthus comes in heights ranging from 6–12 in (15–30cm) and a variety of attractive flower colors. Seeds are small and should be soaked in water before sowing to encourage germination.

Stock (*Matthiola incana*) East Lothian and Brompton stocks are grown as biennials. They give sweetly scented flowers in shades of white, pink, mauve, rose, crimson and purple. The plants are bushy and should be spaced 9 in (23cm) apart.

Sweet William (*Dianthus*) The exquisitely fragrant and brightly colored flowers of Sweet Williams look best grown in a mass rather than dotted about. Heights range from 6 in (15cm), excellent for edging, to 2 ft (60cm) or more, for mixed borders and cutting.

Wallflower (*Cheiranthus*) You will get the traditional blaze of color with mixed wallflowers, but for a more subtle effect try one of the single-color strains. Sow them at the end of the month, thin out or move them to 6 in (15cm) spacings when the seedlings are 2 in (5cm) high. Pinch out growth points to encourage side shoots.

Flowers for the month

The cottage-garden flowers take over in May, with last month's forget-me-nots and wallflowers joined by double daisies (*Bellis perennis*), columbines, graceful, arching Solomon's seal and the first of the peonies. Of the tulips, the small, shy species of early spring have been overtaken by the grand show-stoppers—the Darwin, cottage, Rembrandt and parrot tulips—tall, vigorous and colorful.

Vying for your attention are the pink and white bleeding hearts (*Dicentra spectabilis*) and the bright yellow globe flower. Blue is provided by several cottage-garden classics, notably the flag iris (*I. germanica*), pansies and the pale-blue spikes of veronica (*V. gentianoides*).

Shrubs and trees in the garden are not to be outdone. Lilacs are filling the air with fragrance, overwhelming the lightly scented,

but bright-yellow, laburnum flowers on display now. Adding even more color are the garden forms of thorn—'Paul's Double Scarlet', the pink 'Rosea' and the double-pink 'Rosea Pleno-flore'. Rhododendrons and deciduous azaleas continue their show, but are starting to be challenged by a few of the early roses—*Rosa hugonis* and 'Canary Bird', with single soft and bright-yellow flowers respectively.

Clematis montana will be displaying its white flowers, with the named forms 'Elizabeth' producing pink, 'Rubens' giving soft, rosy-pink and 'Tetrarose', lilac-pink flowers respectively.

The finishing touches to the garden in May are added by wisteria, with hanging bunches of sweet-pea-like flowers, mauve, violet-blue or white. Walls, fences and pergolas are transformed into curtains of color now.

1

4

6

2

3

5

1 *Paeonia delavayi* **2** *Tulipa* 'Oriental Splendour' **3** *Bellis perennis* **4** *Rhododendron schlippenbachii* **5** *Dicentra spectabilis* **6** *Clematis montana* 'Rubens'

A GARDEN IN A BASKET

Towards the end of this month—or early June if you live in a cold area—you should be planting up hanging baskets for a good summer display. Wire baskets for hanging plants are now available made from plastic or metal. Whichever you choose, you will need to line the basket with something to stop the soil from becoming too dry. Sphagnum moss, which is the most attractive, is too porous to use on its own. Try lining the inside of the moss with black plastic or even aluminum foil, to help retain moisture. Make a few slits in the plastic or foil liner, though, because the moss is living and will need a source of water too.

You can dispense with the moss altogether, and line a wire basket with dark-colored plastic alone, or a form of plastic foam which has slits in it which adapt to fit the shape of the basket. Or you can buy ready-made, compressed cellulose basket liners. These can be pierced easily with scissors or a sharp knife where you want to plant trailers—lobelia for instance—in the side, and have the added advantage of looking like soil, but keeping moisture in.

An alternative to wire baskets is hanging baskets made of solid plastic, complete with a fixed saucer underneath to catch any drips. On the minus side, it is not usually possible to plant anywhere but the top, though trailers will soon go over the edge and hang down. Though it has many uses, plastic is not particularly pretty in the garden, especially green plastic, which, by mimicking the color of leaves, seems to draw attention to its unnaturalness.

PLANTING A HANGING BASKET

1 *Support the basket in a bucket. Line it with moss, and fit a plastic lining inside the moss*

2 *Fill the lined basket with soil-based mix, or a mixture of soil and peat-based soil mix*

3 *Make slits in the plastic liner and insert small trailing plants, firming the soil to hold the roots in position*

4 *When planting the top of the basket, put the tallest plant at the center and leave a gentle depression in the soil around it*

5 *Plant trailers near the rim and encourage the stems into place by pegging them with hairpins*

Sit the basket in a bucket and, if it needs lining, put the moss, plastic or cellulose liner in place. Begin filling it with soil-based mixture or, if weight is going to be a problem, a combination of soil- and peat-based mixture. Never use peat alone as it dries out extremely quickly and, once dry, it is very hard to moisten it thoroughly.

Make holes in the side of the liner and put in trailing plants as you go, gently pushing their roots in from the outside and covering them with soil mix. Work your way up to the rim of the basket, putting the tallest plants in the center, trailers and edgers towards the outside. Remember that there is bound to be a bit of settlement, so fill the basket generously with compost to allow for it. Leave a small depression in the center, to help the water sink in, rather than spilling over the edge. Finally, encourage trailers on their way over the side by fixing them in position with large hairpins pressed into the soil.

SITING A HANGING BASKET

Ideally, you should know exactly where your hanging basket is to go even before you buy your plants. Some annuals tolerate, or even prefer, a bit of shade, while others won't even open without plenty of full sun, so pick your plants accordingly. A basket hung in light shade will not lose moisture as quickly as one hung in full sun, and will need watering less frequently. Watering is a factor that must be faced—fully moist soil mix can be surprisingly heavy. If you can, hang your basket with a pulley system, so you can haul it up and down at will. Not only

An attractive hanging basket will brighten up a porch or patio throughout the summer months

helpful for watering, this system allows you to get at the plants for deadheading, general care and tidying up. Or you can buy a special watering kit which includes a lance so you can water baskets above head-height, though water does tend to run back down your arm as you do so.

With all hanging baskets, it is a good idea to take them down regularly—say, once a week—and plunge them in a basin of water until they are thoroughly saturated. If you are careful, no harm will come to the plants growing out of the side of the basket.

Hanging baskets will produce better displays if you can give them a sheltered spot rather than a draughty, windy one – passageways between houses are notoriously windy and plants become desiccated very quickly in such a position. Another consideration is circulation patterns in your garden—what you don't want is a basket that gets bumped every time someone opens a door or gets up from a certain chair on the patio. Either keep them well above head height or tucked out of harm's way.

CONTAINER PLANTS

Many garden and indoor plants can be used to make attractive container-grown displays in summer. Choose from the several species that have both bushy and trailing forms, try a large climber in a spacious tub or trough—give it adequate support—or create a vivid mass of small flowering plants.

Begonia Bushy or trailing plants with flower clusters or single blooms.

Busy Lizzie (*Impatiens*) Bushy plants with a profusion of flowers.

Cherry pie (*Heliotropium*) A large shrub with finely scented flowers.

Chilean glory vine Fern-like foliage and orange-red flowers, climbing up to a height of 10 ft (3m).

Coleus Richly variegated foliage for a window box or tub.

Cosmos The dwarf form grows up to 2 ft (60cm) high, with attractive flowers.

Fuchsia Elegant, drooping growth, perfect for hanging baskets.

Italian bellflower (*Campanula isophylla*) A delicate trailer with blue or white star-shaped flowers.

Livingstone daisy (*Mesembryanthemum*) Prostrate plants in sunset colors.

Lobelia Bushy or trailing growth with a mass of vivid blue flowers.

Marigold Upright plants with long-lasting flowers in sunshine colors.

Pansy Available in dozens of forms, all with rich, velvety blooms.

Pelargonium Fresh, vigorous foliage and bright flowerheads.

Petunia Bushy or spreading flowering plants suitable for all types of container.

Senecio Spreading sprays of attractive deeply-cut, silver-gray foliage.

Slipper flower (*Calceolaria*) The spotted, pouch-shaped flowers do well outdoors in sun or partial shade, provided the plant is sheltered from strong winds.

Verbena Upright plants with bright flower clusters and toothed leaves.

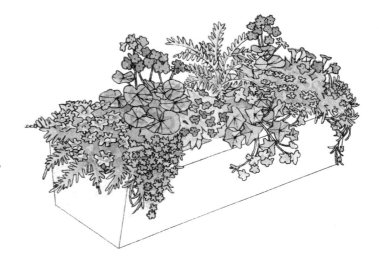

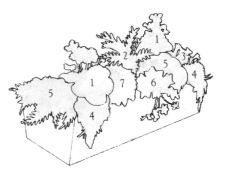

1 Zonal geranium (*Pelargonium × hortorum*) **2** *Centaurea cineraria* **3** Petunia (*P. hybrida*) **4** *Lobelia erinus* **5** French marigold (*Tagetes patula*) **6** Ivy-leaved pelargonium (*P. peltatum*) **7** Busy Lizzie (*Impatiens walleriana*). *There is plenty of variety here in the many shapes, sizes and colors of the flowers and foliage*

CREATING
A FLOWER BORDER

Every bit of a small garden should be so planted that it offers interest and color for as long a period as possible. Traditional herbaceous beds and borders and summer bedding have nothing to offer from late fall to late spring. A return to mixed borders and beds is now popular with a mosaic of shrubs—trees also if there is room— perennial bulbs and annuals.

The backbone of your mixed flower border or bed will be provided by the permanent residents—firstly the shrubs, planted well enough apart to leave plenty of room for plants which are summer guests only. If you think that shrubs have no business in a flower border, think of the displays put on by hydrangeas, shrub roses or camellias, to name a few. If you select your shrubs carefully, they will add a complementary green backdrop to your display even when they are not in flower, providing a foil for bright garden colors.

Next are the herbaceous perennials. These long-term plants usually remain in one spot for four or five years before needing lifting and dividing—or moving elsewhere if they clash with their neighbors. Choose some that are evergreen for winter effect, eg *Bergenia cordifolia* and hybrids, hellebores, tellima, red lungwort (*Pulmonaria rubra*). Bulbs, likewise, can usually be left undisturbed for several years, to multiply in peace. Good bulbs for mixed flower borders include alliums, nerines and summer hyacinths (*Galtonia*) as well as the popular tulips and daffodils.

While choosing and siting shrubs requires the most thought and careful planning, since they are relatively unmovable once established, and herbaceous perennials slightly less so, it is with the annuals and bedding plants that you can take a chance and ring the changes. Try a splash of color here or there, and repeat it or replace it the following summer. Annuals from seed are cheap and easy to grow—hardy ones can be sown *in situ* and left to get on with it. And the range of plants available is much wider when grown from seed than when bought in trays from a garden center.

If you haven't sown your own half-hardy annuals from seed, you can buy these in trays, ready-grown. They are often for sale much earlier in the year than they can be safely planted out. You can either wait to buy them until frost is finished or, if you are worried that all the best ones will be gone, buy now and keep them in a greenhouse or other light, frost-free place for a couple of weeks. You can usually buy bedding plants up to the end of June and into July, and they can be very useful to fill gaps left by spring-flowering biennials, such as forget-me-nots, wallflowers and Sweet Williams. Whether you sow annuals *in situ* or pop in ready-grown plants, make sure the ground is weed-free, or your plants will be fighting a perpetual battle for survival. A few slug pellets will be useful, too, not only around annuals but also tender young delphinium and lupin shoots.

What plants to include and how to arrange them can be perplexing, and also how to strike a balance between a color scheme that is dull and one that looks like the remnants of a jumble sale. As a general rule, go for massing rather than spotting—five or seven plants of a single sort are much nicer than using the same number of different plants. When you have planted large groups, try blurring the boundaries between one group and another, by allowing, or even encouraging, an intermingling of the neighboring plants. This does *not* mean setting them out like a checkerboard, though, as this never happens in nature, and nature is always a good reference point in these matters.

Though it is called a flower border, it is also a leaf border, if you think about it, and plants that have attractive leaves, such as the bold foliage of bear's breeches or the strap-like clumps of African lily leaves, should be chosen over plants that merely have pretty flowers surmounting dull-looking leaves. Dahlias are, sadly, an example, though there are new forms with lovely bronze-red leaves. And sometimes flower colors can be so fierce that they actually need the cooling effect of a gray-leaved neighbour, such as cotton lavender or *Senecio (cineraria) maritima*.

Again, when gardens were grand, whole beds were given to flowers of a single color. You might like to try that on a smaller scale in your own garden; remember white offers little variation in tone.

If you want to try a rainbow mix of flower colors, you will probably have to have several goes at it before you get the scheme just as you want it. A very harsh orange, for example, can ruin a pleasing relationship between pinks, mauves and blues, and it is just a matter of trial and error. One last word: a flower border full of bright color is set off to advantage by a large expanse of a single color, whether it is the dark green of a yew hedge or the bright green of a lawn.

Form is as important as color, if you are interested in overall effect and not just dazzle. Tall, spiky plants, such as delphiniums, larkspur and red-hot pokers, are nicely balanced by the round, flat heads of yarrow, and prickly sea holly by the soft sprays of gypsophila. And some plants, such as lady's mantle and periwinkle, while not being show-stoppers in themselves, quietly weave and mingle through separate clumps of plants in a flower border, creating a unified effect and hiding the soil at the same time.

ALL SEASONS BORDER

1 *Anchusa italica* (B)
2 *Rudbeckia subtomentosa* (C)
3 *Delphinium* (C)
4 *Helianthus decapetalus* (C)
5 *Aster novi-belgii* (C)
6 *Monarda didyma* (D)
7 *Echinops ritro* (D)
8 *Achillea hybrid* (C)
9 *Chrysanthemum maximum* (D)
10 *Kniphofia* (D)
11 *Trollius ledebourii* (C)
12 *Gypsophila repens* (C)
13 *Sedum maximum* (D)
14 *Potentilla atrosanguinea* (C)
15 *Salvia × superba* (C)
16 *Liatris callilepis* (D)
17 *Achillea filipendulina* (C)

SHADE-TOLERANT BORDER

1 *Aconitum arendsii* (D)
2 *Thalictrum glaucum* (**D**)
3 *Eupatorium purpureum* (E)
4 *Campanula lactiflora* (D)
5 *Thalictrum aquilegifolium* (B)
6 *Dicentra spectabilis* (A)
7 *Campanula persicifolia* (D)
8 *Geranium psilostemon* (C)
9 *Lysimachia clethroides* (D)
10 *Anemone japonica* (B)
11 *Liriope graminifolia* (E)
12 *Doronicum caucasicum* (A)
13 *Polygonum milettii* (C)
14 *Doronicum cordatum* (A)
15 *Iris foetidissima* (E)

Note: Flowering times are indicated as follows: spring (A), early summer (B), summer (C), late summer (D), fall (E)

This design for an updated version of the old-fashioned cottage garden retains all the charm of the original, with a profusion of bright colors and heady scents. It is a garden for the enthusiast, who will have to devote some time to upkeep, but whose efforts will be amply rewarded. The vegetable plot, one of the traditional elements of the cottage garden, has been omitted here, but it could easily replace the orchard section.

N

THE COTTAGE GARDEN

Cottage gardens were originally designed to make the maximum productive use of a limited space. There was no room for pure decoration; every plant had to have a purpose – either medicinal, culinary or cosmetic. Lawns were of no practical use, so instead there would have been a collection of flower beds criss-crossed by access paths. The overall effect would have been of a sweet-scented muddle – the perfect setting for a dream cottage.

There's no reason, however, why the same charming, informal effect cannot be achieved in the garden of a modern semi or any terraced house. Haphazard as they may seem, however, today's cottage gardens must be carefully designed to keep maintenance time to a minimum.

This rather long, thin garden is divided into three sections. (The design could easily be adapted to suit a shorter garden by leaving out one of these parts.) Immediately behind the house is a brick-paved area surrounded by sweet-smelling shrubs and herbaceous plants; a lovely scented rose of your favorite variety climbs attractively up the side of the house. The two large flower beds on either side of the garden are packed with plants of varying heights and colors –

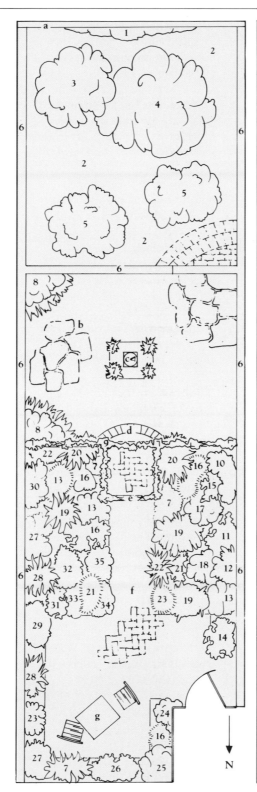

1	morello cherry, fan-trained
2	4 in (10cm) high meadow grass planted with 'wild' flowers, eg poppies, gaillardias, liatris, coreopsis, buttercups, daisies
3	pear tree
4	plum tree
5	dwarf apple trees
6	*Taxus baccata*
7	*Lavandula spica*
8	A rose of your choice
9	A rose of your choice
10	*Stranvaesia davidiana*
11	*Hemerocallis fulva*
12	*Viburnum tinus*
13	*Senecio greyi*
14	*Rosmarinus officinalis*
15	*Lupinus*
16	*Geranium macrorrhizum*
17	*Paeonia* 'Augustus John'
18	*Nigella damascena*
19	*Tiarella cordifolia*
20	*Kniphofia*
21	*Santolina incana*
22	*Verbascum bombyciferum*
23	*Bergenia cordifolia*
24	Any true climbing rose
25	*Ceanothus thyrsiflorus*
26	*Lobelia*
27	*Rosa rubrifolia*
28	*Iris pallida*
29	*Matthiola bicornis*
30	*Anemone japonica*
31	*Papaver rhoeas*
32	*Gypsophila*
33	*Aubrieta*
34	*Salvia officinalis*
35	*Phlomis fruticosa*
a	old 6 ft (2m) brick wall
b	random-patterned paving
c	sundial
d	step with 6 in (15cm) drop
e	wooden trellis with pergola
f	brick paving
g	garden furniture

many of which (peonies, lupins, verbascum, rosemary, hollyhocks) have come to be particularly associated with the old-fashioned cottage garden.

The plants spill over on to the central brick pathway that leads under the pergola of stout chestnut stakes. This forms a pretty garden divider and supports another beautifully scented climbing rose of your choice. The rose's perfume drifts into the peaceful paved area that comes as a relaxing contrast to the busy, colored flower beds. Based on the firm lines of the evergreen yew hedge, this second section of the garden uses only two plants – a white rose (any of your favorites) and lavender – planted in a repeating pattern in each corner to add to the calmer, more ordered atmosphere. The area is paved with flag stone, which is somewhat expensive. Pre-cast slabs make a cheaper substitute. A sundial, decorated with lavender in terracotta pots, provides an interesting visual focus that can also be seen from the house.

Finally, the archway through the hedge, offset to screen the third section of the garden from the house, leads the way to a small fruit garden. Under the young trees, the deliberately unmown grass is dotted with brightly colored meadow flowers – a tiny piece of 'English' countryside in which to relax and while away a sunny May afternoon.

BASIC HARDY PERENNIALS

Anemone (St Brigid or Giant French) Spring-flowering: blue, pink, scarlet, mauve cup-shaped flowers 15 in (37.5cm). Autumn flowering: pink, rose, white cup-shaped flowers 2–3 ft (60cm–1m).

Anthemis* Neat, white daisy-like flowers 6–12 in (15–30cm).

African lily (*Agapanthus*)* Umbels of blue, trumpet-shaped flowers on tall stems 2–2½ ft (60–75cm).

Astilbe* Spiky plumes of white, pink or red flowers 2–3ft (60cm–1m).

Baby's breath (*Gypsophila*) Clouds of tiny white flowers 3 ft (1m).

Bear's breeches (*Acanthus*)* Spikes of white and mauve flowers 2–3 ft (60cm–1m).

Bergenia Trusses of 5-petalled pink or white flowers over large evergreen leaves, 1–1½ ft (30–45cm) tall.

Blanket flower (*Gaillardia*) Yellow or red, daisy-like flowers 2–3 ft (60cm–1m).

Bleeding heart (*Dicentra*) Pink and white, heart-shaped flowers 2–2½ ft (60–75cm).

Bugle (*Ajuga*)* Deep-blue flower spikes 4–12 in (10–30cm).

Campanula Blue, pink or white bell-shaped flowers 8 in–4 ft (20cm–1.2m).

Champion (*Lychnis*)* Bright magenta, scarlet or white flowers, carried singly or in clusters 1–3 ft (30cm–1m).

Carnation (*Dianthus*) Pink, red, white, yellow or crimson flowers; some striped 15 in–2½ ft (37.5–75cm).

Centaurea White, yellow, blue or pink thistle-like flowers 1½–6 ft (45cm–1.8m).

Chinese lantern (*Physalis*) Orange seed pods; invasive 1½–3 ft (45cm–1m).

Columbine (*Aquilegia*)* White, pink, purple, blue or yellow, long-spurred flowers 1½–2½ ft (45–75cm).

Cone flower (*Rudbeckia*) Yellow, daisy-like flowers with black centers 1–3 ft (30cm–1m).

Coreopsis Yellow, daisy-like flowers 2½–3ft (75cm–1m).

Day lily (*Hemerocallis*)* Pink, orange, yellow or red, trumpet-shaped flowers 2–3ft (60cm–1m).

Delphinium Large spikes of blue, mauve or white flowers 2–6 ft (60cm–1.8m).

Fleabane (*Erigeron*) Pink, mauve or blue, daisy-like flowers with yellow centers 1–2 ft (30–60cm).

Foxtail lily (*Eremerus*) Pink, white, yellow or orange, star-shaped flowers on tall spikes 2–7 ft (60cm–2.1m).

Fringecup (*Tellima grandiflora*) Attractive evergreen, maple-like leaves and wands of white to reddish bells 1½ ft (45cm).

Geranium* Saucer-shaped pink, magenta, blue or white flowers 6 in–2 ft (15–60cm).

Geum Yellow, orange or scarlet, saucer-shaped or double flowers 1–2 ft (30–60cm).

Globe flower (*Trollius*) Yellow or orange, buttercup-like flowers 1–2½ ft (30–75cm).

Globe thistle (*Echinops*)* Silvery-blue, ball-shaped flowerheads 3–4 ft (1–1.2m).

Goat's beard (*Aruncus*)* Long creamy white flower plumes 2–6 ft (60cm–1.8m).

Golden rod (*Solidago*) Plumes or sprays of yellow flowers 1–6ft (30cm–1.8m).

Helenium Yellow, orange or red, daisy-like flowers 2–4 ft (60cm–1.2m).

Hellebore (*Helleborus*)* White, green, pink or rose, saucer-shaped flowers 1–2 ft (30–60cm).

Hollyhock (*Althaea*) Red, yellow, pink, white or mauve, funnel-shaped flowers on tall spikes 2–6 ft (30cm–1.8m).

Coreopsis auriculata 'Superba'

Anemone coronaria

Hemerocallis 'Golden Chimes'

Lupinus 'Festival Red'

Scabiosa caucasia 'Clive Greaves'

Pulsatilla vulgaris 'Rubra'

Hosta* White or pale lilac, trumpet-shaped flowers 1–2½ ft (30–75cm).

Iris* -Yellow, white, mauve or blue flowers 8 in–4 ft (20cm–1.2m).

Jacob's ladder (*Polemonium*)* Blue, white or mauve, saucer-shaped flowers 1–3 ft (30cm–1m).

Lady's mantle (*Alchemilla*)* Tiny greeny-yellow flowers 1–1½ ft (30–45cm).

Leopard's bane (*Doronicum*) Yellow, daisy-like flowers 8 in–3 ft (20cm–1m).

Lungwort (*Pulmonaria*) Red, blue and purple tubular flowers and handsome foliage; some species evergreen 10–18 in (25–45cm).

Lupin Tall flower spikes in a wide range of colors 2½–3 ft (75cm–1m).

Mallow (*Malva*) Funnel-shaped, pink or white flowers 2–4 ft (60cm–1.2m).

Michaelmas daisy (*Aster*) White, pink, blue, mauve or purple, daisy flowers 1–4 ft (30cm–1.2m).

Mullein (*Verbascum*)* Spikes of yellow, pink or white, saucer-shaped flowers 3–6 ft (1–1.8m).

Pasque flower (*Pulsatilla* or *Anemone pulsatilla*) White, purple, red or rose, cup-shaped flowers 1 ft (30cm).

Peony (*Paeonia*) Single or double, bowl-shaped pink, red, white or yellow flowers 2½–3 ft (75cm–1m).

Peruvian lily (*Alstroemeria*) Trumpet-shaped orange, yellow or pink flowers 2–3 ft (60cm–1m).

Phlox White, pink, purple, mauve or rose flower clusters 1½–4 ft (45cm–1.2m).

Poppy (*Papaver*) White, pink, or scarlet, single or double bowl-shaped flowers 2–3 ft (60cm–1m).

Pyrethrum White, pink or red, single or double, daisy-like flowers 2–3 ft (60cm–1m).

Ranunculus Yellow, single or double, 'buttercup' flowers 1–2 ft (30–60cm).

Red-hot poker (*Kniphofia*)* Yellow, orange or red tubular flowers 2–5 ft (60cm–1.5m).

St John's wort (*Hypericum*)* Yellow, cup-shaped flowers 1–1½ ft (30–45cm).

Scabious (*Scabiosa*) Large, single blue or mauve flowers with 'pincushion center' 1½–2 ft (45–60cm).

Sea holly (*Eryngium*)* Silvery blue, teasel-like flower heads 1–4 ft (30cm–1.2m).

Sea lavender (*Limonium*) Masses of tubular, blue or mauve flowers 1½–2 ft (45–60cm).

Shasta daisy (*Chrysanthemum*) Single or double, white daisy-like flowers with yellow centers 2–3 ft (60cm–1m).

Solomon's seal (*Polygonatum*)* White, pendant, tubular flowers on arching stems 1–4 ft (30cm–1.2m).

Speedwell (*Veronica*) Spikes of blue, mauve or white flowers 1–5 ft (30cm–1.5m).

Spurge (*Euphorbia*)* Tiny, yellow-green or orange-red 'flowers' 6 in–4 ft (15cm–1.2m).

Stachys Spikes of tubular, pink or purple flowers 6 in–2 ft (15–60cm).

Stoke's aster (*Stokesia*) White, pink, mauve or blue, China-aster-like flowers 1–1½ ft (30–45cm).

Stonecrop (*Sedum*)* Flat heads of star-shaped, yellow or pink flowers 1–3 ft (30cm–1m).

Valerian (*Centranthus*) Sprays of pink, red or white star-shaped flowers 1½–3 ft (45cm–1m).

Violet (*Viola odorata*)* Blue, purple, yellow or white flowers 6 in (15cm).

Yarrow (*Achillea*)* Clusters of small, daisy-like yellow, white or red flowers. In some species the clusters are more compact than others 1½–4 ft (45cm–1.2m).

* attractive foliage

CHRYSANTHEMUMS

The chrysanthemum genus includes a large and complex group of more than 200 annual and perennial plants, some of which are hardy, some not. All are popular, especially the huge show chrysanthemums, but, as with dahlias, the large blooms are really best displayed on the exhibition bench, rather than in the garden. The heavy weight of such blooms, which can be 8 in (20cm) across, is too much for the stems to support and so staking becomes inevitable. Also, disbudding is required, and you tend to sacrifice numbers of flowers – and also lose their natural grace to size.

There are hundreds of chrysanthemums from which to choose, and specialist nurseries provide a wide range for the keen grower. It is worth sending away for their catalogs and attending some of the larger flower shows, staged by horticultural societies, so you can see the flowers 'in the flesh'.

Annual chrysanthemums
These are grown from seed sown in March or April, and many are daisy-like in appearance. *C. carinatum* has single flowers, each marked in concentric rings of bright color – 'Court Jester' is a popular mix. *C. coronarium* has semi-double, bright-yellow flowers, and for window boxes and hanging baskets, the 9 in (23cm) high *C. paludosum*, with its tiny white marguerite flowers, is perfect. *C. parthenium*, sometimes sold as *Matricaria eximia*, is the feverfew of cottage gardens, and though it is a short-lived perennial, it is more often treated as an annual, grown from seed. Its yellow or white flowers are like tiny buttons, and there is a golden-leaved form available, well worth looking out for. And, confusingly, corn marigold is really an annual chrysanthemum, *C. segetum*, with bright yellow single flowers, lovely for cutting.

Hardy perennial chrysanthemums
Several species are included in this category, again mostly daisy-like in appearance and some are tough as nails, coming up year after year in the garden without any prompting at all. The shasta daisy (*C. maximum*) is one, the Hungarian daisy (*C. uliginosum*) is another – the latter is a fine back-of-the-border plant reaching 6 ft (1.8m) in height. The popular pyrethrums are more correctly *C. coccineum*, and it is their pink, rose-red or brilliant cerise flowers that earn them a place in many cottage gardens. The French marguerite, or Paris daisy (*C. frutescens*) is more like a shrub – and, indeed, can be trained as a standard – but is only half-hardy and smaller plants are often treated as half-hardy annuals, grown from seed each year.

Florists' chrysanthemums
These are divided into categories according to flower type, and each of these further sub-divided according to flower size.

Incurved chrysanthemums have fully double, globe-shaped heads up to 8 in (20cm) across. The tightly packed petals curve upwards and inwards.
Reflexed chrysanthemums have globe-shaped heads, up to 8 in (20cm) across. The petals curve down from the center and are much less closely packed.
Intermediate chrysanthemums used to be categorized as incurving, which is what the petals do, but much less tightly. Some have petals which are incurved at the top of the bloom, and reflexed towards the bottom. They can be up to 8 in (20cm) across.
Anemone-flowered chrysanthemums have semi-double flowers, with an 'eye' in the center, made by short, tightly-packed petals, with an outer ring of larger petals. These are slightly smaller than the incurved, reflexed and intermediates, though they can reach 5 in (12.5cm) in diameter.
Single chrysanthemums have one or more rows of long petals around a daisy-like center. Flowers can be up to 6 in (15cm) across.
Pompon chrysanthemums have

Chrysanthemum carinatum cultivar

Chrysanthemum maximum

'Marjorie Boden' (*incurved*)

'Tracy Waller' (*reflexed*)

small, round or button-shaped heads of tightly packed, downward-curving petals. The flowers can be up to 2 in (5cm) across.

Charm chrysanthemums are grown for their massive number of small flowers, rather than for individual blooms.

Cascade chrysanthemums have flexible stems and can be trained to trail downwards. The flowers are small but profuse in number.

Spoon, quill and spider chrysanthemums have uniquely shaped petals. Spider forms have long, thread-like petals. Spoon forms have petals which are broad and flat at one end, narrowing to form a 'handle' towards the center. Quill forms have straight, tubular petals. All have flowers up to 5 in (12.5cm) across.

Spray chrysanthemums can have any one of several types of flower, but all have relatively small flowers, up to 2 in (5cm) across. Spray chrysanthemums give an abundance of flowers rather than single specimens.

'Thora' (*anemone-centred*)

GROWING FLORISTS' CHRYSANTHEMUMS

If you are growing florists' chrysanthemums outdoors, early May is a good time to plant them out – sun and well-drained, fertile soil produce the best blooms, and shelter is advisable in the case of taller-growing forms. Give the soil an additional boost with a well-balanced fertilizer, natural or not. Spacing and staking depend very much on the variety chosen, but 1–1½ ft (30–45cm) between plants should suffice. If you are using stakes, put them in now, one per plant, and as the plants grow, loosely tie them to their stakes.

Protect newly planted chrysanthemums from slugs and birds at this time of year. Pellets based on methiocarb or metaldehyde will sort out the slugs, and black cotton zig-zagged over the plants will deter birds from eating the succulent young shoots. Fine-meshed netting is another anti-bird device.

The growing plants will need regular supplies of water, and

'Mason's Bronze' (*single*)

should be given a feed of liquid fertilizer every ten days from June until the flower buds show.

All chrysanthemums should be stopped – the growing point pinched out – when 6–8 in (15–20cm) tall. This induces the plant to send out strong side shoots, which in turn produce flowers. With spray, Korean and pompon-type chrysanthemums, that is all you have to do in the way of training. If you want huge blooms, you must restrict the number of flowers produced by disbudding, that is, removing all but the central flower bud on each stem, and also any excess stems and side shoots.

If you are growing chrysanthemums in pots, either indoors or for outdoor summer display, plant them in 3 in (7.5cm) pots filled with loam-based soil mix, to start off with. Plant shallowly – a good rule for outdoor planting, too – and not too firmly. Keep them lightly watered and shaded until established, then gradually pot them on as they grow, ending up with 8 in (20cm) pots. Stopping and feeding is the same as for outdoor, open-grown types.

Charm and cascade chrysanthemums are usually treated as half-hardy annuals, sown from seed in January or March to flower in the fall. Other than the initial stopping, charms need no further training, but cascades need quite complicated training to end up with two or three trailing stems covered in blossom.

Provide a sturdy cane for support, tying in new growth as it occurs

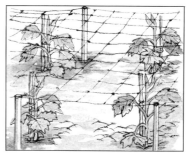

Protect young plants from birds with fine-meshed plastic netting

Pinch out the growing point when the plant is 6–8 in (15–20cm) high

Pinch out side buds to encourage a single large, central bloom

LAWNS

Continue weedkilling, if necessary. Broad-leaved weeds – lawn daisy and plantain, for example – can be treated with lawn sand or sulphate of ammonia now, as long as the weather is dry and calm. The chemicals settle on, and scorch, the broad-leaved plants, but not the narrow grass blades. A second application a couple of weeks later is useful. Hormone weedkillers are a more modern approach to the problem. These are available in solid or liquid form and quickly enter the plant's sap, being absorbed through the leaves. Hormone weedkillers are extremely powerful, so follow the manufacturer's directions precisely.

Adjust the mower to summer cutting early in the month. From now onwards it may be necessary to water the lawn during dry periods. Towards the end of the month apply a light dressing of nitrogenous fertilizer.

Cultivate sites for new lawns for fall sowing now and leave rough during the summer.

ROSES

Continue to control pests and diseases. Watch out particularly for the appearance of aphids, black spot, mildew and rust.

It's a good idea to check roses now for any suckers which may have appeared round the base of the plant. Most roses are grafted or budded onto a rootstock of a wild vigorous species, which means that the roots are from one plant, and the stems, leaves and flowers which comprise the

named variety, from another. Suckering is an attempt by the rootstock to start a life of its own by sending up shoots. These shoots are called suckers, and if they are not dealt with promptly, all the strength of the roots will be diverted into them. The rootstock will take over, and your own chosen rose will die.

How to distinguish a sucker growth presents problems for a beginner, particularly as a number of different roses are used as rootstocks and their shoots vary in appearance. Sometimes a sucker is easy to recognize, as some stocks produce very light green shoots that will probably have several leaflets. They look entirely different from the growth of a large flowered (Hybrid tea) or a cluster-flowered (Floribunda), but this is not an infallible guide. After you have had some experience, you will be able to recognize any sucker immediately, but to be on the safe side, trace the suspected sucker back to its source.

This will probably mean scraping a little soil away from the base of the plant to see where the sucker comes from. If it comes from below the budding union (a thickening of the main stem just above the roots, from which the canes of your rose sprout) it is a sucker. It should be pulled away from the root rather than cut, stopping short, of course, of pulling your rose up in the process.

This is the only way of making sure that no dormant buds are left behind to form new suckers. Never just cut a sucker off at ground level. All you will be doing then is pruning it and encouraging more strong growth. Treated like this, they should come away quite easily, provided that they are dealt

with promptly and not allowed to mature. The only real problem is when one comes from right under the rose, or from the middle of a tangle of old roots. Then there is probably nothing to do except to cut it back as far as possible and to keep an eye open for it emerging again—as it is certain to do.

This bright yellow Rosa xanthina 'Canary Bird' shows how care and attention can be rewarded

The stem of a standard rose is part of the rootstock, and any shoots that appear on the stem are the equivalent of suckers and should be broken off.

REMOVING SUCKERS

In a bush rose, expose the root junction and pull off the sucker

Break off any shoots appearing on the stem of a standard rose

TREES & SHRUBS

Now is the time to deadhead rhododendrons and azaleas as the individual flowers fade, so the plant wastes no energy in setting seed. It looks nicer, too, as some shrubs have a nasty habit of refusing to shed their faded flowers, which give the whole shrub a slightly used look. Go over your late-flowering camellias, and pieris and lilac at the same time, for faded flowers.

You can begin to plant out such tender shrubs as fuchsias and hydrangeas. The latter are as tough as can be, once established, but a newly planted specimen will need cossetting. Keep all newly planted shrubs watered if the weather turns dry. Established plants should be watered and liquid-fed as necessary.

Many of the quick-growing hedges, such as thorn, privet and evergreen honeysuckle (*Lonicera nitida*) will need to be checked for excessive growth. Often and lightly is better than leaving trimming too late, and having to prune drastically as a result. Regular trimming encourages compact, bushy growth, which is exactly what you want in a hedge. Evergreen barberries (*Berberis darwinii, B. × stenophylla*) grown as hedges can be clipped back after the flowers fade. If you have a long run of hedge, it is worth while investing in an electric trimmer which will make the work easier.

TRYING TOPIARY

While you have your shears or trimmer out, you might think about taking up the ancient art of topiary. Most small-leaved evergreens can be trained into fanciful shapes, but yew is considered the best. It can be cut back hard and will send out new growth, even from the woody base. Box is also good for topiary work, but on a smaller scale, and, less often, hol-

The art of topiary – trimming trees and bushes into ornamental shapes – dates back to Roman times. Yew is held to be the best evergreen for this purpose, but box can also be used

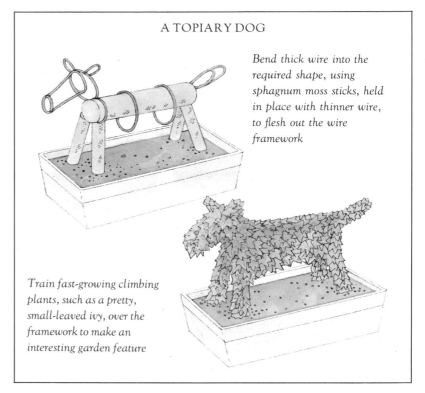

A TOPIARY DOG

Bend thick wire into the required shape, using sphagnum moss sticks, held in place with thinner wire, to flesh out the wire framework

Train fast-growing climbing plants, such as a pretty, small-leaved ivy, over the framework to make an interesting garden feature

ly, bay and firethorn are subjects for topiary. With these larger-leaved evergreens, you start to get the problem of having to trim very carefully to avoid the tatty appearance of leaves, cut in half, remaining on the shrubs. If you are starting your topiary from scratch, buy compact, well-branched shrubs, making sure that they branch from the base. Bigger, older specimens of shrubs, such as yew, are more expensive, take longer to get established, and may even respond more slowly to training.

Whether you are dealing with new or fully established plants, pick a shape that is simple—complicated forms look fussy and are very hard to get right. Pyramids, cones, balls and cubes are good shapes to start with. If you have your heart set on a bird, one of the traditional and more fanciful shapes, then choose a young bush and use stout wires to bend the young stems in the desired direction. Topiary is an art that requires plenty of patience, so don't be tempted to hack out the finished shape at a stroke. If shaping a fully grown bush, use an electric hedge trimmer, beginning at the top and working down. Step back from time to time to get a good look at how the job is going—that way you can correct mistakes before they get too big.

You can also train climbers into various shapes by using a sphagnum-filled wire frame. Variegated ivy or another small-leaved climber is best—indoors you might like to try the creeping fig (*Ficus pumila*). The more plants you use, the quicker the effect—a dog can be made in the space of a season, for example, with four ivies, one trained up each leg.

FRUIT

Established raspberry plants produce many more canes than they need to, so thin them now, to leave six per plant. Remove any weak, diseased or damaged canes first, and any suckers that have sprung up – you will be surprised how far away from the parent plant they can appear. The floppy canes will need supporting, and there are basically two systems. You can either put up two rows of parallel wires, inside which the canes grow and are loosely contained, and fix the wires to strong cross-pieces and posts at each end, or you can tie the canes individually to wires. For the latter you will need three horizontal parallel wires, the lowest 1½ ft (45cm) from the ground, and the remaining two 1½ ft (45cm) apart, again all fixed to strong end posts. Newly planted raspberries should be left to grow for the first season, and only the weakest canes removed.

Mulch summer-fruiting strawberries as soon as the fruit appears. Traditionally the mulching was done with straw, to keep mud off the fruit as well as keeping weeds down and the soil moist, but plastic sheeting or special strawberry matting will do just as well, and nowadays are easier to come by. Scatter slug pellets around the plants at the same time, and continue to protect them from night frosts. If mildew or graymold have been troublesome, dust your strawberry plants with a suitable fungicide, according to manufacturer's instructions (see page 184).

Continue your spraying regime from April, giving follow-up sprays as necessary. Again, try to

MULCHING STRAWBERRIES

As an alternative to mulching with straw or special matting, grow *strawberries on a raised bed through plastic sheeting*

avoid spraying when flowers are open (see page 57).

Pear and apple trees that stubbornly refuse to flower can be bark-ringed in May. Cut a thin strip, ¼ in (6mm) wide, half-way around the trunk, and repeat the

BARK RINGING

Remove a narrow strip of bark from each side of the tree. Bind the cut tightly with adhesive tape

exercise on the other half of the trunk next year. This reduces the flow of sap and slows down woody and leafy growth, hopefully encouraging flower production. It doesn't always work, but is worth a try. Remove any malformed and

under-sized fruits where trees have set very heavy crops, to relieve branches before the 'June drop'.

Thin shoots of established espaliered plums and cherries. Cut back the leaders of mature apples and pears grown as cordons, espaliers and dwarf pyramids. Begin thinning gooseberries.

Melons sown earlier in spring can be planted out towards the end of May, in a sunny spot or, preferably, a cold frame. Provide a rich soil and plenty of water, and pinch out the growing point when six leaves have formed.

Newly-planted grape vines will be producing shoots from the three buds left after initial pruning (see page 172). These will eventually need to be trained along wires spaced 16 in (40cm) apart, but for the first season simply tie them to a stout cane or post for support. All vines will benefit from applications of liquid fertilizer now and continued feeding throughout the growing season.

Melons sometimes need the protection of a cold frame when they are planted out. This is done towards the end of the month

VEGETABLES

Continue successional sowing of salad crops to keep up a regular supply. Lettuce sown from now on–and spinach, too–should be given light shade. Salad cucumbers, zucchinis, pumpkins, squash, chicory and marrows can be sown now–these love rich soil and should be given plenty of space to grow, 3 ft (1m) between plants. Next winter's staples, broccoli, cauliflower, cabbage and Brussels sprouts can be started off outdoors, together with root crops, such as rutabagas, turnips and carrots, and sweetcorn. To get the best pollination, plant sweetcorn in blocks, not rows–this also lessens the chance of wind damage. Basil, sweet marjoram and edible pod peas may also be sown outdoors.

Self-blanching celery seedlings can be planted out towards the end of the month, also in blocks, with 9 in (23cm) between plants. This close spacing helps them shade and blanch each other–put some earthed-up soil, wooden boards or

black plastic around the outside of the planting, to keep light off the end plants.

Harden off such half-hardy plants as eggplants, peppers and tomatoes. In the northern US they can go out at the end of the month, in extremes early June. Don't forget to pinch out the growing points of the first two, at about 6 in (15cm), to get bushy plants.

Continue to earth up potatoes as they grow, so no young tubers are exposed to the light, or they will become green and inedible.

As soon as the top cluster of flower buds has formed, pinch out the growing tips of broad beans. This helps keep down aphids, which are particularly partial to the succulent shoots.

Runner beans and shell beans can be sown now or planted out from the middle of the month. Prepare the supports for runner beans and climbing shell beans

Black plastic sheeting is used around dwarf shell beans as a mulch suppressing weeds and keeping the soil moist. Weigh down the sheeting to keep it in place

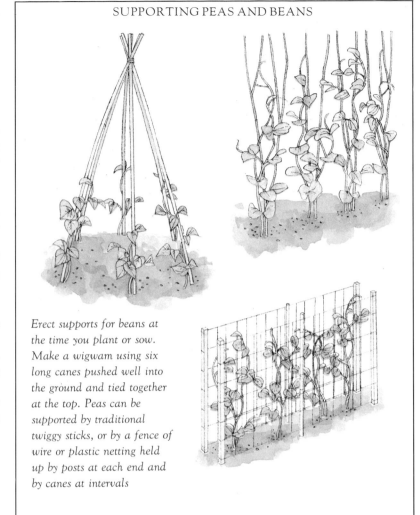

SUPPORTING PEAS AND BEANS

Erect supports for beans at the time you plant or sow. Make a wigwam using six long canes pushed well into the ground and tied together at the top. Peas can be supported by traditional twiggy sticks, or by a fence of wire or plastic netting held up by posts at each end and by canes at intervals

at the same time, so you don't disturb growing roots. The most decorative way of growing beans is to make a wigwam with six tall bamboo canes pushed into the ground, then lashed securely together at the top. Wigwams are easier to erect than the traditional rows of canes, and are less likely to be blown over in high winds.

Now is the time to provide support for growing peas as well– use traditional twiggy pea sticks or erect a temporary fence made from wire netting held in place by posts at each end of the row. Give

the netting additional strength by inserting bamboo canes through it at regular intervals, pushed well into the ground.

Thin the vegetable seedlings sown last month–carrots, turnips, onions and leeks, for example. Young lettuce thinnings can be transplanted elsewhere, if they are watered in thoroughly.

Tomatoes will need feeding– there are special proprietary liquid fertilizers available–and the unwanted shoots forming where the leaf stalks meet the main stem should be pinched out.

June

Summer is here at last
and the days are filled with the color and scent of
flowers. The salad season begins in earnest and the
first strawberries appear. Work in the garden is
tempered with enjoyment as the long, warm days
and light evenings give us time for leisure. Except in
the north, this is the month of the rose.

*A riot of color in a
summer flower garden (left), from the pink and
red roses in the foreground to the elegant white lilies,
the scarlet poppies and the yellow evening
primroses in the background*

Jobs for the month

General
Continue watering and weeding
Keep the greenhouse well
ventilated and shaded as necessary
Take softwood and leaf cuttings
Protect against insects and birds
Place the hardier house plants
outdoors

Flowers
Continue sowing biennials
Sow perennials and calceolarias,
cinerarias and fairy primroses
Continue planting out bedding
plants
Lift and divide bearded irises and
primulas after flowering
Continue training sweet peas
Move chrysanthemums outside
Stake tall-growing flowers
Propagate pinks from cuttings
Cut back or deadhead spent
flowers

Lawns
Keep Bermuda grass in place
Water during dry spells
Continue mowing

Roses
Disbud if large blooms wanted
Protect against pests and diseases

Trees and shrubs
Continue trimming hedges
Remove laburnum seed pods
Prune early-flowering clematis
Deadhead and prune shrubs that
have finished flowering

Disbud gray-leaved shrubs
Apply an acid compound to
hydrangeas if soil is alkaline

Fruit
Layer strawberries and remove
unwanted runners
Thin apples, plums and pears
Continue tying in the young
shoots of cane fruit
Summer-prune gooseberries and
red currants at the end of the
month
Train and pollinate melons
Continue training and tying in
grape vines
Begin harvesting gooseberries and
strawberries

Vegetables
Continue sowing salad crops,
including Chinese cabbage
Make a final sowing of peas and
snap beans
Thin carrots
Plant out tomatoes and pumpkins
(see page 45)
Transplant brassicas and leeks
Plant winter celery in trenches
Expose shallots to ripen
Continue pinching out tips of
marrows, cucumbers, broad beans
and side shoots of tomatoes as
necessary
Finish earthing up potatoes
Harvest new potatoes, fall-sown
peas
Stop picking asparagus
Begin harvesting herbs

Weeds will need attention in the shrubbery and flower beds as well as the vegetable and fruit gardens—more so if the weather has been warm and wet. Seed beds, with their expanses of bare earth, can easily be over-run with weeds, if you let them get a foothold. Watering newly planted, young and particularly thirsty plants—tomatoes and dahlias spring to mind—may become a daily routine in hot, dry weather.

Conditions in the greenhouse can become tropical—much to the detriment of most plants inside—this month, so keep it well ventilated and apply shading paint or screens if you haven't already done so.

Taking cuttings can keep you busy, but in the nicest possible way, as no heavy work is involved and the end results—new flowers, house plants and shrubs for free—are so rewarding.

Insects and birds will be after ripening fruit and succulent, young leaf growth, whether vegetable or ornamental plants, and your skills in outwitting them will certainly be tested this month.

HOUSE PLANTS

Some house plants appreciate a spell outdoors during the summer, and during June is a good time to put them out. Sun and heat will ripen the growth of plants like bougainvillea and cacti, and this improves their flowering in the coming year. It also gives you a chance to clean up the windowsill or greenhouse bench. If you keep your house plants on saucers or in waterproof containers, give these a thorough scrub as well.

Outdoors, choose a level spot, warm and draught-free, for the

This plunge bed houses a large number of pots, but the principle is exactly the same on a smaller scale in your own garden

house plants, and out of traffic's way on a patio or balcony. Some house plants, such as the sweetly scented angel's trumpets (*Datura suaveolens*) and agaves, revel in full sun. Others, such as aspidistra, begonias and Indian azaleas need protection from strong sunlight, and a lightly shaded spot suits them better.

Plants in pots dry out very quickly, so be prepared to water them, possibly on a daily basis. As a rough guide, the smaller the pot, the quicker it dries out, and peat-based mixtures dry out more quickly than loam-based ones.

You can also turn the plants out of their pots and use them as bedding to replace gaps left by flowers that have finished—wallflower and sweet Williams, for instance. Again, take the opportunity to scrub out the empty pots, and store them away.

A half-way solution is to plunge

the pots directly into the soil up to their rims, or into an old-fashioned plunge bed. Make one out of a wooden frame, filled with coarse sand, weathered boiler ash or peat. Pots in plunge beds are much less affected by sudden temperature changes, and need watering less frequently than they would standing in the open.

Remember to spray your house plants, whether indoors or out, with tepid water, to keep red spider mite at bay. This pest tends to be troublesome in hot, dry weather. Bronzed, netted leaf undersides are sure signs of infestation, and spraying will be necessary (see page 184).

FLOWERS

Continue sowing biennials (see page 66) and add forget-me-nots and Brompton stocks to the list, for sowing at the end of the month.

If you have the room, try sowing perennials as well. Some of them—columbine (*Aquilegia*), for instance—are very easy to grow from seed, and there is always a special pleasure to be had from raising a plant yourself. Most seed catalogs have a range of the more popular perennials, or you can collect seed from your own plants, or from a friend's or neighbor's garden.

Sowing perennials indoors in trays or individual pots is fairly straightforward (see page 10) and is best for fine seed. Outdoors, seed drills should be spaced 6 in (15cm) apart and $\frac{1}{4}$–1 in (5mm–2.5cm) deep—the smaller the seed, the shallower the drill. Primulas, violas and pansies can be sown now, too, but at this time of year it is best to provide the seedlings with light shade. And whether sown in sun or shade, seedlings may need protection from birds—zig-zagging black cotton over the beds is one method of protection.

Once your tall bearded irises have finished flowering, lift and divide any clumps of rhizomes that have become overcrowded—once every four or five years should suffice. Carefully lift the clump with a fork, and remove and discard the old, central section. Select strong growths with at least a 4 in (10cm) long piece of rhizome and cut the leaves back by half. Arrange the rhizomes so that their leaves are all angled in the same direction and then plant them firmly, barely covering the rhizomes with the soil.

For a good display in the greenhouse or house next winter, begin sowing calceolarias (C. × *herbeohybrida*), cinerarias (C. *cruenta* hybrids) and fairy primroses (*P. malacoides*) under glass. The seeds are very fine, so give the lightest possible dusting of soil mix or sand to cover them.

The purple-blue and gold of the Iris xiphioides provide a splash of deep and dramatic color in a summer garden

Continue bringing out tender bedding plants and half-hardy annuals that have been hardened off, and plant them in their permanent positions. The colder and more exposed your garden, the later in June this should be done. Keep a close watch on the local weather reports, as a double check.

DIVIDING RHIZOMES

1 *Lift the overcrowded plants from underneath with a fork*

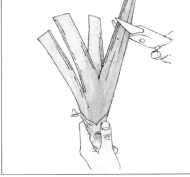

2 *Cut off the outer sections, each with a length of rhizome attached*

3 *Cut the foliage tips so the new plant forms a blunted fan shape*

4 *Replant each section with the rhizome showing above the soil*

Red roses here provide a contrast with light gray stone

Primrose clumps that have finished flowering can be lifted and divided now. This goes for polyanthus and the lovely, old-fashioned auriculas as well, but most polyanthus are best raised annually from seed. This is because they can degenerate after a while, becoming prey to several pests and diseases, including viral infections. If you have an unusual polyanthus that you want to propagate vegetatively, or large clumps of primrose or auricula, gently tease it apart with the fingers. Make sure that each piece of rhizome has plenty of strong roots and bed them out in a lightly shaded spot to grow on.

Continue training cordon sweet peas—once you have pinched out the growing tip and selected one strong side shoot to train on, keep removing any further side shoots that form, and tendrils. Be careful, though, not to remove the flower shoots in your enthusiasm—they

should be starting to form now, and even when quite small have tiny flower buds showing. Make sure the plants get plenty of water, or the buds may wilt and drop off before they open. Feed regularly with liquid fertilizer and apply a mulch of damp peat, well rotted manure or lawn clippings to conserve soil moisture.

If you haven't yet done so, you should move the greenhouse chrysanthemums in pots outdoors for the summer.

Border carnations tend to get a bit lanky now, with their long stems and heavy flowers, so give them some gentle support. The stems' arching growth is part of the charm of the plant, and if you tie them too tightly to supports, they look unnatural and distinctly ill at ease. For large flowers, remove any side shoots that form on the stems and remove all but the terminal flower bud.

Garden pinks can be propagated from cuttings, or pipings, at the end of the month (see page 90), and cuttings can still be taken of pelargoniums and fuchsias (see page 34).

Wherever practical, deadhead annuals, to keep fresh supplies of flowers through the summer. If you want them to self-seed, or want to save seed to sow elsewhere in the garden, stop deadheading towards the end of the season. Unless you are fanatic, deadheading small-flowered plants—lobelia and ageratum are two—is not worth the time and effort involved.

Herbaceous perennials that have finished flowering can be cut back now to just above the basal foliage, unless you want the seed for sowing or seed pods for their beauty.

Flowers for the month

Roses take pride of place now—the species roses, large-flowered and cluster-flowered—and garden pinks (*Dianthus plumarius, D. × allwoodii*) add to the scent and old-fashioned feel of the garden. In the herbaceous border, delphiniums raise their tall spikes in every shade of blue, mauve and cream, together with rainbow-colored lupins, some of the lilies—the turk's cap lily (*Lilium martagon*) and the red-spotted, lilac-pink *L. cernuum*. The fiery-red oriental poppies (*Papaver orientale*) in the garden will be echoed, on a more modest scale, by wild field poppies (*P. rhoeas*).

All your hard work on bedding plants should be paying off now—ageratum, begonias (*B. semperflorens*), Canterbury bells (*Campanula medium*) and fall-sown antirrhinums will be filling window-boxes, pots and flower beds with bright color and the promise of much more to come. And don't forget the fuchsias and pelargoniums, fresh from cuttings or lovingly over-wintered and hardened off, which add their own charm to the scene.

Many of the rhododendrons, including the naturalized wild rhododendron (*R. ponticum*) and its hybrids, together with other hybrid rhododendrons, will be providing the traditional blaze of

color. On a smaller scale, the rock rose and sun rose (*Cistus* and *Helianthemum*—though their common names are frequently interchanged) will be showing their paper-thin, open-faced flowers. *Magnolia sieboldii*, with its downward-turning, saucer-shaped flowers is in bloom, and the first of the buddleias (*B. alternifolia* and *B. globosa*, the orange ball tree) will be attracting butterflies. The laburnum is draped with yellow pea-like flowers. Care must be taken with the latter, however, as all parts of them are poisonous.

Flowering plants, more appreciated for their foliage than their flowers, and which are looking good now, include *Senecio* (*cineraria*) *bicolor* and *S. leucostachys* (both included in seed lists under *Cineraria*), and *Ruta graveolens*, better known as rue. Other foliage plants making a contribution to the garden at this time of year are *Eucalyptus gunnii* and *E. perriniana*, whose leaves are much prized by flower arrangers, and *Stachys byzantina* (*lanata*). *Gypsophila paniculata*, with its tiny, star-like flowers, also looks attractive as a cut flower.

Vertical color will be added by the large-flowered hybrid clematis and the climbing honeysuckles (*Lonicera × brownii, L. japonica* and *L. periclymenum* 'Belgica').

1 *Rosa* 'Constance Spry' 2 *Rosa*
'Dainty Bess' 3 *Campanula
cochlearifolia* 4 *Delphinium* (garden
hybrid) 5 *Begonia semperflorens* 6
Fuchsia 'Swingtime' 7 *Pelargonium
× hortorum* 'Irene Cal' 8 *Buddleia
alternifolia*

CARNATIONS AND PINKS

These charming summer flowers are all members of the genus *Dianthus*. Besides tender and hardy perennials, it includes Sweet Williams, a wide range of rock garden plants, hardy and half-hardy annuals. The parentage of carnations and pinks is quite complex, but what they have in common is their narrow, evergreen, often gray-tinged leaves, and their, usually fragrant, flat or rounded, single or double flowers. There is a special language for the markings and forms of carnations and pinks, which is useful to know if you are ordering plants or seed from catalogs. 'Selfs' are flowers of one color; 'bicolors' have a second, contrasting color in the center, or 'eye'. 'Picotees' have a contrasting narrow rim or edge, 'fancies' have contrasting markings in the form of stripes or flecks, and in 'laced' forms, the petals are bordered with a second color.

Cultivation of carnations and pinks varies according to the type you are growing, but all share certain likes and dislikes. Neutral or limy soil is best, and one that is well drained. Most *Dianthus* are very prone to rotting if there is excess moisture about, particularly if it is coupled with cold temperatures. Outdoors, they should have full sunlight and an airy spot—never low-lying sites which could easily become frost pockets.

Shallow planting is called for, again to avoid any possible rotting, and it is for this reason that carnations and pinks are not mulched.

Feeding and watering have to be done in moderation. Carnations and pinks need nutrients to survive and grow, particularly when they are producing flower buds, but it is all too easy to give them too much in the way of nutrients. This leads to sappy, weak growth and—particularly in the case of excessive nitrogen—delayed or diminished flowering. Fertilizers rich in potash and phosphates should be used, and sparingly. Carnations and pinks need a little less water than many other garden plants. In the open ground, watering is only necessary in severe droughts, if the plants begin to wilt—though you should keep an eye on newly planted carnations and pinks in spring, as they are vulnerable to drying out. When grown in pots, watering on a regular basis becomes a necessity, but even then, allow the soil to dry out between waterings and ensure that the pots are free-draining.

The enemies of carnations and pinks include aphids and red spider mites, as well as rabbits and pigeons, which go for the young shoots.

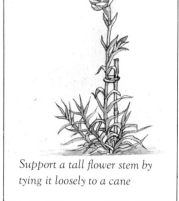

Support a tall flower stem by tying it loosely to a cane

For larger flowers, remove all but the terminal bud on each stem

Dianthus has a characteristic five-petalled flower and in certain hybrids it has a typically flat face

Old-fashioned pinks are a garden favorite: this is a white, single-petalled form

Despite their delicate shape and coloring, Dianthus hybrids are very hardy, vigorous plants

This pink, named 'Prudence', has unusually bold coloring. It is a dense, compact, free-flowering plant

Border carnations

These are descended largely from the wild carnation (*Dianthus caryophyllus*), sometimes called clove pink or gilliflower. Border carnations can reach a height of 3 ft (1m) and put on their main, and only, display in July. Staking is a must (see page 86) and disbudding the traditional method of ensuring blooms 3 in (7.5cm) or more across.

Some border carnations are treated as half-hardy annuals, grown each year from seed sown in winter. These include the F₁ hybrid 'Knight' strain. At 1 ft (30cm) high, they are more manageable than the taller forms, and staking is unnecessary.

Perpetual-flowering carnations

These are also called florists' carnations and are well-known in button-holes and bouquets at weddings or other social events where formal flower arrangements are called for.

Also descendants of *D. caryophyllus*, they differ from border carnations in being largely grown under glass, to provide flowers all year round. Growing taller than border carnations, 4 ft (1.2m) high, perpetual-flowering carnations need a minimum winter temperature of 50°F (10°C) to flower – if cooler they will grow very slowly or not at all.

Old-fashioned pinks

Old-fashioned pinks are largely derived from *Dianthus plumarius* and are delightfully fragrant. The lovely gray foliage forms wide-spreading mats, and the flowers range in height from 8 in (20cm) to 16 in (40cm) or more. The flowers can be single or double, with the typical carnation range of colors and markings, and smooth or frilly-edged petals. Though the flowers are smaller than carnations, more are produced per plant, and as they have a naturally branching habit, no stopping or disbudding is done. Old-fashioned pinks flower in June, a few weeks earlier than border carnations, and flowering is not repeated until a year later.

Modern pinks

These plants share the characteristics of border carnations and old-fashioned pinks, which is not surprising as these two were crossed to produce *Dianthus × allwoodii*, the collective name for modern pinks. In height and spread they tend to resemble old-fashioned pinks, but have the quick growth – and more frequent need for replacement – of border carnations. They are very free-flowering, both in sheer numbers of flowers carried and the flowering period – through June and July, and again in the fall.

Dwarf-growing forms of modern pinks are delightful in rockeries or as edging plants. They have grass-like, silvery gray foliage which forms cushion-like mats, and heavily scented, single flowers, from June until September. From 3–6 in (7.5–15cm) high, they are hardy and sturdy little plants, and can grow undisturbed for many years.

Indian pinks

Sometimes called the Chinese pink, these hardy annuals, biennials and short-lived perennials are derived from *Dianthus chinensis* var. *heddewigii*, also sometimes confusingly called Japanese pink. Originally from East Asia, it is represented in gardens nowadays by its many named forms. The flowers are usually single and come in a wide color range, as self, bicolors or laced. Heights range from 5 in (12.5cm) to 1 ft (30cm).

Rock pinks

Perfect for rock gardens, dry stone walls, troughs and sink gardens, as well as for the front of borders and even cracks in pavings, these little, mat-forming evergreen plants require little in the way of care. They are very hardy and attractive, and tend to be free-flowering over several weeks, or months in some cases.

Cheddar pink (*D. gratianopolitanus*) is an English plant, with single, deep-pink flowers in spring and early summer. 'La Bourbille' is similar, but dwarfer and neater, in pink or white.

The maiden pink (*D. deltoides*) is another English plant, which is usually found in one of its many named forms. 'Albus' is a lovely white, crimson-eyed form; 'Wisley' has dark-red flowers with a purple eye.

The glacier pink (*D. neglectus*) is a popular rock plant, with its large, single blooms in midsummer.

There are many other choice rock pinks, including the rich green-leaved *D. alpinus*, and a specialists' catalog, a trip to an alpine flower show or a large garden center, will give you a better idea of their range.

This subtle shell-pink is one of the most delightful colors. The plant is a hybrid modern pink

These single-petalled mauve flowers are also a form of Dianthus × allwoodii, the modern pinks

TAKING CUTTINGS

Now is a good time to increase your stock of plants–and replace those which have become old and woody–by taking softwood, tip cuttings from unripened stems. There are other types of stem cuttings, too, but these are usually done at other times of the year. Semi-ripe, or semi-hardwood cuttings, for example, are taken towards the end of summer, when the new growth from last spring has started to 'ripen', or become hard (see page 119). Ripe, or hardwood, cuttings are taken from the middle of the fall onwards, once the growth has become woody and hard (see page 153). A rough-and-ready guide to distinguish between the two is to bend a shoot–if it is pliant and bends easily, it is semiripe, and if it snaps, it is hardwood. There are, of course, exceptions.

There are also leaf cuttings, which can be taken any time during the growing season, and root cuttings, usually taken in winter (see page 177). Which type of cutting is best depends partly on the plant – Cape primrose (Streptocarpus), for example, lends itself only to leaf cuttings, while Begonia masoniana and B. metallica are equally happy propagated from leaf or soft stem cuttings. The time of year also determines the type of cutting you are taking–fuchsias can be propagated from soft, semi-ripe and hardwood stem cuttings depending on the time of the year.

Because cuttings are sections of root, stem or leaf, taken from the parent plant and encouraged to form roots and shoots of their own, the new plant formed will be identical to its parent. This is a distinct advantage over propaga-tion from seed, which usually results in a wide–and unpredict-able–range of variation in the seedlings. Also, they are virtually free, and you save time because you are starting with already formed growth.

However, any disease or pest infestation the parent plant has, is likely to be transmitted to the new plant. This is particularly so in the case of virus infections, which are, from an amateur gardener's viewpoint, incurable. Make sure the parent plant is healthy before taking cuttings.

Many cuttings will happily form roots if suspended in a jar of water–tradescantia, fuchsia, busy Lizzie or African violet are a few examples. Some, such as tradescantia and busy Lizzie, can be potted up in peat- or loam-based soil mix, once roots have formed, with no ill effects; others, such as African violet, have a high mortality rate when transferred from water to soil mix. It is certainly worth trying as an experiment, though, especially if you have a full load of cuttings rooting in soil mix in a propagating case at the same time.

SOFT CUTTINGS

Besides fuchsia, pelargonium, chrysanthemum and dahlia (see pages 21 and 34), many other house plants and herbaceous perennials lend themselves quite easily to soft cuttings. Busy Lizzie, tradescantia, lupin and delphinium are just a few. The first two will root almost any time of the year, as all their growth is soft, but with lupins and delphiniums, you have to take the young shoots early in spring, while they are soft and about 4 in (10cm) high. April to June are the usual months, depending on the plants' development.

Cuttings to take now–on the softwood principle, although at this time of year they are referred to as greenwood cuttings–include tarragon, rosemary, sage and thyme from the herb garden, and the tips of lavender, fuchsia, hydrangea, cotton lavender (Santolina) and the shrubby artemisias (A. arborescens, A. abrotanum, A. absinthum). If you are pushed for time, simply take semi-ripe cuttings from them in late summer (see page 119).

Greenwood cuttings are softwood shoot tips taken after the main burst of growth has died down. They are therefore a shade firmer than true softwood cuttings.

Because soft plant tissue quickly loses water and wilts, speed is of the essence. Cut a shoot 2–4 in (5–10cm) long immediately below the base of a leaf joint, or node. Avoid long, spindly shoots–those with short distances between the leaf nodes are better. Use a clean, sharp knife or razor blade to make the cut, and at the same time cut back the shoot remaining on the parent plant to just above the next leaf node. This is because it will die back anyway, and there is no point in leaving an unsightly, disease-prone stump on the plant.

Cut off the leaves on the lower half of the shoot–breaking them off can leave ragged edges which would rot in root mediums. Dip the cut edge of the shoot into hormone rooting powder–it contains a fungicide as well–and, using a dibber, or pencil, make a hole in the medium. If you just push the cuttings into the firmed medium, you are likely to snap or otherwise bruise them. One-third to one-half of the cutting should be buried.

A medium for cuttings can be one of several combinations–a mixture of peat and sand, a soil-based loam, or even vermiculite–the main criteria are that it is free-draining and well-aerated. No nutrients are necessary.

You can pot the cuttings singly, or place several in a larger pot–three or four in a 3 in (7.5cm) pot. Moisten the medium–but do not soak it–using a watering can with a fine rose or a mister. To keep the air around the cuttings moist, enclose the pot in a plastic bag or put it in a propagator. If the propagator is a heated one, so much the better, as a bit of bottom heat encourages rooting. One thing you must not do is expose the containerized cuttings to bright sunlight–the temperatures inside will soar and the plants will roast.

Cuttings of pinks, both the old-fashioned and the modern sorts, are called pipings, and now is the time to take them. Choose non-flowering side shoots – cuttings should always be taken from non-flowering shoots, if possible, and any flowers that develop during rooting should be removed. The pipings should be about 4 in (10cm) long, and they are inserted, 1 in (2.5cm) deep, into sandy soil.

LEAF CUTTINGS

Leaf cuttings are fascinating, because a whole new plant is formed from a single leaf or, in some cases, a tiny section of a leaf. African violet is a suitable subject, and the same treatment can be used for other house plants – begonias, peperomias and gloxinias–with slightly fleshy leaves. Cut a healthy newly matured leaf, with its stalk

SOFTWOOD CUTTINGS

1 *Choose a healthy tip or side shoot and cut it cleanly with a sharp knife just below the leaf joint*

2 *Sever the lower leaves on the shoot and dip the cut end of the stem in hormone rooting powder*

3 *Make deep holes in a fresh root medium and insert the cuttings, firming it around them*

LEAF CUTTINGS

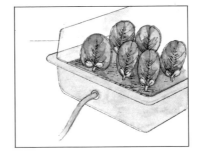

Whole leaf cutting 1 *Sever the leaf at the base of the plant*

2 *Insert the leaf stalk into a tray of fresh potting medium*

3 *A heated propagator encourages speedier rooting of the cutting*

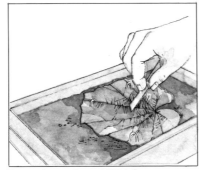

Sansevieria cutting *Cut sections across the leaf and pot them up*

Begonia cuttings 1 *Weight or peg the leaf and slit the main veins*

2 *Keep the leaf warm and moist until new plants are established*

attached, from the parent plant. Place it in a seed tray or pot filled with a mixture of peat and sand. Obviously, several leaves can be done at the same time, but make sure they are well spaced out and not touching each other. The leaf stalk is the bit that is buried, leaving the leaf blade exposed.

Mother-in-law's tongue (*Sansevieria*) and Cape primrose (*Streptocarpus*) have long leaves which can be cut crossways into sections, 2 in (5cm) long, and each of these sections will produce new plants. Push them vertically into the medium, in the same direction as they grew—the veins should point upwards from the central rib in the case of Cape primrose, and in the case of mother-in-law's tongue, stack them the right way up as you cut them.

Leaf cuttings from begonias can be done in two ways. You can insert the leaf stalk into the medium and rest the leaf on the surface, holding it in place with hairpins or small pebbles. With a sharp razor, make several slits across the main veins, and a new plant should appear at every cut. Alternatively, cut the leaves up into 1 in (2.5cm) squares, and place every square that has a section of vein running through it firmly on the rooting medium.

Leaf cuttings are vulnerable to both drying out and rotting before they root, so a balancing act is involved. A bit of bottom heat should hurry the rooting along, while occasional misting and a propagator lid or plastic bag should keep the air around them moist and the leaves from wilting. Once the young plants appear, they can be potted up separately into a soil mix containing nutrients to meet their growing needs.

LAWNS

June is a good month to use lawn sand or hormone weedkillers against broad-leaved weeds—from midsummer onwards, there really is less growing season left for the grass to recover and replace the dead weeds. Hand weeding can also continue.

You will probably be much more concerned with watering than weeding, though, at this time of the year. Never put off watering in the hope that it will rain 'tomorrow', because the dryer the soil becomes, the harder it is for water to penetrate, and most of the rain in heavy summer storms simply rolls off the surface. If your lawn is on thin, sandy or acid soil, or has a high proportion of bents or annual meadow grass, then it is especially vulnerable. Lawns based on fescues are much more drought-tolerant, because their inrolled leaves expose less blade surface to the sun and air, and thus reduce transpiration. But whatever the composition of your lawn, if it is allowed to become brown and dry, it is likely to be overrun by coarse weeds.

If the soil is compact and bone-dry, spike the lawn before watering, to allow the water to penetrate. And the deeper the penetration the better, so one good watering, say 2 gallons per sq yd (9 liters per sq m) is far better than several light sprinklings adding up to that amount. Light waterings lead to shallow-rooting grass, which becomes even more vulnerable to drought, and also encourages the growth of moss. Most of it evaporates before it can do any good, anyway.

Use a fine spray, not a torrent, especially in the case of new lawns, or you may inadvertently wash the seedlings away, and create mini-gulleys on the soil surface.

It is sometimes said that you shouldn't water lawns, or plants generally, in full sun, because the drops of water act as magnifying glasses and scorch the leaves. There is not a grain of truth in this, either in the greenhouse or outside. It is far better to water in full sun than not to water at all.

Mowing will be a regular task, but raise the blades high in dry weather and leave the cuttings on the lawn—they are largely composed of water and act as a protective mulch.

ROSES

If you want top-quality large-flowered (Hybrid tea) rose blooms, for exhibition or just for cut flowers, start to disbud them now. By restricting the number of flowers to the central—or crown—bud on a stem, you produce larger and better, but fewer, blooms. Simply nip off the side buds as soon as they are large enough to handle.

The same process, in reverse, is sometimes used with cluster-flowered (Floribunda) roses. The crown bud, being the strongest-growing, may come into flower well before the smaller, weaker-growing side buds, and be over by the time they open. By nipping out the crown bud, the remaining buds get more nourishment, and flower at the same time.

If you are growing your roses for a pretty display in the garden, rather than for the perfection of single blooms or clusters, leave disbudding to the exhibitors, and confine yourself to deadheading

June sees gardens in mild areas bursting with a profusion of roses

DISBUDDING A ROSE

To encourage larger blooms, pinch off all but the central flower bud on each stem or side shoot, where the stem divides

faded blooms. This is not so important for roses that flower for a week or two and not again until the following year—'Albertine' and 'Paul's Lemon Pillar' are two non-recurrent climbers—but it is very important in the case of large-flowered, cluster-flowered and recurrent roses. Removing the spent flowers prevents seed from setting and encourages the production of more flowers. Leave the heads on, though, if you are saving seed for propagation or, more likely, if you are growing roses which have pretty hips. *Rosa moyesii* and *R. glauca* (*rubrifolia*) are examples with bright-red hips that add color to the garden in the fall.

Roses will need all the protection you can give them now, against aphids, beetles, mildew and blackspot. Be on the lookout and take precautions or rearguard action as necessary (see page 142).

SPIKING A LAWN

An aerator is a labor-saving tool for even and rapid spiking

Alternatively, plunge a fork into the lawn at regular intervals

TREES & SHRUBS

Continue trimming hedges—formal and informal, evergreen and deciduous—to keep the growth dense, right down to the base, and, in the case of flowering shrubs, to encourage the growth of new shoots to provide next year's flowers. Don't forget to hand-weed along the bottom of your hedge – brambles, nettles and ground elder have a terrible stranglehold effect, if you let them get established in a hedge, and couch grass is always a threat to adjacent beds and borders.

If children play in your garden and you have a laburnum, pick off all pods within a child's reach and sweep up any that fall, as they are poisonous and some children are fascinated by them.

Wall-grown shrubs that have finished flowering need hard pruning to keep them within bounds. Spring (early summer-flowering) ceanothus (C. *dentatus*, C. 'Delight' and C. *thrysiflorus* are three) and japonicas (*Chaenomeles*) should both be cut back to within 2–4 in (5–10cm) of the old wood. With ceanothus, though, be particularly careful not to cut into old wood, or it may respond by dying, instead of putting on new growth. The main exception to this prune-after-flowering rule for wall shrubs is firethorn (*Pyracantha*). This is because it is the bright berries, rather than the white flowers, that make this shrub so popular for wall training, and if you prune it hard after flowering, the net result is virtually no berries in the fall and winter following. Giving the shrub a big enough expanse of wall to grow un-

restricted for a few years is part of the solution, and pruning in late winter, after the berries have finished, is also beneficial. Sadly, the older a wall-trained firethorn gets, the less fruitful it tends to be, but their display when young and early-middle-aged makes up for it.

Water shrubs and climbers—indeed all plants—growing against walls, if the weather is warm and dry. Water newly planted trees, shrubs and climbers generously at this time of year, too, as a severe dry spell can kill them. Keep the ground around them free of grass, so they do not have to compete for water and food.

Many gardeners break out into a cold sweat whenever pruning clematis is mentioned, but as long as you know the name or, failing that, the type of clematis you have, there is no need to worry. Now is the time to prune the early-

Above Hydrangea macrophylla *'Blue Wave' grows well in a semi-shade and makes an excellent informal screen or hedge*

Left Hydrangea paniculata *enlivens the summer garden scene with its bright green leaves and large pyramidal flowers*

flowering clematis—the evergreen C. *armandii*, C. *montana*, C. *alpina* and C. *macropetala*, and their named forms. But they don't necessarily need pruning every year, only when they start to overcrowd their neighbors. This is most likely to be the case with C. *montana*, which can be totally dominating, and C. *armandii* if grown in a particularly favorable spot. The others tend to be well behaved, even modest, in their growth rate. Cut out all the old and weak growth, and shorten the remaining growth by about half. By pruning now, you give the plant the whole summer to form new shoots, which will carry masses of blossom next spring.

Continue deadheading lilacs, rhododendrons and azaleas as they finish, to keep the garden tidy and to conserve the plants' strength. Leave the faded flowers

on if you are saving seed or, as in the case of guelder rose (*Viburnum opulus*), the flowers are followed by pretty, red, translucent berries later on.

There are some gray-leaved shrubs, notably Senecio × 'Sunshine' (syn. S. *laxifolius*, S. *greyi* of gardens), artemisia (A. *arborescens*) and cotton lavender (*Santolina chamaecyparissus*) which may have their flower buds removed as they form towards the end of June. Once these shrubs flower, the leaves lose their fresh, silvery sheen and the growth generally becomes lax and floppy. Either hand-pick the silver-bauble flower buds, or take a pair of shears to them.

If your soil is limy and your heart is set on blue hydrangeas, then you must apply aluminum sulphate, sequestrene or a proprietary acidifying compound to the soil now, in liquid form, where they are growing. Otherwise the flowers will come out a muddy pink, no matter how blue they were when you bought the plant. Digging in plenty of moist peat when you plant a blue hydrangea in a limy soil helps, too, Sequestrene and acidifying compounds must be used according to the manufacturer's instructions. Aluminum sulphate is applied weekly from bud break to flowering, using a solution of $\frac{1}{4}$ oz (7g) per 1 gallon (4 liters) rainwater at 2 gallons (8 liters) per bush each time.

The main display of deutzias, weigelas and bridal wreath (*Spiraea* × *arguta*) will be over by the end of the month. Cut out any old, dead or crowded wood, and remove some of the flowered shoots at ground level to make way for new growth.

FRUIT

Strawberries will be producing runners now, and unless you want them for layering, nip them off at the base of the parent plant. If you do want to start new plants—and remember that strawberries tend to weaken after a few years' cropping and become prone to virus infections – then select strong plantlets for layering. Those closest to the parent plant are best, and no more than three or four should be layered from any one plant. Either peg them down into the soil, using an unbent paper clip or small stone to keep them in position, or peg them down into 3 in (7.5cm) pots filled with good-quality potting mixture. Sink the pots into the ground up to their rims, and remember to keep them well watered, as they will dry out relatively rapidly. The rooting plantlets may themselves send out runners—nip these off, as well as any others that are sent out by the parent plant, as they only sap the plants' vigor.

Pests will be working overtime—aphids wherever they find succulent young growth, codling moth and woolly aphid on apple, sawflies on gooseberries, and maggots in the ripening fruit of raspberries. Spray at the first sign of infestation, and follow up as necessary, according to manufacturers' instructions (see page 184).

The gradual thinning of apricots and peaches should be finished by this month or next (see page 57), so turn your attention to your apple, plum and pear trees. These, too, produce many more fruitlets than they can carry, and one fruit per spur, or two at the most, is a good guide. Again, keep your enthusiasm in check and make thinning a gradual exercise. This makes sense because you will be left with some fruit after the natural fruit-fall that takes place later this month and in July. Always remove small, discolored and misshapen fruits first.

Cane fruits—raspberries, loganberries and blackberries—will be putting on rapid growth, so keep tying in the young shoots as they grow.

You can begin summer-pruning gooseberries and red currants at the end of the month, but not blackcurrants. Gradually, over a couple of weeks, shorten the tips of the side shoots to about 3 in (7.5cm) from the stems, or just above the fifth leaf on new growth. Because American gooseberry mildew is partial to the soft, new, tip growth, summer-pruning gooseberries now reduces the chance of infection.

As your strawberries, soft and cane fruit ripen, your struggle against birds may reach fever pitch. Fruit cages are the only permanent solution, though strips

The prudent gardener can protect strawberry plants from birds with nylon mesh netting

of foil can offer temporary relief if moved from bush to bush—if you leave them in one place, the birds quickly learn that they are harmless. Strawberries can be protected with lightweight plastic netting stretched over short posts.

Melons growing in frames or under cloches will need your attention. After the growing point has been pinched out (see page 80), side shoots will form. Allow four per plant, pinch out any others, and spread these four out in opposite directions. Pinch out the growing tips of these side shoots when each has produced five leaves, to get sub-laterals and flowers.

Fruiting will be more certain if you hand-pollinate melons—not at all difficult to do. Wait until seven or eight female flowers have formed—these are the ones with a tiny bulge on the stalk behind the flower. On a sunny day, from late

LAYERING STRAWBERRIES

1 *Select a sturdy plant and pick three or four of the healthiest runners*

Draw them free of other runners and leaves

2 *Sink a pot of soil mix into the soil and peg down the runner*

3 *Wait four to six weeks before severing it from the parent plant*

POLLINATING A MELON

female flower

male flower

Strip the petals from a male flower and press the central tip against the female flower

VINES

One satisfactory system of training grape vines is called the double guyot system, and it involves regular training and tying in this month. Two side shoots are trained, horizontally along wires and in opposite directions, from a main stem. A third side shoot is cut back to three buds, in early spring, and it is these buds that will provide next year's side shoots.

The three replacement shoots will be growing strongly now, and should be trained up the center and then along the top wire. The horizontally trained side shoots will by now also have produced five or six strong-growing shoots, and you should train these vertically, tying them to the wires as they grow. Once they reach the top wire, pinch out any further growth. Pinching out at the top wire leads to side shoots forming all the way up the vertical laterals. These are called secondary laterals and should be stopped after one leaf, or the vine will rapidly become an unmanageable thicket.

HARVESTING

Towards the end of June, some fruit may be ready for picking. If your gooseberry bushes are carrying a heavy crop, start thinning the fruits when they are a little larger than peas. You can use these small berries in pies, tarts and jams, and the berries remaining on the bush will grow that much bigger. In sheltered gardens, the early and maincrop strawberries will be ripening quickly now. Pick over the rows daily, and take the berries with the stalk still attached. At the same time, remove any rotting or diseased berries.

morning to early afternoon, break off the male flowers, remove their petals and brush them onto the central knob-like stigma of a female flower. When the fruits start to swell, select no more than four—one per side shoot—and remove the others. Also remove any flowers that appear later, as they have no purpose, and cut off the shoots two or three leaves beyond each developing fruit. Melons grown under frames or indoors will always need hand pollinating to ensure that pollination takes place.

PRUNING VINES – THE DOUBLE GUYOT SYSTEM

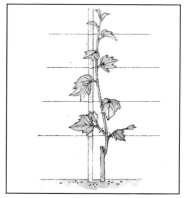

First year *Train a single shoot against a vertical stake and pinch back other shoots that appear*

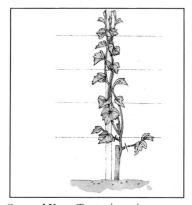

Second Year *Train three shoots only on the vertical support and trim back any other shoots*

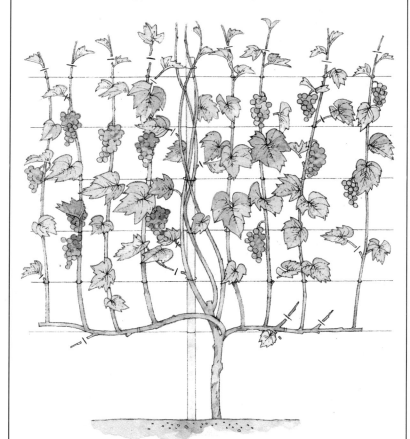

Third and subsequent years *Tie two of the shoots to horizontal wires. Train fruiting stems vertically up parallel wires. Pinch out tips as they rise above top wire. Allow three new shoots to grow at the center, two of which will become next year's laterals*

VEGETABLES

Weeding should be taking less of your time now, with vegetables filling out nicely and over-shadowing any weed seedlings that appear. If the weather has been wet, weeds will be more trouble-some, and in the case of onions and leeks, whose own leaves are thin and unlikely to keep down competition, weeding is a must. Other areas that may need atten-tion are seedlings from late sowings, in seed beds, and ground cleared of early salad crops.

Watering may become impor-tant, depending on the weather. If it is hot and dry, give vegetables a thorough soak with a good stream every few days–do not tease the thirsty plants with a light sprin-kling that sits on the surface of the soil and does more harm than good. If you haven't got enough time–or water–to go round, seed-lings should have first priority, along with plants growing in pots, tubs, growing-bags and frames. Certain vegetables, such as toma-toes, lettuce, celery and radishes, are less tolerant of drought than others–parsnips, Brussels sprouts and Savoy cabbages, for example–so water accordingly.

Continue successional sowing of salad crops, and make a late sowing of lettuce. Use an early cultivar, which matures quicker than a maincrop one, to harvest it before the chill nights of the fall. If you have cloches, choose a dwarf-growing form–you can prolong the season by giving cloche protec-tion when the weather turns cool-er. Make a later sowing of snap beans, too, for a fall crop, and continue sowing root vegetables–

Watering may be essential if the early summer is hot and dry

carrots, beet, kohlrabi, rutabagas and turnip–to provide winter crops. Winter salads can be had by sowing chicory and endive to-wards the end of this month, and those sown last month can be thinned. June is also a good month to sow Chinese cabbage (see page 61).

Thinning, planting out and transplanting to final positions will start to overtake sowing as the main activity on the vegetable front. Deal with tender crops first, if you are pushed for time. Lettuce and tomatoes have a much shorter life cycle than brassicas, for exam-ple, which can wait for a little, if need be. If you live in a cold area, or have an exposed garden, once you are confident that frosts are over, plant out, or set out, your tomatoes, eggplants, peppers, sweetcorn, runner and snap beans.

Tomatoes should be 6–9 in (15–23cm) tall, with the first flower truss just showing. Give them the sunniest, most sheltered spot you can find, and if you are not grow-ing bush cultivars, provide a tall stake for each plant. You can now buy rolls of special perforated transparent film, in tubular form, for outdoor tomato bushes. You

place a length of tubing over each plant, tying the top to the top of the cane, rather like a sleeve. As the plant grows, the tubing ex-pands, protecting it from cold and wind, like a tiny individual greenhouse.

When thinning carrots, make sure you firm the soil around the remaining plants–carrot flies are on the look-out for loose soil near carrots for egg-laying (see page 184). Carrot thinnings are not worth transplanting–root vegeta-bles do not move well–but the later thinnings can be used in the kitchen. Don't leave the thinnings lying on the seed bed, as that seems to attract carrot flies, too.

Transplanting brassicas – broc-coli, kale, Brussels sprouts, cauli-flower and cabbage–can be done as soon as the young plants have made four or five true leaves. Wet weather is best, but that can't always be arranged, so liberal use of a hose or watering can may be necessary. If the soil is dry, water the plants in the seed bed thor-oughly, so you can lift them with plenty of soil sticking to the roots. Discard any that are lacking a growing point, or growing blind,

---

MOVING BRASSICAS

1 *Lift the seedlings when four or five true leaves have formed*

2 *In dry weather, water the plot well and puddle in the seedlings*

3 *Draw up the soil around the plant, leaving a depression to catch water*

as it is called, or those that have a distinct blue tint to their leaves—that indicates that the roots are damaged or otherwise defective. Dig individual holes in the new positions, spaced roughly 2–2½ ft (60–75cm) apart in each direction, then if the weather has been dry fill each hole with water.

Because brassicas have a system of very fine roots, they are planted slightly deeper than they originally grew in the seed bed for initial stability. Put the plant in the moistened hole up to its lowest leaf, and draw the soil up and around it. A depression in the soil surface will be left around the plant, but it will gradually fill with soil and in the meantime acts as a tiny receptacle for water. Finally, firm the soil thoroughly round each plant.

Newly transplanted brassicas will need protection against birds—especially pigeons—so net the rows, or use strips of aluminum foil as temporary bird scarers.

Leeks can be put into their final position now. There are several methods of growing leeks, to provide the blanching they need. They can be grown in well-manured trenches, 1 ft (30cm) deep; the trenches are gradually filled with soil as the leeks grow. You can plant them 'on the flat', later providing paper, plastic or drain-pipe collars and earthed-up soil to blanch the leeks. Lastly, you can simply plant them in holes, made with a stout wooden dibber, 8 in (20cm) apart. For 8 in (20cm) high plants, make the holes 6 in (15cm) deep and proportionally shallower for shorter plants. Trim any long straggly roots back to about 1 in (2.5cm) and trim the leaves a little. Then water the plants into their holes, as for

brassicas. If you didn't have time to sow your own leeks and brassicas, you can often buy young plants from nurseries or garden centers. Select plants that are fresh-looking, and get them into their new home as soon as possible.

If you are growing winter celery, then trenches are a must–the trenches are gradually filled in to blanch the celery–and you can use the earthed-up soil between the trenches for catch crops (see Glossary). Celery is a particularly thirsty crop, and must not be allowed to dry out. Keep your eye open for celery fly now–brown blisters on the leaves are a sure sign of infestation–and spray as necessary (see page 184).

Towards the end of June, shallots planted in spring will start to swell. Gently scrape away the soil from the necks of the bulbs, to expose them to warmth and light.

Continue tying in runner beans and check that all is well with pea supports. Jerusalem artichokes may need staking now, if they are growing in a very windy spot.

Continue pinching-out operations, as and when necessary–the growing tips and side shoots of

trailing marrows and of cucumbers, the side shoots of tomatoes and the tips of beans if necessary.

Most vegetables will benefit from a feed of quick-acting, complete fertilizer in liquid form.

Gradually finish earthing up maincrop potatoes this month, and you can start lifting the early potatoes. Don't lift more than you need for any one day, as their lovely fresh flavor is soon lost. Japanese onions planted out last fall will be ready–again, only take what you need for one day.

Fall-sown peas can be picked now. Harvest them while they are young and tender, to encourage a steady supply. If pea moth maggots have been a nuisance in the past spray about one week after the first flowers open. The tiny maggots must be killed before they tunnel into the pods. Pea moth is a pest that must be dealt with as a precautionary measure. Once an infestation has started there is no easy cure.

Towards the end of the month stop picking asparagus, and allow the pretty, fern-like foliage to grow. If you don't, the plant will soon exhaust itself.

HARVESTING HERBS

If the weather has been hot and sunny, you can start harvesting herbs towards the end of June, and continue well into summer. Pick them before the flowers open, on a dry, sunny day. Always inspect them first for signs of pests or diseases, and discard damaged leaves as necessary. Pick only a little from each plant and you will continue to get fresh growth for another three months.

Fresh herbs taste and look better than their dried counterparts, which, however, last longer.

To dry large-leaved herbs, strip the leaves from the stems and lay them out on wire trays, so air can circulate around them. Alternatively, spread them out on sheets of newspaper. Small-leaved herbs should be tied in bundles, then loosely wrapped in a porous material, such as muslin, to keep dust off. Hang them upside-down to dry in a warm, dark, airy place– a temperature of 65–70°F (18–21°C) is ideal. Or you can spread them out in a single layer on a tray and place it in the oven at a low temperature. Leave the oven door open so the temperature does not rise above 90°F (32°C). Once the herbs are completely dry and crisp, crush them between two sheets of paper, then store in labelled, airtight containers away from the light.

Mint, basil, chives, tarragon and parsley freeze well, too. Blanch them for 30 seconds in boiling water then plunge them into ice-cold water for another 30 seconds. Drain carefully and freeze in sealed plastic bags. Parsley is best frozen without being blanched. It will lose its color after a month or so but you can use it for cooking.

PLANTING LEEKS

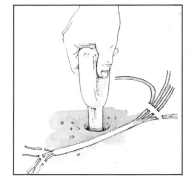

1 Trim back the leaves and any long straggly roots on young leeks

2 Place the plants in the hole and gently water into position

July

Hot summer days are here
and though there are still jobs to be done in the
garden, they are easy-going, pleasant ones—
disbudding roses, dahlias and carnations, tidying
up herbaceous borders, watering the lawns and
flower beds in the evening—that hardly qualify as
work at all. And there is no more pleasurable July
'task' than harvesting your own luscious
strawberries, raspberries and currants, all with that
garden-fresh flavor.

Color and variety
in the vegetable garden (left).
Standard roses and several varieties of
lavender surround an unusual bed
of ornamental cabbages

Jobs for the month

General

Continue watering and mulching
Apply quick-acting fertilizers
Layer woody and herbaceous plants
Save seed for future sowing
Check for pests and diseases

Flowers

Disbud chrysanthemums, dahlias and carnations
Deadhead flowers not wanted for seed
Lift and store tulip and hyacinth bulbs in a cool place
Start tender cyclamen plants into growth
Continue feeding sweet peas, chrysanthemums and dahlias, and tie in new growth
Thin or prick out seedlings of annuals, biennials, perennials and winter-flowering house plants
Sow pansies
Check house plants for aphids, whitefly, red spider mite and other pests
Layer border carnations

Lawns

Mow regularly
Continue mulching
Weed as necessary
Apply fertilizer

Roses

Deadhead and disbud
Continue feeding
Spray against black spot and mildew
Propagate by budding

Trees and shrubs

Layer shrubs and climbers
Continue pruning shrubs after flowering
Summer-prune wisteria
Clip hedges
Remove reverted branches
Continue taking cuttings

Fruit

Tidy strawberry beds under the hill system and remove runners
Harvest strawberries, currants, raspberries and gooseberries
Summer-prune bush and tree fruit
Cut back old raspberry canes after fruiting
Thin apples, pears and grapes
Continue pollinating and training melons
Support fruit-tree branches
Check plums for silver leaf

Vegetables

Lift and dry shallots, garlic and fall-sown onions
Harvest globe artichokes, runner, broad and shell beans
Mulch beans and salad crops
Harvest young beets, turnips, kohlrabi and carrots
Continue harvesting herbs
Sow parsley for winter use, plus salad crops (including endive, winter radish and corn salad, see page 61), root crops and spring cabbage
Thin or transplant seedlings sown last month
Protect potatoes from blight
Continue training, tying in and feeding tomatoes

If the weather makes watering necessary—and July can be the hottest month of the year—do so regularly and thoroughly. If there are water restrictions where you live, or simply restrictions on the amount of time you can spend watering, give top priority to plants growing against walls, seedlings and young plants, and plants growing in containers. Window boxes are often overlooked, but you will find that, even after a heavy rain, they may still be dry, because the overhang of the roof, windowsill above, or guttering, may deflect whatever rain there is. Dense foliage cover will also deflect much of the rain to the outside of the container. Check hanging baskets every day in dry weather; even twice a day may not be overdoing it.

In terms of watering, the greenhouse should be thought of as a huge container, too, as the plants growing there depend entirely on artificial watering. Damping down the greenhouse—by watering the floor and benches—will help keep the atmosphere moist and the temperature bearable inside.

Mulching can be used with watering to get the most benefit from the water supplied to the plants. Trees and shrubs—both fruit and ornamental—flowers and vegetables, and lawns, too, will be grateful for such treatment. The second, long-term benefit from mulching is the provision of nutrients to the soil—and eventually, the plant—in the form of slowly decomposing organic matter.

Plants in full growth, whether flowering or cropping, will need steady supplies of quickly available food now from inorganic fertilizers, applied as a powder which is watered in, or in liquid form.

MULCHING

Apply peat or compost on the soil surface in a circle covering the area of the root spread. Leave the stem base free of mulch as it can be rotted by it

Propagation of plants, especially in the form of cuttings and layering, can continue at a leisurely pace, and collecting and saving your own seed for sowing later in the year can start this month, too (see page 104).

Pests and diseases in the garden will need watching out for and treating at the earliest possible stage. Mildew is especially problematical in hot, wet weather, and red spider mite can be a real nuisance (see page 184).

Planning changes and improvements in your garden is part of the fun of having one, and you might set aside one or two evenings to look ahead to later in the year and to plan which bulbs to plant for autumn color (see pages 106–7).

FLOWERS

Disbudding may or may not become part of your July routine—if you want exhibition-size chrysanthemums, dahlias and carnations then pinch out the unwanted side buds around the central, large bud on each stem. It is a routine chore, involving little in the way of thinking or time, but many gardeners would rather have larger numbers of smaller blooms, and the choice of whether or not to disbud is entirely up to you.

Watering plants must be done, each according to kind. Generally speaking, gray-leaved plants from Mediterranean regions need less water than 'soft', lush plants such as dahlias, but wilting leaves are a sure sign that any plant needs watering. Occasionally, wilting can be caused by pests feeding off the plants' roots or by certain diseases, but watering usually does the trick, especially when the weather is dry, as it is likely to be at this time of the year.

PRUNING AND DEADHEADING

Deadheading of flowers not needed for seed production (see page 104) is much the same as for last month. If you are quick enough removing the faded flower spikes of delphiniums and lupins, they may put on a second, smaller display later in the season. And flowers that have a long period of display—scabious, gaillardias and achilleas, for example—will be encouraged to continue producing more flowers by the removal of fading blooms.

Flowers produced on bare stems—red hot pokers (*Kniphofia*) and African lilies (*Agapanthus*), for example—should be cut right back to the base. Those produced on leafy stems, such as peonies and delphiniums, should simply have the flower-head or spike cut off, leaving the leafy growth intact.

Some rockery plants may begin to look a little under the weather this month, straggly and with brown edges appearing on the leaves. Trim them ruthlessly for a fresh display of leaves, and sometimes even of flowers.

BULBS

Tulips, hyacinths and other spring-flowering bulbs can be lifted now from where they flowered or were heeled in temporarily. Lay the bulbs out in a single layer in a cool, airy place to dry, then store them in similar conditions until planting them next fall. You may find that small bulbs have been produced at the base of the larger bulbs—these can be detached and planted in a nursery bed to grow to

At the height of summer, a flower border is at its colorful best

flowering size, before you transfer them to a prime position in the garden.

While you are lifting and storing some bulbs, you will be starting off others. Tender cyclamen house plants that have been resting after their winter display may start to send out tiny leaves—a sign that they will need potting up in fresh soil mix, watering and exposure to light and warmth. Fall-flowering bulbs, too, will need to be planted at the end of the month (see pages 106–7), for a seasonal garden display.

CHECKING SUPPORTS

Continue feeding sweet peas in bloom, as well as chrysanthemums and dahlias. Check, as you do so, that any supports, in the form of stakes, wire circles or netting, are in good condition and doing their job properly. Continue tying in new growth to the supports, using soft twine or perhaps special strips of coated wire. Make the ties firm enough to prevent the plants from flopping about, but not so tight that growth is constricted.

Flowers for the month

July is one of the busiest months of the flowering year, and if you have planned your garden carefully, you shouldn't be left 'high and dry' when last month's display of perennials has finished. Red hot pokers (*Kniphofia* spp) should be blazing away, in shades of cream ('Maid of Orleans') and yellow ('Brimstone') as well as the more familiar orange and red.

African lilies (*Agapanthus*) will be taking up the blue theme from last month's delphiniums, and many of the campanulas (*C. glomerata, C. lactiflora, C. persicifolia*) will be on display, too. Day lilies (*Hemerocallis*) add contrast in shades of yellow, salmon, orange, pink and deep browny bronze.

Hardy and half-hardy annuals– in beds, window boxes, tubs and hanging baskets–put on a pretty show, with lobelia, alyssum and nasturtiums hopefully concealing any remaining bare earth. Cherry pie (*Heliotropium*) and tobacco plant (*Nicotiana*) will be adding scent, as well as color, to the scene, but it is the roses that still rule the garden on both fronts.

The California tree poppy (*Romneya coulteri*)–really a woody-based perennial, never a tree– carries its huge, white, gold-centered flowers now, paper-thin and delicately fragile. Shasta daisies (*Chrysanthemum maximum*) add to the white theme, with their cottage-garden charm and great endurance. Daisy-like, too, are the flowers of the daisy bush (*Olearia × haastii*) and anthemis, both on display this month.

July is good for flowering shrubs and trees, from the hugely grand tulip tree (*Liriodendron tulipfera*), with its long, yellow-green flowers, and evergreen magnolia (*M. grandiflora*) to the hydrangeas, St John's wort (*Hypericum*), philadelphus and shrubby potentillas. Summer-flowering heathers (*Erica cinerea, E. tetralix*) add color closer to the ground. In the climber department, late-flowering clematis such as 'W.E. Gladstone' are joined by Russian vine (*Polygonum baldschuanicum*) – excellent for using as screening – and summer-flowering jasmine (*Jasminum officinale*).

1

2

3

4

5

6

7

1 *Kniphofia sparsa* 2 *Agapanthus* 'Headbourne Hybrid'
3 *Campanula glomerata*
4 *Hemerocallis* 'Stafford'
5 *Heliotropium arborescens*
6 *Magnolia grandiflora* 'Exmouth Variety' 7 *Hypericum calycinum*

THINNING

When uprooting a seedling, press down the soil around it

SEEDLINGS

Thinning and pricking out of perennials and winter-flowering house plants—calceolaria, cineraria and fairy primrose—sown earlier in the season should be done this month, and check any annuals sown directly where they are to flower, as some judicious thinning may be needed here, too.

Biennial seeds sown last month may need thinning, and you can make a sowing of pansies now, to flower next winter and spring.

TREATING PESTS

Indoors, check house plants for aphids and for whitefly, easily spotted as a cloud of white 'flecks' that flies up when you move a plant or inspect it. The leaves of house plants are also vulnerable to red spider mite if conditions are hot and dry, so spray as necessary (see page 184).

Outdoors, the usual pests— aphids, spider mites, and so on – will be troublesome, with leaf miners a particular problem for chrysanthemums. Wallflower seedlings may fall prey to flea beetles this month, so treat them

with a suitable pesticide at the first sign of trouble (see page 184). Various caterpillars will be on the move, and it is up to you to outflank them, either by hand-picking—admittedly not a task for the squeamish—or by spraying (see page 184).

On the disease front, Michaelmas daisies may suffer from mildew, and fungal rust can infect a wide range of plants, including carnations and pinks. Spray at the first sign of infection, or, if you have had the problem in previous years, spray preventatively.

LAYERING CARNATIONS

Border carnations can be propagated this month by layering, and the new plants should be fully rooted and ready for planting elsewhere by September. Choose a young, non-flowering side shoot

that will bend easily. Strip off some of its lower leaves by pulling them downwards towards the base—make sure you leave a growing tip with at least four pairs of leaves at the top. Next, slice through the stem with a sharp knife, about 1½ in (4cm) below the leafy shoot tip, and cut downwards through the stem, passing through a joint and finally coming out through the side of the stem to form a tongue. Make the tongue on the side of the stem that will be in contact with the soil. Dig a small hole where the stem is to be layered, and fill it with a mixture of equal parts sharp sand, soil and peat.

Open out the cut gently and bend the stem down, pushing the tongue into the special soil mix, and cover it with more of the mix. Try to get the end of the stem to point straight up, and anchor it in this position. To keep the stem

Spray pinks, such as the Dianthus chinensis, against fungal rust

vertical, you could also tie it to a small stick. Keep the plant well watered, and once rooting has occurred, in about two months, sever the new plant with a sharp knife (see page 129).

LAYERING CARNATIONS

1 *Select a vigorous non-flowering side shoot with a springy stem. Strip lower leaves by pulling them downwards, keeping at least four pairs at the top of the stem*

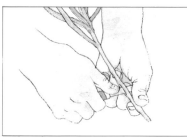

2 *Slice the stem, cutting downwards and out through a leaf joint*

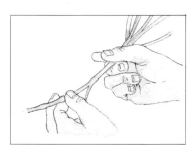

3 *Flex the stem so the cut section forms a tongue on the lower side*

4 *Bend the stem and push the tongue into a hole in the soil*

5 *Cover the stem section with soil and anchor it with a wire loop*

SAVING SEED

Flowers of all sorts of plants—trees, shrubs, perennials, annuals, even bulbs—can be left to set seed, rather than being deadheaded. As soon as they are ripe, you can begin to collect them for sowing at a future date. The best seed to save is that from named species rather than F_1 hybrids or special strains or cultivars. This is because these last seldom breed true to type, and the seedlings are likely to have lost the qualities—vigor, dwarfing, color or form—that made the parent plant special.

Why save seed at all, rather than let the plant get on with it and the seed fall where it will? Collecting the seed and sowing it under controlled conditions, be they under glass or in a seed bed, will give you far better results in terms of germination than leaving it to nature. Besides, you may want those plants in a different part of the garden, or to give them to a friend or neighbor.

Collect the seed on a still, dry day, when the pods are just about to open. If you can collect the seed over the span of a couple of weeks, so much the better—that way, if you have miscalculated their ripeness on one occasion, all will not be lost. Larger seeds can be tipped directly into your hand or a paper bag. Some—all species of *Impatiens*, for example—actually expel the seeds if the ripe pods are touched, however lightly, so be prepared for this to happen.

Smaller seeds need a slightly different approach. Fix a paper bag over the just-ripe seed head, cut the flower stalk, and shake the head, upside-down, in the bag.

No matter what the size of the seed, it must be absolutely dry before being stored. If there is any hint of dampness, spread the seeds out on paper on a sunny windowsill for a few days. Once dry, store them in envelopes—don't forget to label and date them—which can in turn be stored in jars or tins with tight-fitting lids. Keep them in a cool, dry place—about 41°F (5°C) is ideal.

How long you can keep them is another matter. Some seed will only germinate if it is freshly ripe—cyclamen seed, for example. Alpine plants, too, should be sown from just-ripe seed, though germination can take a year or more, and some true alpines, which grow naturally in high altitudes, need to be exposed to low temperatures during winter before they will germinate. This process is called stratification, and is applied to most tree and shrub seeds to soften the hard seed coating.

As a general guide, very tiny seeds and seeds that are soft and fleshy or oily within do best sown as soon as ripe—camellia and magnolia seed are classic examples. Those that are slightly bigger and hard-coated can be kept for some time—often several years—before sowing, providing the storage conditions are right.

1 *As large, ripe seed pods open, shake the seeds into your hand*

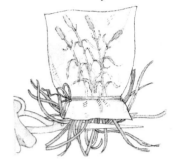

2 *Place a bag over smaller seedheads, tie it and cut the stems*

3 *Turn it upside down and shake it, to collect the seeds in the bag*

4 *Spread the seeds to dry and then store them in labelled envelopes*

Care of established lawns is much the same as for June, with regular mowing being given priority. If the weather is hot and dry, the growth rate will have slowed down slightly, so set the blades high. Again, make the grass cuttings do double duty as a mulch for the lawn, to keep moisture in. If you water the lawn and it is compacted, remember to spike it over first, for better penetration.

Check the mower is not set to cut too close when the weather is hot

If the weather has been dry, you may find that yellow annual trefoil clover is a problem. Hand-weed it as soon as you see it, and certainly before it has time to set seed and so perpetuate the problem for another year. Pearlwort is another weed that revels in hot, dry summers, and its low habit of growth means that it can set seed in spite of being mown regularly. Again, quick action on the part of the weeder is called for.

Apply a light application of fertilizer—sulphate of ammonia is ideal—to established lawns, to see them through the growing season.

ROSES

Continue deadheading and disbudding roses, and you can lightly prune large-flowered–the old hybrid tea–roses, to keep them neat, trim and flowering. Cut back the stems without buds showing on them by about half their length. Feeding your roses with a good, general fertilizer now will also encourage them to continue producing flower buds. At this time of year, especially if it looks as if the weather is going to be dry, use a liquid fertilizer, for rapid results.

Black spot and mildew might be troublesome, in which case spray with a suitable fungicide as soon as the problem declares itself (see page 184).

Most people buy their roses 'ready made', from a garden center, or grow them from cuttings or layering, as, on the whole, they root easily. You might like to try another method of propagating roses–budding–which, although usually left to commercial growers, is fascinating nonetheless. This method combines a bud from the desired rose with the strong rooting system of another, well established rose. There are special rootstocks used commercially, but the dog rose (*Rosa canina*) or Japanese rose (*Rosa multiflora*) will do very nicely.

Make a T-shaped slit, as close to ground level as possible, in the bark of the rootstock, and gently peel it back a little. Select a bud on a strong young shoot of the rose you want to propagate, and cut it, and 1 in (2.5cm) of the surrounding wood, out of the shoot. Next, carefully remove the wood from behind the bud–or 'eye', as it is known in the trade. Be careful not to damage the bud or the green 'shield' around it. Quickly place the shield, bud-outwards, into the T-shaped split in the rootstock and secure it with twine.

Next spring, cut the host rose back to about 1 in (2.5cm) above the bud, which by then should be growing away strongly. Standard roses are produced this way, only the bud is inserted into a cut about 4 ft (1.2m) above ground level, usually on *Rosa rugosa* stock. If you are making your own standard rose, try the commercial practice of inserting two buds, on opposite sides of the stock, for a full head.

R. canina, the dog rose: ideal rooting stock

R. rugosa 'Blanc Double de Coubert'

Large-flowered variety 'Alexander'

PROPAGATING ROSES

1 *Make a T-shaped slit in the bark of the rootstock near ground level*

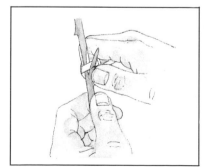

2 *Select a bud for propagation and slice the section of stem around it*

3 *Remove the bud with its 'shield' and take out the wood behind*

4 *Insert the bud in the T-shaped slit and bind it securely*

PLANTING LATE-FLOWERING BULBS

Although your garden is packed with flowers now, and putting in more is the last thing on your mind, it is time to look ahead to the fall and plan for color then. There are bulbs to plant now that will take over when the annuals and bedding plants are past their best, and provide brightly–even exotically–colored flowers at a time of year when they are much appreciated.

Autumn crocus (*Colchicum*) Not a crocus at all, in the strict botanical sense, the common name refers to the fact that it closely resembles a true crocus. Its alternative common names–naked boys and naked ladies– come from the pale, flesh-pink flowers, that appear without the 'clothing' of their leaves. The lack of leaves are the one big drawback of autumn crocus. Rather like tulip leaves in shape and size, they appear in spring and add their large presence to the garden until July, when they die back. They take a long time dying back, too, so you are left with messy, yellowing leaves and the knowledge that if you give in to your temptation to cut them off, you will permanently damage the plant. So . . . rough grass or in among shrubs is the best spot for these plants–lawns are out of the question as normal mowing regimes would remove the leaves. Rockeries are another

possibility, and indoors, they are sometimes grown 'dry'– simply placed on a saucer without any soil or water and left to get on with flowering, but they must be planted immediately the flowers fade.

Select a sunny or lightly shaded spot outdoors, and dig in plenty of leaf-mold or a mixture of sand and peat, especially if the soil is on the heavy side.

Plant the bulbs 3 in (7.5cm) deep and 8–10 in (20–25cm) apart, and as they are perfectly hardy, you can leave them in the ground for some years. Eventually, you may have to lift and divide them, in much the same way as daffodils.

The goblet-shaped flowers are usually 6–8 in (15–20cm) high–it is the 16 in (40cm) leaves you have to remember– and are available in several colors. *C. autumnale* is a species with soft-lilac, rose-tinged flowers. Its named forms include the white 'Album' and the double-flowered white 'Album Plenum'. *C. byzantinum* has rosy-pink blooms early in the fall. *C. speciosum*, lilac-rose, has named forms in white ('Album') and deep reddish-purple ('Atrorubens'). Dutch hybrid colchicums include a wide range of colors–'The Giant' is a striking dark-violet, with a contrasting white center, 'Lilac Wonder' is a lovely lilac-rose shade with white stripes, and 'Waterlily' really does resemble an exotic waterlily, with its fully double, mauve flowers.

Colchicum 'Lilac Wonder'

Colchicum autumnale

Amaryllis belladonna

Belladonna lily (*Amaryllis belladonna*) The belladonna lily is related to the immensely popular flowering house plant, amaryllis (*Hippeastrum*). Its trumpet-shaped bright-pink flowers are unforgettable. Much more particular about the amount of warmth and sunshine they receive than autumn crocuses are, belladonna lilies should be planted only in sheltered, warm gardens in the most northern states of the US and in Canada. Be prepared, especially in colder areas, to give them protection from frost in winter with a layer of straw or dry peat, ideally with a cloche on top.

Plant the bulbs, which are very large, deep enough to give a good 4 in (10cm) layer of soil above the bulb. It is a good idea to line the hole with a layer of sharp sand or peat when planting, as badly drained or waterlogged soil means death to belladonna lilies–in fact, most of these fall-flowering bulbs are extremely sensitive to soil moisture.

Despite this cossetting, you will be more than glad you made the effort when the lilies reward you with their fragrant, pale-pink flowers on bare stalks in September and October. Their long, strap-shaped leaves do not appear until early the following year.

Crocus You have to look hard to spot the differences between the true crocus and the *Colchicum*—the crocus has flowers with three stamens, while *Colchicum* has six. Both fall-flowering, true crocus and *Colchicum* also produce flowers before the leaves arrive. But when they do come through the ground, you will find the sparse, grassy foliage much less of a problem than that of *Colchicum*. Some species are quite happy in a lawn, and in the expanse of green, their pretty flowers—on the whole, smaller than *Colchicum*—are shown to advantage. Both the true crocus and the autumn crocus naturalize if happy where they are growing, and the broad sweeps of color provided by a mass of crocus in a lawn can be very dramatic. There are several species as well as named forms available and bulk buying keeps the costs down.

C. *speciosus* is an easy one to start with—its mauve flowers, pale-throated and purple-veined, appear early in the fall. The named forms—'Albus', which is a pure white, the deep, sky-blue 'Conqueror' and the fragrant, blue-violet 'Globosus'—flower a bit later. C. *kotschyanus*, sometimes listed as C. *zonatus*, is worth looking out for—the lilac-pink flowers are attractively marked with white and yellow. Another beauty, and a very fast naturalizer in moist soils, is C. *nudiflorus*, with large, deep-purple flowers in early fall. To extend the crocus season in your garden, plant C. *laevigatus*, with usually lilac-purple flowers in late October, and sometimes even later.

Plant crocus about 3 in (7.5cm) deep and the same distance apart, but to avoid an artificial look, especially on lawns, drop them, from hand-height, on the ground and simply plant them where they fall. Special tools are available for removing plugs of turf to plant bulbs individually in lawns, but lifting the turf with a spade is almost as easy, and you can plant several at once if you use this method.

Nerine There is only one species, N. *bowdenii*, which is hardy enough to be grown outdoors even in the mild areas, and a sunny, sheltered and relatively dry spot is essential. If you can offer these conditions, this South African plant will produce clusters of long-lasting, pale-pink, trumpet-shaped flowers on leafless stalks, up to 3 ft (1m) high, in September and October. The form 'Fenwick's Variety' has larger and darker pink flowers, and 'Pink Triumph' is silvery pink. Strap-like leaves are present during the summer and at flowering time.

Whether in the open ground or in pots, the soil or pot mix must be well drained, preferably gritty or sandy. Plant shallowly in pots, 4 in (10cm) deep in the open ground, and about 6 in (15cm) apart. They are not keen on rich soils and, once planted, resent disturbance. To be on the safe side, protect them from frost, as for belladonna lilies.

Sternbergia Thought by some scholars to be the 'lily of the field' referred to in the Bible, sternbergia looks far more like bright-yellow crocus. And just to make matters even more confusing, it is sometimes called the 'autumn daffodil', and it is botanically related to belladonna lilies and nerines. The flowers, slightly larger than those of crocus, open in September and October, and the deep-green, strap-shaped leaves keep their color through the winter. These plants are from the Middle East, and the hotter, sunnier and drier their environment, the better their flowering will be. Try them in south-facing rockeries or borders.

Plant the bulbs 4 in (10cm) deep and roughly the same distance apart. Once established, they can be left undisturbed for years. S. *lutea* is the most common form, with 6 in (15cm) high flowers, blooming with or sometimes before the leaves. S. *clusiana* does not produce leaves until the spring.

Crocus speciosus 'Oxonian'

Crocus sativus

Nerine bowdenii

Sternbergia lutea

TREES & SHRUBS

Keep shrubs and trees well watered during periods of drought.

LAYERING

Though increasing plants by layering is often done in spring (see page 52), now is as good a time as any, if you have a few minutes to spare. And a minute or two is virtually all it takes, though the actual root formation can take a year or more. And don't forget that climbers can be layered, too, and, with the abundance of long flexible stems they produce, make perfect candidates. Try layering wisteria, clematis, Virginia creeper (*Parthenocissus quinquefolia*), honeysuckle or the beautiful *Trachelospermum jasminoides*, with its sweetly scented flowers. Climbing roses are worth trying, too, and indeed any climber you have and want to make more of. One of the glories of layering is that the parent plant continues to grow, so that in the unlikely event that something goes wrong with your layering, and roots don't form,

nothing has really been lost and you can try again, perhaps at a different time of the year, and using a slightly riper–or less ripe–stem or branch.

The method for layering climbers is much the same as for layering shrubs, though you may want to refine it a bit by sinking pots, filled with good-quality soil mix and sharp sand or grit, into the soil, so their rims are level with the soil surface. The reason for this is that there will be much less root disturbance when the time comes to move the newly rooted plants to a different location, if you layer them into the pots now. Another variation on the layering theme, useful if you want quite a few more new plants from supple-stemmed climbers, is serpentine layering. Pick a young, long trailing shoot and repeat the nicking and burying process several times along its length, using the open ground or soil mix-filled pots. Be very careful, when nicking the undersides, that you do not cut the stem in two, and if the stem in question is thin or slightly brittle, omit the nicking step entirely. Leave at least one pair of leaves above the ground between each buried section and remove any leaves that

The clean lines of a box hedge are a perfect frame for brightly colored summer flowers

would be buried in the process. Keep the stem well watered, especially if you are using pots, and leave it for a year before testing to see if roots have formed. A gentle tug at the base of the stem will give you your answer, and rooted sections can be cut apart and planted separately.

PRUNING

Summer pruning of shrubs that have finished flowering is an ongoing process–the exact timing depends on what the weather has been like, as well as the number of other garden tasks needing doing. Mock orange, botanically *Philadelphus* but sometimes called syringa, just to confuse matters, may need pruning now, together with *Weigela*, the beauty bush (*Kolkwitzia*) and any deutzias that have finished flowering. Cut out old flowered shoots back to a strong new shoot, and take the opportunity to cut out any crowded, old wood completely.

Wisterias need keeping in check, if they are not to take over your garden. Cut back the long,

twiny side growths to about six leaves from the main stems.

Hedges, especially quick-growing ones, such as privet (*Ligustrum*) will need clipping back this month, and the slow-but-steady hedges, such as yew (*Taxus*) can have a once-over-lightly, too. Check for weeds growing along the hedge bottom at the same time. If your privet is a golden-leaved form, you may find that a few branches carry deep-green, rather than yellow, leaves. This is called reversion, and it is the same thing if you find a branch on a variegated shrub producing solid-green leaves. In both cases, cut the reverted branch right back, or it will inevitably take over from its weaker, variegated neighbors.

Continue taking soft cuttings from shrubs you want more of (see page 90). If the weather has been hot and sunny, though, the wood should be ripening nicely, and you can take semi-hard cuttings instead (see page 119).

SERPENTINE LAYERING OF CLIMBERS

Nick the underside of a long shoot at intervals. Peg down and bury each

nicked section, in garden soil or in sunken, soil mix-filled pots

FRUIT

As maincrop strawberries finish, begin tidying up the beds. Runners will be growing thick and fast now, and unless you need them for propagating (see page 94), snip them off. An old-fashioned–and very dramatic–method of clearing strawberry beds is to set fire to the straw. This destroys most of the pests and diseases likely to be troublesome, and burns away the old foliage, but not the crowns. These quickly recover and send up fresh, new growth. Alternatively, rake up the straw or remove the protective sheeting and cut off the old foliage with shears. If your plants are past their prime, though, dig them out and replace them with rooted runners from earlier in summer. After two or three years' cropping, strawberry plants start to degenerate, and it is worth the small effort needed to replace them. Ideally, make your strawberry bed elsewhere in the garden, not on the site of the previous bed.

Everbearing strawberries should be left to flower without disturbance now, for your late summer and fall crops.

Melons growing under any sort of protection should be pollinated and trained in the same way as last month (see pages 94–5).

PRUNING AND LAYERING

Soft fruit–currants, raspberries and gooseberries–should be cropping nicely now, so check your defences against birds. Continue pruning gooseberries (see page 94) to keep both excessive foliage growth and mildew in check, and

SUPPORTING FRUITING BRANCHES

Heavily laden branches can be tied with ropes radiating from a central pole, or supported individually on sturdy, forked stakes. Padding prevents damage to the tree bark

spray against sawfly as necessary. When one-crop raspberries finish fruiting, cut out all the old growth at ground level, and begin tying in the new shoots that will provide next year's fruit.

Late in the month is the time to start layering blackberries, loganberries and blackberry hybrids. Simply bury the tip of a young shoot about 2 in (5cm) into the soil, first making sure that no leaves are buried. If you have ever struggled with brambles in your own garden, you will know that the plants are more than happy to oblige by sending out roots from the tip.

THINNING FRUIT

Thinning of fruit–apples, pears and grapes–continues this month. The procedure for apples and pears is the same as for June (see page 94) and should be finished by the end of July–in fact, some of the early cultivars of both may be ready for picking then, if the summer weather has been good.

Thinning grapes results in nicer-looking bunches and fewer, but larger, berries. As with fruit trees and bushes, thinning should be done gradually. Once the berries have started swelling, remove any obviously diseased or small ones first, and from the center of the bunch outwards–you can get special scissors for this. Then gradually, and starting from the bottom, reduce the number of berries so that those remaining are not crowded. Leave a slightly denser concentration of berries at the top of the bunch, but with heavy-cropping vines, a good third, or even more, of the berries should be removed.

Even after thinning, you may find it necessary to support some of the more heavily laden limbs of fruit trees–the weight of the fruit can cause the limbs to break. Use strong, vertical stakes which are forked at the top, to cradle the limbs. Alternatively, tie a stout pole to the tree trunk and run strong cords from the top of it to support the heavier branches. Such supports should always be padded where they come into contact with the branch to prevent damage to the bark.

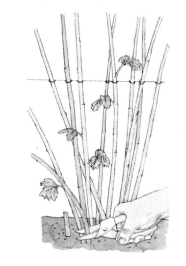

PRUNING RASPBERRIES

1 When fruiting is finished, cut back the old canes that have fruited to ground level

2 Make sure new canes are tied in securely and will be firmly supported for the following season's growth

PRUNING FRUIT TREES

Summer pruning of fruit trees can start this month, and continue into early fall. Take it slowly and easily, for the trees' benefit as well as yours. On the whole, summer pruning is more often done to trees trained to a particular shape—espalier, cordon, wall-trained or bush trees—than to large, fully established fruit trees, simply because of the scale of the work involved. An espalier-trained tree consists of a vertical central stem which has horizontal fruiting branches running from it. It is often used to form a natural boundary in a garden or to hide walls. Cordon-training requires less space, and is convenient as it means that fruit trees can be planted fairly close together. Leave the leading shoots alone, but prune back the side shoots, or laterals, to leave 6 in (15cm), or three or four leaves. With fruit trees trained against walls, you can combine summer pruning with training and tying in, removing shoots growing at right angles to the wall, and any diseased, weak or crossing wood.

PESTS AND DISEASES

Pests and diseases can still be troublesome. Keep a look out for the persistent ones—woolly aphid, various caterpillars, red spider mite, and mildew—and spray as necessary (see page 184).

Plum trees should be inspected for silver leaf—a particularly nasty fungal infection which shows up as a silvery sheen on the infected leaves. Cut out and burn any infected branches, and paint the wound with a fungicidal paint. Apple and pear trees can also suffer, especially in the Northwest US.

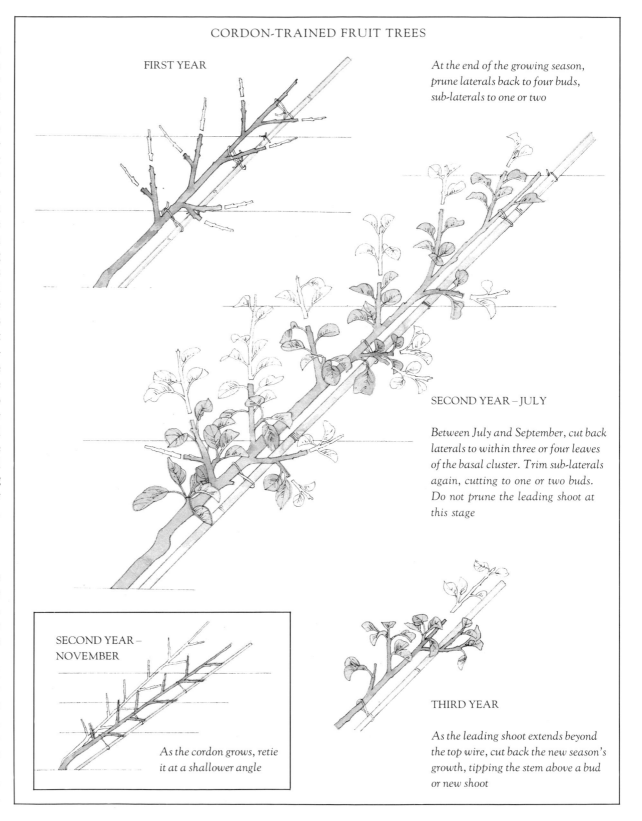

CORDON-TRAINED FRUIT TREES

FIRST YEAR

At the end of the growing season, prune laterals back to four buds, sub-laterals to one or two

SECOND YEAR—JULY

Between July and September, cut back laterals to within three or four leaves of the basal cluster. Trim sub-laterals again, cutting to one or two buds. Do not prune the leading shoot at this stage

SECOND YEAR—NOVEMBER

As the cordon grows, retie it at a shallower angle

THIRD YEAR

As the leading shoot extends beyond the top wire, cut back the new season's growth, tipping the stem above a bud or new shoot

ESPALIER-TRAINED FRUIT TREES

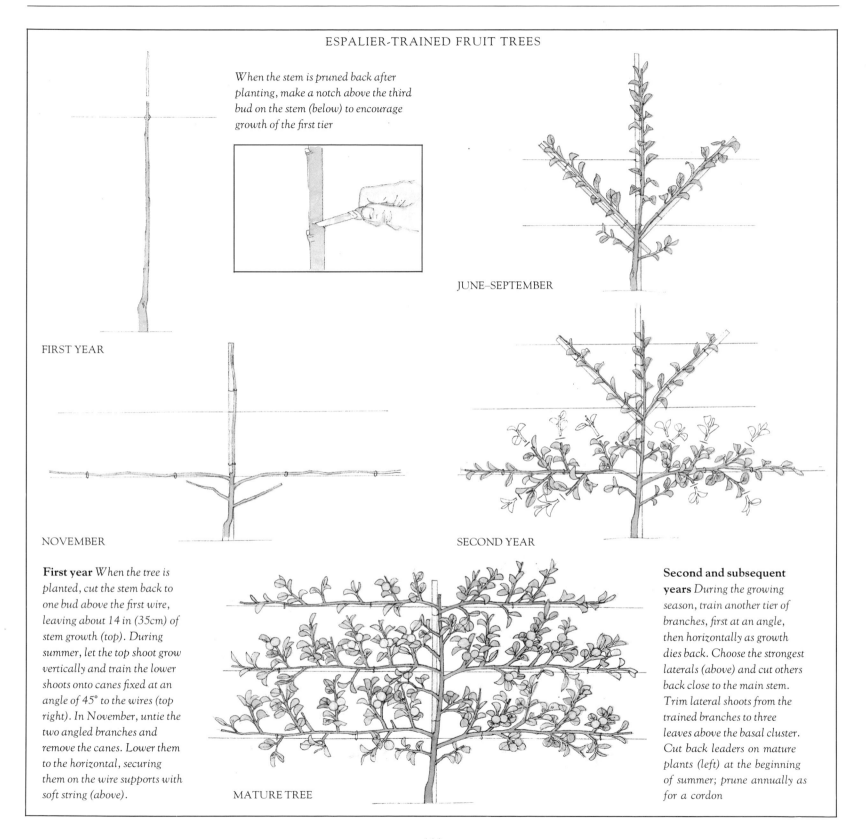

When the stem is pruned back after planting, make a notch above the third bud on the stem (below) to encourage growth of the first tier

FIRST YEAR

JUNE–SEPTEMBER

NOVEMBER

SECOND YEAR

MATURE TREE

First year *When the tree is planted, cut the stem back to one bud above the first wire, leaving about 14 in (35cm) of stem growth (top). During summer, let the top shoot grow vertically and train the lower shoots onto canes fixed at an angle of 45° to the wires (top right). In November, untie the two angled branches and remove the canes. Lower them to the horizontal, securing them on the wire supports with soft string (above).*

Second and subsequent years *During the growing season, train another tier of branches, first at an angle, then horizontally as growth dies back. Choose the strongest laterals (above) and cut others back close to the main stem. Trim lateral shoots from the trained branches to three leaves above the basal cluster. Cut back leaders on mature plants (left) at the beginning of summer; prune annually as for a cordon*

VEGETABLES

Once the leaves of your shallots turn yellow, lift them carefully and leave them out in the sun to dry. When fully dry, rub them over to remove any remaining particles of soil or loose outer skin. Save some of the best small bulbs for planting next spring, and store the rest in a cool, airy place until ready to use. Any garlic and onions you planted in the fall should be ready as well, and should be given the same treatment.

Globe artichokes—one of the most ornamental vegetables—should be ready for picking now. The best time to cut them is just as the leafy scales start to open—leave it too long and you will have an attractive, blue-flowered thistle that is completely inedible. If you take the artichokes on the ends of the main stems first, smaller, but still edible, artichokes will be produced lower down the stem.

BEANS AND SALAD CROPS

To get a good 'set' with runner beans—that is gardener's terminology for successful fertilization of flowers—the weather must be warm which in turn stimulates the insects which pollinate them. Experimental evidence shows that the old practice of spraying the plants with water in the evening has no effect. Once the plants have reached the top of their supports, pinch out the growing tips. Towards the end of the month, you may be able to start harvesting the first of the runner beans, as well as some broad and shell beans. All of these leguminous plants will need a steady supply of water,

augmented by mulching, if the weather is hot and dry.

Mulch salad crops, too, if the weather calls for it, or you may find that your lettuce, radish and spinach have bolted. New Zealand spinach is the one exception. Though not a true spinach, botanically speaking, it has a similar taste and thrives in the hot sunny conditions that would ruin a normal spinach crop.

HARVESTING HERBS AND VEGETABLES

Young beets, turnips and kohlrabi should be ready for harvesting—and tender carrots, too—but pick only as much as you need for the immediate future, to keep that splendid, fresh-from-the-garden taste. As with dahlias and chrysanthemums in the flower garden, there is always a temptation to grow the biggest you can, when it comes to growing vegetables, and often the size is in inverse proportion to its flavor. Huge marrows are never as tasty as young, tender ones, though they may win prizes in local horticultural shows.

Celery dug from a trench shows the depth of the soil covering in the final stage of earthing-up

In this bed, beets and onions sown side by side in rows are well-grown and ready for harvesting

You can continue to harvest and dry herbs, or freeze them, whichever suits you better, but don't forget to take advantage of their color and fragrance when fresh, and use them in the kitchen whenever you can. And to get a supply of fresh parsley in the darkest winter months, sow parsley seed now, in a sheltered spot. Make the seed drills $\frac{1}{2}$ in (15mm) deep, and don't despair if nothing seems to be happening—parsley is slow to germinate and it can take six weeks for the seedlings to show if the weather is abnormally cool. Thin the seedlings to 6 in (15cm) apart when they are large enough to handle, and protect them with cloches when the weather turns cold. Another alternative is to sow them in a cold frame, if available.

SOWING VEGETABLES

Other vegetables to sow at the end of the month include salad crops, both summer and winter, root crops and spring cabbage. Start the cabbage in a seed bed, and sow little and often, over the next month or so, to get crops next spring in the southern areas. And while you are working in the seed bed, check that the seedlings from last month's sowing (see page 96) are coming along, and thin or transplant as necessary.

EARTHING-UP

Potatoes will be vulnerable to blight, a fungal infection that seems to be more troublesome in cool, wet summers. Brown markings on the leaves, and discolored patches on the potato flesh, are tell-tale signs, so spray with a suitable fungicide (see page 184) if necessary.

BLANCHING CELERY

For blanching, celery stems are tied or encased in a paper collar.
Layers of earth, added every two weeks, eventually cover the stems

Only the top leaves should show above the earthed-up trench

Earthing-up winter celery can start this month. Fill in the trenches with a 4 in (10cm) layer of soil, first encasing the young plants in protective paper collars to keep the soil from getting into the hearts. Tying the stalks together with soft twine accomplishes the same thing. Continue the earthing-up process once every two weeks.

Earthing-up leeks, if you are growing them 'on the flat' or in trenches, is another July chore. Proceed in stages, rather than burying the vegetable at one stroke.

TOMATOES

Tomatoes, whether soil-grown or in containers, will need feeding now, with a good vegetable fertilizer. A steady supply of water is crucial, especially for those growing in containers, and you can count on their needing 2 pt (1.2 liters) a day in hot weather. An uneven supply of water will lead to split fruit, and all your hard work would be wasted, so put them at the top of your watering list.

Tall-growing cultivars of tomato should be given support, and have the little side shoots, where the leaf stalk joins the main stem, nipped out. Once the plant has made six flower trusses, pinch out the main growing tip two or

Overcompensating by heavy watering of a dried-out plant will cause the ripening tomatoes to split

To stop tomatoes, pinch off side shoots growing between leaves and main stem

After six flower trusses have set on the plant, take out the growing point two leaves above the top truss

three leaves above the top truss. If left to grow on, more flower trusses would continue to be produced, but would have no chance of ripening, or even filling out, before the cold weather sets in.

Tomatoes grown in a greenhouse need much the same care, but you must also make sure that there is plenty of ventilation and shading, as well as sufficient water and liquid fertilizer. If the air is close and stagnant, a whole host of diseases—molds and mildews—are likely to appear, and lack of protection from fierce summer sunlight, intensified by the magnifying action of glass, will lead to scorched leaves.

Bush tomatoes are treated just as generously when it comes to food and water supplies, but you need not bother with stopping the main stem—there is no single main stem, in any case—or removing the little side shoots.

In general, it isn't necessary to pollinate the flowers yourself, as wind and insects will do it naturally. You can release the pollen though, by giving the support a light tap.

August

Lazy summer days are here and many
of us go away this month, thus missing the results of
our hard work in the garden. For those who remain
at home, there are still flowers and fresh crops to
enjoy, but some garden chores to do as well.
Fall is not far away, and the first bulbs need
planting for a good display next spring.

Fuchsias (left) are among the most versatile
of flowering shrubs. In mild areas they can be
grown as hedging plants; where winter frosts are sharper,
they can still be used as summer bedding plants,
to be lifted in the late fall and moved
into a cool greenhouse

Jobs for the month

General
Water the garden as necessary, and make arrangements for watering while on vacation
Continue weeding and tidying up
Treat pests and diseases
Keep the greenhouse ventilated
Continue harvesting
Consider the use of ground-cover plants

Flowers
Support dahlias and trap earwigs
Sow butterfly flower (*Schizanthus*) and stocks indoors
Plant Madonna lilies
Pot up house-plant seedlings
Start arum lilies
Rest hippeastrums and tuberous-rooted begonias for indoor use
Take pelargonium cuttings
Continue deadheading
Continue disbudding dahlias, carnations and chrysanthemums
Cut flowers for indoor display and for drying

Trees and shrubs
Summer-prune hydrangeas

Take semi-ripe cuttings, and leaf-bud cuttings of camellias
Pot up rooted cuttings taken earlier in the season
Continue deadheading
Start training standard fuchsias

Lawns
Continue mowing
Prepare areas for sowing next month
Treat newly sown lawns with weedkiller

Roses
Finish budding
Continue disbudding and deadheading
Spray against black spot and mildew

Fruit
Make a new strawberry bed, continue removing runners from established plants, and protect fall-fruiting cultivars
Finish pruning gooseberries
Prune blackcurrants
Prune loganberries after cropping

and tie in new canes
Harvest tree and soft fruit; protect against birds and wasps
Water swelling melons and expose fully grown melons to sunlight
Continue training fruit trees against walls and fences
Clear up around bush and cane fruit after cropping
Spray grapevines against mildew

Vegetables
Sow Japanese onions, scallions, lettuce, summer and winter radish, turnips, stump-rooted carrots, spring cabbage and winter spinach
Thin and transplant last month's seedlings
Harvest runner beans, sweetcorn, second early and maincrop potatoes, onions and salad crops
Harvest herbs and collect ripe seed for sowing
Blanch endive
Continue earthing up leeks and celery
Continue training, tying in and feeding tomatoes
Clean up after harvesting

Routine summer chores—watering, tidying up, weeding and mowing—are much the same as for last month, but you may notice a decrease in your work load, and things in the garden will seem a little less hectic. This is because the plants are responding to the lower light levels and cooler evenings that late summer brings. For the most part, pests, diseases and weeds have slowed down, too, though you may be troubled by earwigs and mildew.

In the greenhouse, whitefly and red spider mite are just as active, and graymold may put in an appearance, so be ready with appropriate pesticides and fungicides. Keeping the greenhouse well ventilated, and the humidity and the temperature equable will contribute towards preventing these problems.

Harvesting of fruit, vegetables and herbs will be your first priority, if you grow them. Flowers are 'harvested' now, too, freshly cut for flower arrangements or dried for use in the winter season.

Make arrangements for watering the garden if you're going on vacation.

If keeping the garden in order has kept you busier than you expected, and you are looking for a way to cut down, then now is the time to think about planting ground cover. These pretty but tough and undemanding plants will mat up to form a carpet in your garden and give you years of trouble-free cover. They include evergreen and herbaceous perennials, shrubs, especially low-growing conifers, climbers, ferns and even ornamental grasses, all relatively low-growing and dense enough to exclude weeds, even when dormant.

FLOWERS

Make sure that dahlias, particularly large-flowered sorts, are well staked, as late summer gales can be very damaging. Even without gales, the weight of the flower-heads can snap the stems, especially when wet with rain, so staking is necessary to give support. At this time of year earwigs may prove to be a nuisance. A traditional method of trapping them is to place a flower pot, filled with straw or grass, upside down on a stake near the dahlias. The earwigs collect inside the pot, as they hide from the light, and the pot can be emptied of its contents into hot water every morning. Alternatively, spray with malathion or dust hiding places with carbaryl.

SOWING

For color in the greenhouse next spring, now is the time to sow seeds of the exotic-looking butterfly flower or poor man's orchid (*Schizanthus pinnatus*). Borne in elegant sprays, the somewhat orchid-like flowers come in a wonderful array of colors and patterns. Sow the seeds in trays of seed mixture, but don't give them any artificial heat, or you will end up with weak, sappy seedlings that won't last the winter. Stocks, too, can be sown now to give a greenhouse display next spring. Treat the seed as for the butterfly flower.

LILIES

Madonna lilies (*Lilium candidum*) should be planted this month. It seems an odd time of year to do so,

Dahlias should be staked firmly. Set a flowerpot to trap earwigs

but Madonna lilies begin growing new roots and leaves from late August, so you should get them in the ground now if possible. Choose a sunny spot and well drained soil. Plant them shallowly–barely 2 in (5cm) of soil to cover them is more than enough–and add a little lime to the surrounding soil for good measure.

PLANTS IN CONTAINERS

The house-plant seedlings – calceolaria, cineraria and fairy primrose–that were thinned last month (see page 103) may well have grown large enough to need potting up individually. Use good-quality soil-based mixture, and 2½–3 in (6–7.5cm) pots. There is no need at all for larger pots at this stage in the proceedings.

If you haven't started your tender cyclamen into growth (see page 101), do so immediately. Start the rhizomes of arum lily (*Zantedeschia aethiopica*), too, either newly bought for planting, or existing plants which have been

resting through the summer. They need big pots–say, 10 in (25cm) across–and a rich, soil-based mixture. Keep the soil mix on the dry side until signs of growth appear, then increase watering.

One of the most interesting aspects of gardening is its cyclical nature–how each plant develops according to its own schedule. Meeting the various needs of plants, whether in the garden or indoors, can be quite a challenge. While you are starting some plants into growth, you are putting others 'to bed'. Hippeastrum (*Amaryllis*) is a case in point. It should now be gradually dried off. Early-flowering tuberous-rooted begonias can be grown indoors and need the same treatment.

CUTTINGS AND PRUNING

Pelargonium cuttings can be taken now, and they should be well rooted by the time the cold weather comes. Follow the same method as for cuttings taken in spring (see page 34). If your pelargoniums are good sized, you should be able to take plenty of cuttings without disfiguring the plants. In fact, the plants will respond to this pruning by sending out fresh side-shoots.

Watering depends, as always,

on the weather, but be prepared to water regularly. Deadheading and disbudding–of chrysanthemums, dahlias and carnations in particular – will continue as for last month (see page 101).

Keep cutting sweet peas, to fill your house with scent and to keep the flowers coming on the plants. Most of the bigger dahlias are too cumbersome for flower arrangements, but smaller ones combine well with other summer flowers.

Start cutting everlasting flowers for drying now. Besides the ever-popular honesty (*Lunaria annua*) and straw flower (*Helichrysum*), try drying the lovely green calyces of bells of Ireland (*Molucella laevis*). If you haven't grown special flowers for drying, try experimenting with what you do have. Hydrangeas dry very well, for example, and you can try drying ferns, flowers belonging to the daisy family, and ornamental grasses. The flowers or foliage you intend to preserve must be bone dry and in peak condition to start with. Hang them upside down, either singly or in bunches, in a dark, airy place. Do not make the bunches too big, or the air won't be able to circulate freely.

Bright helichrysum are a popular choice for dried flowers

Flowers for the month

Roses and bedding plants still provide a dazzling backdrop of color, but there are newcomers to the garden, too. Among the shrubs, it is a good month to enjoy the hardy hibiscus (*H. syriacus*), with trumpet-shaped flowers, that looks almost as exotic as its tropical cousin. In sheltered gardens, the scented, pure-white flowers of myrtle are on display. More dramatic still are the spikes of New Zealand flax (*Phormium tenax*) and yucca–up to 6 ft (2m) tall–carrying bell-shaped flowers in creamy white, sometimes pink-or red-tinted in bud. Blue spiraea (*Caryopteris × clandonensis*), hardy plumbago (*Ceratostigma willmottianum*) and Russian sage (*Perovskia atriplicifolia*) add a blue note to the garden, joining the already-flowering ceanothus (*C.* 'Burkwoodii' and *C. caerulus*).

Brilliant orange and scarlet are the new colors for climbers in August. The trumpet creeper (*Campsis radicans*) combines wisteria-like foliage and scarlet, trumpet-shaped flowers. More delicate are the nasturtium flowers of flame creeper (*Tropaeolum speciosum*), which makes its graceful way through shrubs and other climbers. Lastly, the Chilean glory flower (*Eccremocarpus scaber*) livens up sunny walls and fences with its racemes of tubular scarlet flowers.

All manner of daisy flowers are out now, from the huge sunflower (*Helianthus*) to the little Swan River daisy (*Brachycome*). Mid-way between the two are the cosmos (*C. bipinnatus*), black-eyed Susan (*Rudbeckia*) and helenium (*H. autumnale*). An unlikely member of the daisy family is dahlia, working overtime this month to rival the roses for your attention. With its wide range of dramatic shapes and colors, dahlia is excellent for garden display and as a cut flower.

In garden ponds, water lilies (*Nymphaea*) will be in full flower, displaying waxy, perfect blooms above their glossy leaves. On dry ground, Peruvian lilies (*Alstroemeria*), with their pinky-orange, trumpet-shaped flowers, join the true lilies (*Lilium speciosum, L. auratum, L. henryi*) to complete the scene.

1 *Helenium autumnale* **2** *Caryopteris × clandonensis* 'Kew Blue' **3** *Perovskia atriplicifolia* **4** *Eccremocarpus scaber* **5** *Cosmos bipinnatus* **6** *Nymphaea alba* **7** *Alstroemeria* Ligtu hybrids

TREES & SHRUBS

There are no dramatic differences between the care of shrubs and trees last month and this month. You should keep in the back of your mind, though, an awareness that the growing season does not stretch indefinitely ahead. The evenings are already growing shorter and the odd cool spell is a forewarning of more to come. For this reason, get any hedge trimming done as early in the month as possible. Later trimming encourages even later new growth, which may fall to early frost.

Hydrangeas that have almost finished flowering can have deadheading combined with a bit of summer pruning. Cut back the flower stem to a healthy bud, and remove any weak or crowded stems while you are at it.

TAKING CUTTINGS

This is a good month for taking semi-ripe cuttings of shrubs. You should be using this season's new wood for cutting material, and it should be soft and green at the growing tip, but slightly tougher and browny-green or brown at the base. The procedure is the same as for soft cuttings taken earlier in the season (see page 90), though wilting is likely to be less of a problem. Cuttings to take now include hydrangea—pot them up individually to avoid root disturbance later on—evergreen ceanothus, cornus, buddleia, philadelphus, deutzia, garrya and berberis. Though it does seem extravagant, individually potting cuttings taken now means you don't have the problem of teasing the roots apart next

spring, when they may have grown together into one huge mass.

Keep the pots outdoors in a lightly shaded cold frame and remember to water the soil mix from time to time. Late next spring you should be able to plant them out where they are to grow.

Try taking camellia cuttings now. They may be slow to root, but are not difficult. Select semi-ripe shoots, about 4 in (10cm) long, each with three or four leaves. Carefully remove the bottom leaves and cut the upper leaves in half crossways—it looks odd but reduces transpiration. Insert the almost-leafless stems into a mixture of half-peat, half-sand, so that half the stem is buried. A bit of bottom heat helps, but is not absolutely necessary, and a cold frame will give you rooted cuttings, but takes longer to do so.

Commercially, camellias are propagated from leaf-bud cuttings taken at this time of year. Although you are unlikely to be interested in the vast number of new plants obtained by this method, you might like to try it for

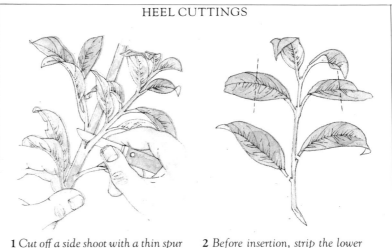

HEEL CUTTINGS

1 *Cut off a side shoot with a thin spur of wood from the main stem*

2 *Before insertion, strip the lower leaves and cut across the upper leaves*

fun. Select leaves growing on semi-ripe wood, and a growth bud visible where the leaf joins the stem. With a sharp knife, cut the stem just above the bud (in the leaf axil) and 1–1½ in (2.5–4cm) below. Insert the cuttings into a mixture of peat and sand, so that the leaf and bud rest at soil level. Keep in a propagating frame or plastic bag, and give bottom heat to encourage rooting.

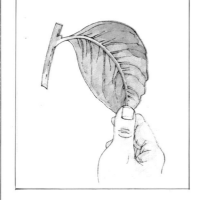

LEAF BUD CUTTINGS

1 *Remove a shoot from the plant and cut a short section of stem, including a single leaf with axil bud*

2 *Insert several cuttings around the pot rim, each bud just showing above the peat and sand mixture*

While you have cuttings on your mind, check any soft cuttings you may have taken last month. Those that have produced flowers should have them firmly nipped off, but any showing signs of new leafy growth should be checked for rooting. The gentlest possible tug at the base should give you the answer, and if they have rooted, pot them up individually. As the cuttings are now in a position to absorb nutrients, make sure you give them a reasonably rich soil mix. Once potted up, keep them watered, and out of direct sunlight for a few days.

DEADHEADING

Deadheading is still a general job in the garden. Some flowers, such as buddleia, look particularly untidy when they are on the way out, and spoil the appearance of the rest of the bush. If practicable, go over it with pruners. On a smaller scale, lavender may also need deadheading. Use the flower-heads for making potpourris—they have a delicious fragrance.

FUCHSIAS

There is still time to start off some standard fuchsias from cuttings. They won't be ready for display until next year, but given good care and treatment, a standard fuchsia will carry on flowering summer after summer.

Fuchsias are particularly suitable for training in this way, being relatively quick growing, and with long-lasting floral displays. Other plants that respond well to this treatment include pelargoniums, marguerites (*Chrysanthemum frutescens*) and cherry pie (*Heliotropium*). Bay, too, can be trained into lollipop-shaped standards, but the training of standard roses is slightly different and involves budding (see page 105).

Take cuttings from non-flowering shoots and root them as for fuchsia cuttings taken in spring (see page 34). Once the cuttings have rooted, pot them up separately and provide sturdy canes, one per plant. Tie each plant to its stake, using ties or soft twine, and adjust them and provide more as the plant grows. Remove any side shoots but be careful not to damage the growing tip.

Once growth slows down, in the fall, give the plants as much light as possible, but cut down on watering, so that the soil mix is barely moist.

When growth starts up, next spring, increase watering and feed regularly. Provide larger pots once the roots become pot-bound, and pinch out the growing tip when the desired height has been reached. At the same time, remove all the side shoots from the stem except those from the top two to three leaf pairs. These will make the bushy top to the standard. When they are about 4 in (10cm) long, pinch out their tips as well, to encourage the production of even more side shoots, until the head fills out and becomes dense with foliage and shoots.

If you want to train the fuchsia into a weeping standard, first select a normally lax-growing cultivar, e.g. 'Red Spider'. Erect, robust cultivars never look right and are liable to snap during the training period. Tie strings of cotton to the ends of the shoots and peg them down into the soil in the pot, using hairpins. Eventually, the weight of the flowers will cause them to hang down naturally, and the strings can be removed.

Standard fuchsias in pots need much the same treatment as other fuchsias, but be on the look-out for shoots forming on the stem or from the base, and remove them to encourage a bushy head.

Every spring, when starting your standard into growth, you should prune back the side shoots that form the head by a third or half of their length, so plenty of new wood can form—which will carry the flowers—without the plant losing its bushiness.

Double-flowered fuchsia hybrids are vivid and ornamental plants (above)

A bushy, well-trained standard fuchsia rising on a slim, strong stem is an elegant focal point (below)

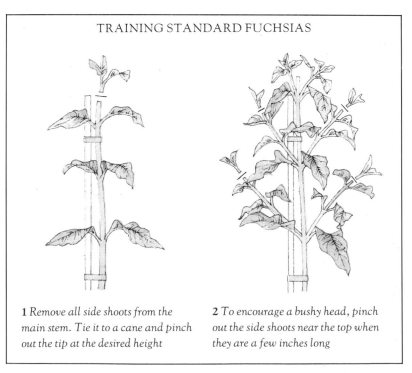

TRAINING STANDARD FUCHSIAS

1 *Remove all side shoots from the main stem. Tie it to a cane and pinch out the tip at the desired height*

2 *To encourage a bushy head, pinch out the side shoots near the top when they are a few inches long*

GROUND COVER PLANTS

Bugle (*Ajuga reptans* 'Burgundy Glow') An attractively variegated purple, gray, green and creamy mat-forming plant, bugle can be invasive if grown in rich, moist soil and sun or light shade.

Campanula (*C. portenschlagiana*) Happy in sun or partial shade, this campanula forms mats of heart-shaped leaves and has violet, bell-shaped flowers in summer.

Common juniper (*Juniperus communis*) There are several ground-hugging named forms of common juniper. Try *J.c. depressa*, *J.c.d.* 'Aurea' or *J.c.* 'Hornibrookii'.

Creeping Jenny (*Lysimachia nummularia* 'Aurea') An invasive ground cover for light shade, the buttercup-like flowers appear along trailing stems in summer.

Creeping juniper (*Juniperus horizontalis*) There are several first-class forms of creeping juniper, usually growing to a height of 6 in–1 ft (15–30cm) and with an eventual diameter of up to 10 ft (3m).

Epimedium (*E.* × *rubrum*) The heart-shaped leaves of epimedium are glossy-green when mature, red-tinted when young and are usually evergreen. Wands of yellow flowers appear in spring.

Ivy (*Hedera helix* 'Variegata') This ivy has large leaves striped and edged in silvery gray and white. It should do well in all but the most exposed or cold gardens and is fine for deep shade.

Norway spruce (*Picea abies* 'Reflexa') 'Reflexa' is a ground-hugging form with rich-green foliage, and it can cover 6 ft (2m) or more horizontally.

Periwinkle (*Vinca minor* 'Aureo-variegata') Greater periwinkle (*V. major*) takes time to become established, but can be highly invasive. Lesser periwinkle (*V. minor*) may spread over 3 ft (1m) or more. 'Aureo-variegata' has creamy leaf markings and mauve flowers.

Savin juniper (*Juniperus sabina*) The form 'Tamariscifolia' forms a mound of densely packed, blue-green foliage.

Stonecrop (*Sedum spathulifolium* 'Cappa Blanca') Stonecrop has evergreen fleshy, light-gray leaves and bright-yellow flowers in summer. Full sun and dry, even poor, soil suit it best.

Thyme (*Thymus serpyllum* 'Annie Hall') A low-growing thyme with pale-pink flowers and pale-green leaves, this does well in full sun.

Yew (*Taxus baccata* 'Repens Aurea') The young leaves of this low-growing yew are edged in yellow. Grow it in full sun.

Ajuga reptans

Epimedium × *rubrum*

Campanula portenschlagiana

Vinca minor 'Aureo-variegata Alba'

Lysimachia nummularia

Sedum spathulifolium 'Cappa Blanca'

WATERING

How much water does your garden need? This question becomes a crucial one when you are planning to go away on vacation and worried about the fate of the plants in your garden and, indeed, in your house. Apart from weather, which we can't do much about, there are various factors that influence the amount of watering needed in times of drought, especially aspect and soil type.

Aspect is important. An exposed, windy garden will dry out more quickly than a sheltered one. A shady garden overhung with trees, or overlooked by high walls, tends to keep moisture longer, since the sunlight cannot get at the soil. At the same time, these trees and walls act as a shield, preventing rain from reaching the soil in the first place. Additionally, the roots of large trees can regularly take up thousands of quarts of water from the soil, leaving it bone dry. And the crown of a tree in full leaf acts in much the same way as an umbrella, keeping the ground beneath it dry. In short, once a shady garden is provided with water, it should be slow to evaporate, but you have to make extra allowance for water if the shade comes from nearby trees.

Soil is another factor to be considered. A free-draining, sandy soil needs more water than a clay one. Once clay has really dried out, though, and sun-baked cracks appear, it takes a lot of watering to really moisten it right through. In both cases, the addition of well-rotted organic matter – garden compost, leafmold or peat – to the soil improves its ability to retain moisture. Besides digging organic matter into the soil – not a particularly pleasant prospect at this time of year – you can use it as a mulch, spreading it on the surface of the soil, to cut down evaporation.

Remember, though, that you can't keep in what you haven't got in the first place, so mulching dry ground is fairly counter-productive, and the mulch can even act as a waterproof coating, keeping light rain from reaching the dry soil. So if a drought threatens, and certainly if you are going away on vacation, water and then mulch your garden.

Ideally, the mulch should be 1–2 in (2.5–5cm) thick. Unless you've got a tiny garden – or a huge family – your own compost heap, made from vegetable scraps from the kitchen, lawn clippings, and soft vegetable matter from the garden, is unlikely to yield as much as you need. You can 'buy in' mulch, in the form of spent mushroom compost, peat, leafmold, fine straw, or bags of farmyard manure. This can be expensive for large-scale mulching. A compromise solution is to select the most vulnerable plants, and give them generous rings of mulch round the area of their root spread. Don't let the mulch

touch the plants' stems, or they may rot (but this is rare).

Though there is much to be said for home-made garden compost, it isn't always a pretty sight used as a mulch, especially if it has not had time to rot down completely. If your garden is small, fastidiously tidy and eminently visible, you may find paying the extra money for bought-in mulches – dark brown and earthy looking – preferable to partially decomposed potato peelings, orange peels and so on featuring heavily in your garden scheme!

Watering systems
Except in the tiniest of gardens, trying to provide the amount of water plants need – $4\frac{1}{2}$ gal per sq yd (17 liters per sq m) per week – with a bucket or watering can is impossible. A hose certainly improves the situation, but it is fairly time-consuming if you have to stand in the garden holding it. And nothing is more off-putting than having to fix a hose, through an open window, to a sink tap. Watering a garden via an indoor tap means that you can't leave the house, because of the open window. Tap connectors tend to come adrift, too, if they are under any pressure, so a hose fitted to an outside tap is worth the initial expense involved in installing it. You then can fit snap-together connectors part-way along the hose, if you want to use it for short-distance watering, or for filling a watering can. An alternative to

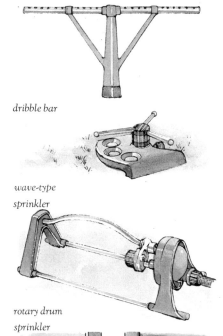

dribble bar

wave-type sprinkler

rotary drum sprinkler

flat hose in cassette

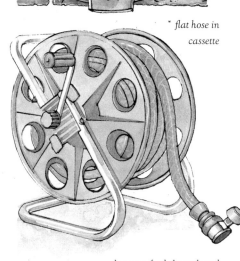

hose on feed-through reel

a hose fixed permanently to a tap is a cassette type of hose, made from a flexible material that lies flat when rolled onto a reel, which makes storage neat and easy.

Whichever type of hose you buy, treat it as a long-term investment and buy the best you can afford. Some are available with a ten-year guarantee, well worth the extra you may have to pay.

There is a wide range of hose attachments available. Sprinkler heads can be had from most garden centers and chain stores. For a little more money, you can buy a system that will automatically change position, 'walking' around the lawn for you, and vary the pitch and height of the water, at the same time.

You can buy handle attachments for hand-held sprinklers that automatically cut off the water supply when you release your grip—this is quite a bonus when you consider those awkward, long walks back to the tap with a fully-on hose.

A commercially popular system of watering which could be scaled down to small gardens is the drip-feed system. Though originally done with metal piping, you can buy high-quality plastic pipes that are perforated, to allow water to trickle out along its length. Ideal for between rows of vegetables, it is available, usually in 100 ft (30m) lengths, with T and Y connectors, to take it round corners or join it to other lengths of pipe.

LAWNS

Care of the lawn in August very much depends on the state of the weather. If it has been hot and dry, there won't be much new growth, so set the mower blades high and leave the clippings to act as a mulch to preserve what little moisture there is. If the weather has been wet and growth generally lush, lower the blades and collect the clippings. Be on the look-out for weeds, too, in wet weather, and remove them as soon as you can identify them as the unwanted visitors they are.

If you have roughly prepared a bare patch of garden for sowing next month—the procedure is much the same as for spring sowing (see page 40)—break up any rough clods, and hand-weed, paying particular attention to perennial weeds, and any weeds showing ripe seed. Pick up any debris or stones on the surface, and break it down to a fairly even tilth.

Spring-sown lawns may be showing signs of weed invasion and you may be able to treat them with a selective weedkiller now, but check the instructions on the packet carefully to make sure that the particular chemical can be used late in the growing season.

A rose arch is part of the fantasy of a cottage garden – an avenue of roses (below) is all the more delightful. Keep the stems clear of deadheads and unhealthy leaves

In dry weather lawn clippings can be left to lie as a mulch (above) which will preserve what moisture there is. In a wet spell, rake up clippings and get rid of weeds

ROSES

If you didn't finish budding roses in July, you can still do so during the first half of August (see page 105). After this, the bark becomes more difficult to peel away for bud insertion, and there may not be enough time left for the bud to become established on the parent plant, before cold weather sets in. Check that any budded roses from last month are not being strangled by the twine or tie that keeps the bud in position.

You should also stop giving fertilizers to roses now. Any new growth encouraged to form would still be young and soft when the weather turned cold, and would never make it through the winter unscathed.

Disbudding and deadheading continues (see page 92).

Continue spraying against black spot and mildew, if necessary.

FRUIT

If you didn't get a chance last month, detach young strawberry plants from their parent plants to make new strawberry beds. Check that new roots have formed by gently pulling on the runner. If the new plant remains firmly in position, then you can assume that it has rooted successfully. Cut the runner with a sharp knife, and a couple of days later, move the plant to its new home–ideally a sunny, sheltered spot with fertile, well-drained soil. Keep them well watered at this stage.

Continue removing runners from established strawberries, and give protection to fall-fruiting cultivars, in the form of netting against birds, and strawing down against mud splash.

PRUNING AND TRAINING

Finish summer-pruning gooseberries, and be on the look-out, still, for mildew and sawfly.

Blackcurrants, when they have finished fruiting, will benefit from a late-summer pruning. Prune right back to ground level one or two of the oldest fruiting canes, and tip back the other branches to a healthy new bud. Leaf spot can be a problem, and may require spraying.

Loganberries–very much like blackberries in growth habit–should be cropping nicely now. Once they have finished, cut back the old cropping canes to ground level, to give this year's canes–next year's fruiting canes–a chance to get away strongly. If the new canes are crowded, it's advisable to remove all but four or five

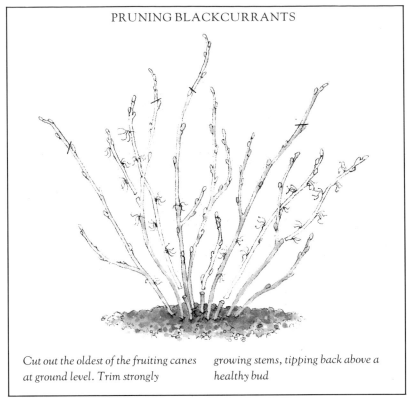

PRUNING BLACKCURRANTS

Cut out the oldest of the fruiting canes at ground level. Trim strongly growing stems, tipping back above a healthy bud

of the best looking, and train them along the wires as they grow.

Tree fruit–pears, plums, apples, cherries, peaches and apricots–will need picking, as soon as ripe. In the interests of tidiness and good gardening, rake up and put on the compost heap any fruit rotting beneath the trees. Birds, as usual, will be after your fruit, and wasps are a particular menace this month. Short of destroying their nests–which may not be easy to find–there is little you can do, though the old-fashioned trap of jars filled with beer or honey and water sometimes proves effective. If a nest is found, apply carbaryl or derris dust to the entrance after dark when all the wasps are inside.

Melons should be swelling and will need regular supplies of water. If they have reached their full size and have stopped swelling, stop

watering them and move aside, or cut off completely, any leaves which are shading the fruit. The plant may still be producing flowers and young shoots and these should be nipped off.

The training and summer-pruning of fruit trees grown against walls (see page 110) should continue through August.

If you have the time, summer clean the area around bush and cane fruits that have finished cropping. Weed round the bases and between the rows. The ground may very well be compacted from heavy picking, so break up the soil surface by hoeing. A thorough watering followed by mulching completes the job.

Mildew may be a problem on grapevines, so spray with an appropriate fungicide (see page 184) to get rid of it.

VEGETABLES

In mild areas there is still time for sowing crops to be harvested the next couple of months, and those that carry on over winter to provide vegetables next spring. Choose a sheltered spot for sowing Japanese onions and scallions, in rows 9 in (23cm) apart. Lettuce sown now will give you crops in mid-to-late fall, but you should be ready to give them cloche protection when the night temperatures drop.

Both winter and summer radishes can be sown now, but give summer radishes a partially shady spot, or they may bolt. Winter radishes will remain happily in the ground until you are ready to lift them for cold-weather salads, or can be lifted in late fall and stored, like other root vegetables, until needed.

Less exotic root vegetables than the winter radish, but still very useful, are stump-rooted carrots and turnips. Make sowings of both, and in the warm climates another sowing of spring cabbage. Winter spinach is another sensible choice if you want greens through fall followed by fresh new growth in spring. Sow the prickly seeds now, in a sheltered spot which gets plenty of sun.

Thin and transplant last month's seedlings, and keep them well weeded and watered.

HARVESTING VEGETABLES

Harvesting should be taking up quite a bit of your time, but what an enjoyable task. Check your runner beans every day, and pick them before the beans begin to bulge, or they will be tough and stringy. Picking them regularly encourages the plants to continue flowering and therefore producing more and more beans, so it is doubly important. In a hot summer, sweetcorn may be ready at some time this month The silky tassels should have turned from yellow to brown, but don't leave it until the tassels have withered up, or the sweetcorn will be past its best and tasteless.

Second early and maincrop potatoes can be lifted, as and when you need them. Onions, too, will be ready for harvesting. Lever them out of the ground with a garden fork, and spread them out on the surface of the soil for a few days to dry. Once dry, any caked earth can be brushed off, and they can either be stored in shallow boxes or made into pretty, old-

fashioned ropes, saving valuable space in garden sheds.

Salad days are here, with heavy crops—perhaps even gluts—of carrot, beets, lettuce, cucumbers, tomato, radish, pepper, self-blanching celery and endive. Pep up your salads with fresh herbs—basil, summer savory, sorrel and tarragon—and collect the ripe seeds of some *Umbelliferae* herbs—fennel, dill and caraway—for sowing.

BLANCHING AND EARTHING-UP

Start blanching endive, to make them less bitter. The blanching process takes about two weeks,

Regular harvesting of runner beans encourages continuing crops. Pick the largest beans, before they become coarse-skinned and swollen

Onions stored on ropes look very attractive, and also save space in boxes and on shelves needed for other purposes

and the easiest way to go about it is to cover each plant with a large, upturned flower pot. Cover the hole in the pot with a stone or cap of aluminum foil, to keep out all light. Blanch the endive a few at a time, over several weeks, rather than all at once.

Other vegetables to continue blanching include leeks and celery (see page 113); with leeks, you want a good 10 in–1 ft (25–30cm) of nice, white stem. Don't forget, especially with celery, to take precautions against soil getting into the heart of the plant when you are earthing up.

TOMATOES

The treatment of tomatoes this month is much the same as for July (see page 113), with training, tying-in and feeding a regular routine.

CLEARING UP

A mundane but necessary task at this time of year is cleaning up and tidying after harvest. If you do keep a compost heap, try to put all healthy vegetation left over from clearing—spent cucumber plants, for example—on the heap, rather than burning it or consigning it to the trash. The few exceptions to this general rule are very woody, tough, vegetation, such as brassica or globe artichoke stems, and anything that looks diseased. These should go straight onto the bonfire. Don't despair, though, as bonfire ash is an excellent source of potash, and your garden will be all the better for it.

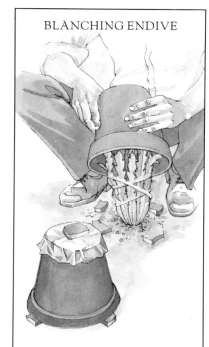

BLANCHING ENDIVE

Place a pot over the tied endive, on crocks with the hole covered

September

As harvest time approaches,
the garden takes on the glow of fall. The foliage
trees later turn to crimson and gold, matched by the
brilliant display of berries and the last of the
summer flowers. Time now to choose roses for next
year and, in the vegetable garden, make provision
for winter.

Apples ripen in the orchard (left),
while the pelargoniums continue to display
their scarlet blooms in the slanting
sunlight of a fall evening

Jobs for the month

General
Remove debris from garden pools
Clear spent crops and flowers
Weed and water as necessary
Remove shading from greenhouse

Flowers
Sow hardy annuals
Transplant biennials
Plant lilies outdoors and in pots
Take cuttings of pelargoniums,
fuchsias, violas, pansies, anti-
rrhinums, Livingstone daisies
Take in house plants and late-
flowering chrysanthemums
Thin butterfly flower and stock
seedlings
Repot calceolarias, cinerarias and
fairy primroses
Sever and plant out rooted
carnation layers
Plant certain spring-flowering
bulbs outdoors and in containers
for forcing

Lawns
Make a new lawn from seed or turf
Make repairs to existing lawns

Roses
Continue spraying against mildew
and black spot
Prune rambling roses and newly
planted weeping standards
Consider buying more roses

Trees and shrubs
Plant nursery-grown evergreen
shrubs

Continue deadheading
Water as necessary
Take semi-ripe cuttings
Weed shrub beds
Take in any tender tub-grown
shrubs

Fruit
Spray against mildew
Fix grease bands round fruit trees
Finish planting strawberry beds
Harvest fall-fruiting strawberries,
raspberries, grapes, apples, plums,
pears, figs, peaches, melons
Continue pruning wall-trained
fruit trees
Prepare planting sites for new trees
and bushes
Thin figs

Vegetables
Sow lettuce, summer radish,
spring cabbage and onion where
possible
Sow parsley and borage
Transplant parsley and chives to a
cold frame
Pot up chives for taking indoors
Thin, weed and transplant
seedlings
Cloche peas, shell beans and
tomatoes that still have fruit
Harvest tomatoes and salad crops
Lift maincrop potatoes
Continue blanching endive, celery
and leeks
Spray against cabbage white
butterflies and protect crops from
slugs and snails

The weather is the key to September. It will determine how much work you need to do, and how fast it has to be done. Some Septembers seem like an extension of summer, while others can bring cold—even frosty—nights. Be on guard, and if frost threatens, protect tender plants as necessary. This may mean cloching some vegetables, harvesting others, bringing in perennial bedding plants and giving temporary cover to permanent, but vulnerable, residents of the garden. Container-grown plants should be given first priority, as their roots are more vulnerable than those grown in the open ground. Remember newly germinated seedlings, too.

Garden pools should be cleared of any dead or decaying vegetation lying on the surface of the water. Peg down a cover of fine plastic netting over the top. It allows light to penetrate but collects dead leaves and other debris and prevents them from polluting the pool. The netting can then be taken up, cleared and replaced as necessary.

Tidying up generally, clearing spent vegetables and flowers and making way for new ones, seeing one season out and another in, sets the tempo for September. If the weather is wet, then cleared ground will quickly become weedy ground, and the temptation to 'leave it till spring' will be a strong one. Resist it, if you can, and clear the weeds as they appear. If the weather is dry, weeding will be replaced by watering.

In the greenhouse, the protective shading on the glass can come off now. With the coming of cooler weather, damping down should be done less frequently, and stopped entirely by the end of the month. Ventilation can be tricky, and depends very much on the temperature and its rapid changes. On hot, sunny days, there should be plenty of air circulation, but the odd cold day, and cold nights, call for watchfulness.

FLOWERS

In the sowing department, there are many hardy annuals that can be sown now, where they are to flower. It gives them just enough time to germinate, so they will over-winter as young plants and flower a few weeks earlier than their spring-sown cousins. Sow them as early in September as possible, and they can take advantage of the last of the summer warmth. Though there are many more you can try, a good selection of annuals that can be treated this way includes alyssum, annual chrysanthemum, annual scabious, candytuft (*Iberis*), cornflower (*Centaurea*), godetia, larkspur (*Delphinium*), love-in-a-mist (*Nigella*), pot marigold (*Calendula*) and Shirley poppy (*Papaver*). During severe winter weather, cloche protection may ensure the survival of the young plants.

Biennial plants started from seed earlier in the season can be transplanted to their final positions. This is usually an end-of-the-month task, as the ground is likely to be occupied by summer bedding plants or annuals until September is almost over.

LILIES

At the end of the month many lilies can be planted. Stem-rooting lilies, such as the gold-rayed lily (*L. auratum*), the Easter lily (*L. longiflorum*) and the regal lily (*L. regale*) should be planted a good 6 in (20cm) deep. Basal-rooting lilies, such as the panther lily (*L. pardalinum*) and the Turk's cap lily (*L. martagon*) can be planted 6 in (15cm) deep. If you have lily bulbs to spare, pot some up for forcing in the greenhouse (see page 134). Again, stem-rooting lilies should be planted well down in the pot, and covered with more and more soil mix as the shoot grows, while basal lilies may be planted nearer the surface. Keep the lilies in a cool place until they have formed strong roots and green shoots.

Lilium longiflorum (above) is best potted or repotted now to ensure the best flowers next year. L. auratum (right) is at its peak this month

TAKING CUTTINGS

There is still time to take cuttings of pelargoniums, fuchsias and other half-hardy plants (see pages 34 and 117). An old-fashioned method of propagating violas, pansies, antirrhinums, and Livingstone daisies (*Mesembryanthemum* or *Doreanthus*) is taking cuttings, though nowadays few people bother. You might want to try it, especially if there is a particularly attractive plant that you'd like more of. Use young, non-flowering shoots, found near the base of the plant. They should be 2–3 in (5–7.5cm) long, and you may find that there are a few fine roots already sprouting from the bottom. Remove the lower leaves and pot the cuttings in a mixture of damp peat and sand or free-draining loam-based soil mix. If your garden soil is sandy, use that. Keep the cuttings in a cold frame or a sheltered, lightly shaded spot. Don't let them dry out, and give them a bit of protection from frost, but otherwise they can fend for themselves.

PLANTS IN CONTAINERS

House plants that have been basking in the summer sun for the last couple of months should be brought indoors. Inspect them first for insects and other pests—snails and slugs have a nasty habit of taking up residence in succulent, tightly packed leaves, and woodlice are fond of the little crevices in amongst the crocking at the bottom of the pot. Check for mildew, too, and pick off any dead or diseased leaves.

Late-flowering chrysanthemums will need taking in towards the end of the month. Give them a once-over, as above, and put them in a well-ventilated greenhouse. The ventilation is extremely important because if the atmosphere is still and warm, you are encouraging disease. If the chrysanthemums are growing in the open ground, as opposed to containers, lift them carefully, with plenty of soil attached to the roots, and plant them directly in the greenhouse border. When you are finished with the move, water well.

THINNING SEEDLINGS

The butterfly flower (*Schizanthus*) and stock seedlings sown last month are certain to need thinning. Space them 1½–2 in (4–5cm) apart. The calceolaria, cineraria and fairy primrose seedlings that were moved to small pots last month (see page 117) can move into slightly larger ones, 3 in (7.5cm) in diameter.

CARNATIONS

If you layered carnations earlier in the summer (see page 103), they should be ready for separating from the parent plant and moved to their permanent homes. Leave a few days between the two operations, to minimize the shock.

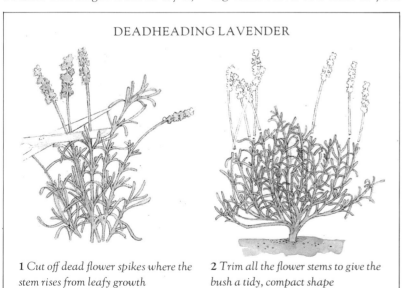

DEADHEADING LAVENDER

1 *Cut off dead flower spikes where the stem rises from leafy growth*

2 *Trim all the flower stems to give the bush a tidy, compact shape*

Flowers for the month

With the arrival of the fall, and sunny, but slightly cooler, weather, many of the flowers that were subdued by the summer heat and dryness are taking on a new lease of life. Dahlias become more colorful than ever, and their brilliant flowers will carry on until cut by the first hard frost. The shorter days and longer nights bring chrysanthemums into flower, with their rich colors echoing the tints of the first coloring autumn leaves.

Berries and rose hips will be starting to color, from the homely fishbone cotoneaster (*C. horizontalis*) to the bright-red hips of *Rosa moyesii* 'Geranium', and the red and yellow fruit of the ornamental crab (*Malus* 'White Angel').

The fall-flowering bulbs that were planted in spring and early summer are displaying their finery now. The bright-pink belladonna lily (*Amaryllis belladonna*) and nerine (*N. bowdenii*) join the fall-flowering crocus (*Colchicum autumnale*) and the hardy cyclamen (*C. purpurascens europaeum, C. neapolitanum*). Other newcomers to the fall scene include the crimson kaffir lily (*Schizostylis coccinea*) now in several shades of pink and crimson.

Of the climbers, clematis are out in full force. Besides the popular purple *C. × jackmanii* and its cultivars, the unusual, yellow-flowered clematis are also in bloom. *Clematis orientalis*, with thick, yellow-orange petals—it is sometimes called the orange-peel clematis—is joined by *C. tangutica*, with bright-yellow, downward-facing flowers and the smaller, pale-yellow bells of *C. rehderana*.

The slightly cooler weather suits fuchsias, and you will find them producing flowers with renewed vigor. It is almost as if they are racing against time, with the possibility of frost not far away.

1

3

5

7

2

4

6

1 *Dahlia* 'Highgate Torch' 2 Mixed single spray chrysanthemums 3 *Cotoneaster horizontalis* 4 *Rosa moyesii* 5 *Clematis orientalis* 6 *Malus hybrid* 7 *Schizostylis coccinea* 'Major'

PLANTING BULBS FOR SPRING

Though next spring seems far away, now is the time to ensure a good display of daffodils. They start growth earlier in the season than most other spring-flowering bulbs, and putting them in soon means that you will have strong-growing plants and fine blooms.

Another bulb to plant now is the cheerful, yellow winter aconite (*Eranthis hyemalis*). Only 3 in (7.5cm) high, winter aconites are tolerant of heavy soils and shade, which makes them perfect for planting under trees and shrubs. They are as pretty in flower pots and window boxes as they are in lawns and shrubberies. October is, however, the month when most of the spring-flowering bulbs should be planted. Though their initial cost may seem relatively high, bulbs are one of the best gardening investments you can make. As long as your choice of bulb is roughly matched to your site and soil, it is almost impossible to fail. Besides providing an annual display of color over years to come, many will increase in number as well.

Strictly speaking, a number of 'bulbs' are more correctly described as corms or tubers. The differences are botanical, and they are all food storage organs which have the same growing needs. Most significant of these is the need for a period of rest, or

dormancy, during which many bulbs can be lifted out of the ground and stored. This ability to be packed away makes bulbs ideal for small gardens.

The structure of a true bulb is like that of an onion—a central stem and bud surrounded by scales or outer layers—and a typical example is the daffodil bulb. Bulbs form offsets, or bulblets, at their base. These will eventually form flowers, but may take several years to do so, and are often detached from the parent plant and grown on separately.

A corm does not have a series of layered scales surrounding a central bud, but is simply a thickened stem, with an outer, bulb-like cover. The growing points or buds are on the surface, mainly at the top and sides, but sometimes also near the base. The crocus is a typical example, and so is the freesia. Corms produce new corms on the top and sides of the old ones, which then die.

Tubers are botanically either a thickened root or a thickened stem. Stem tubers have buds on their root surfaces, root tubers do not. The potato is the classic example of a stem tuber and the dahlia of a root tuber.

Fall planting of bulbs is rewarded in spring with bright flowers

Buying bulbs
Since bulbs are an investment in the future, buy the best ones you can afford. It is safer to buy bulbs you can actually see—either loose in boxes or pre-packed in clear plastic—rather than those pre-packed in opaque brown paper. Go for bulbs which are plump and firm, smooth-skinned and of average size. Though you can save money by buying large quantities, beware of the suspiciously cheap job lot. They may have a high failure rate or include a lot of small offsets or cormlets. Another, equally grim, possibility is that

they are simply not what they are sold as. By the time, many months later, that you find out that the parrot tulips you bought are really very tall and nondescript yellow ones, you have wasted a whole growing season. In the South buy only cold-treated bulbs or store six weeks in the refrigerator.

Having bought your bulbs, handle them with care. If they are packaged, open the packages immediately, to allow the air to circulate. If you are not planting them in the next few days, spread them in a single layer in boxes or shelves in a cool, dry, airy place.

hyacinth   *narcissus*   *tulip*   *crocus*   *snowdrop*

Planting bulbs outdoors
One thing most bulbs need is well-drained soil. Heavy, wet soils may lead to rotting, though most daffodils and narcissi are tolerant and *Leucojum aestium* and *L. vernum* positively revel in moisture. You can lighten heavy soils and improve their drainage by digging in peat or well-rotted compost before planting bulbs. Another trick is to set each bulb on a little bed of sharp sand, and work it up round the sides of the bulb as well.

Different bulbs need different planting depths. As a general rule, the larger the bulb, the deeper it needs to go, and light soils call for deeper planting than heavy soils.

Packaged bulbs usually come with instructions on planting, but a good rule of thumb is to plant a bulb so that its top is two or three times its depth below the soil surface. In almost all cases, deeper is better than shallower and again, in almost all cases, the pointed end of the bulb goes uppermost.

Make sure the bulb is sitting firmly at the base of the hole, and that there are no air pockets beneath it—in a clay soil these could fill with water and rot the bulb.

Spacing is largely a matter of taste, but spacing dimensions are usually suggested on packages, as well as in catalogs. In general, dense areas of closely-planted bulbs look prettier, and more natural, than bulbs planted out in single lines.

PLANTING GUIDE TO BULBS

Bulb	Depth of hole	Distance apart	Flowering height
Crocus	2–3 in (5–7.5cm)	3–4 in (7.5–10cm)	3–6 in (7.5–15cm)
Crown imperial (*Fritillaria imperialis*)	6 in (15cm)	12 in (30cm)	2–3 ft (60cm–1m)
Daffodil (*Narcissus*)	4–6 in (10–15cm)	4–8 in (10–20cm)	1–1½ ft (30–45cm)
Dog's tooth violet (*Erythronium dens-canis*)	4 in (10cm)	4 in (10cm)	6 in (15cm)
Glory of the snow (*Chionodoxa*)	2 in (5cm)	3 in (7.5cm)	4–6 in (10–15cm)
Grape hyacinth (*Muscari*)	3 in (7.5cm)	3 in (7.5cm)	6–10 in (15–25cm)
Hyacinth	6 in (15cm)	8 in (20cm)	6 in–1 ft (15–30cm)
Iris (*I. danfordiae*, *I. reticulata*)	2–4 in (5–10cm)	2–4 in (5–10cm)	3–4 in (7.5–10cm)
English, Dutch and Spanish iris	4 in (10cm)	8–10 in (20–25cm)	1½–2 ft (45–60cm)
Miniature daffodil (*Narcissus*)	3–4 in (7.5–10cm)	3–4 in (7.5–10cm)	4 in–1 ft (10–30cm)
Snowdrop (*Galanthus*)	3 in (7.5cm)	3 in (7.5cm)	6–8 in (15–20cm)
Spring squill (*Scilla sibirica*)	2–3 in (5–7.5cm)	2–3 in (5–7.5cm)	4–10 in (10–25cm)
Tulip (*Tulipa*)	3–8 in (7.5–20cm)	4–8 in (10–20cm)	6–30 in (15–75cm)

FLOWERING HEIGHTS
1 *Crocus 3–6 in (7.5–15cm)*
2 *Grape hyacinth 6–10 in (15–25cm)*
3 *Hyacinth 6 in–1 ft (15–30cm)*
4–6 *Daffodils 1–1½ ft (30–45cm)*
7–11 *Tulips 6–30 in (15–75cm)*

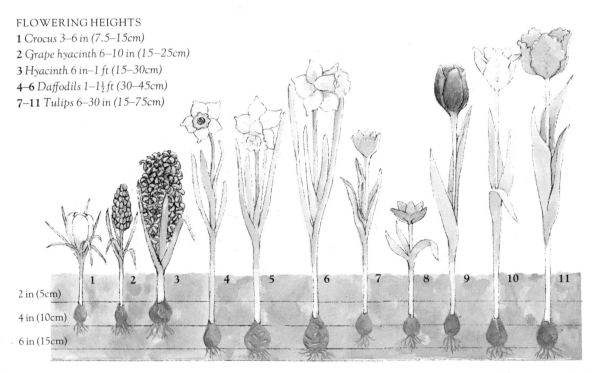

2 in (5cm)
4 in (10cm)
6 in (15cm)

Planting bulbs indoors
If you plant now, you can have bulbs in flower from Christmas onwards, to brighten up the winter months. Though bulbs are often sold– and can be grown successfully–in decorative bowls without any drainage holes, it is really better to grow them in a container which does have adequate drainage. To get the best of both worlds, why not grow the bulbs in flower pots which are then placed inside a larger, decorative bowl?

The growing medium may also need changing–though bulb fiber is very popular, and bulbs are often sold planted in it, there are some drawbacks when compared to a good, loam-based potting mixture. Because bulb fiber is so light, tall-growing or top-heavy bulbs may topple over. In addition, watering can be trickier with soil-less mixtures, which dry out quickly. The ideal mixture is loam-based, with sharp sand and peat added to it, plus a little bit of charcoal to keep the mix 'sweet'.

For best results, restrict each container to one type of plant. Work out the planting depth, then put a layer of drainage material in the bottom, followed by a layer of growing medium. Sit the bulbs on top, quite close together but not touching. As a rough guide, you should be able to poke a pencil between them. Fill the container with soil until the tops of the bulbs are just visible. To allow adequate space for watering, the level of the growing medium should be $\frac{1}{2}$ in (15mm) below the level of the rim.

One of the major pitfalls of growing bulbs indoors is getting the temperature right. All too often, bulbs are killed by kindness, and the false assumption that a lovely warm place will bring them on nicely. This is absolutely the reverse of what is needed. Cool, dark conditions are vital if the bulb is to form a strong root system, which will, in turn, lead to a good display of flowers. Putting them somewhere warm will encourage the bulb to make top growth–leaves and flowers–before it has the root system to support them. Sometimes, bulbs given too much warmth fail to flower at all, so when it comes to forcing bulbs, keep them cool and take your time.

A good eight-to-ten weeks, sometimes more, should be allowed for root formation. Water the soil mix well, then place the container in a plunge bed outdoors, and cover it with a layer of sand or ash. Alternatively, use a dark corner of a cellar, shed or garage. Check the plants towards the end of the waiting period, and once 2–3 in (5–7.5cm) of new growth shows, including the flower bud, gradually bring them into light and warmth. Flowering should take place 3–6 weeks later.

1 *Position the bulbs on a layer of drainage material covered with growing medium, so the tips will just show when you add soil mix to $\frac{1}{2}$ in (1cm) below the rim*

2 *Keep the bulbs cool and dark, in a box inside a black plastic sack, until roots are well established*

Hyacinths are a consistent favorite among pot-grown bulbs, providing clear colors and light fragrance indoors; cool conditions are needed to start them into growth

Forcing times for indoor bulbs
Daffodil
12–16 weeks

Crocus
14 weeks

Grape hyacinth
18 weeks

Hyacinth (specially prepared)
10–11 weeks

Iris
10–12 weeks

Snowdrop
16 weeks

Squill
14 weeks

Tulip
single early cultivars
7–10 weeks
later-flowering cultivars
14–16 weeks

Bulbs for outdoor containers
While there is never any trouble in filling flower pots, window boxes and tubs with bright color through late spring and summer, there are times of the year—early spring comes to mind—when most outdoor plant containers are displaying soil and nothing else. Try spring-flowering bulbs to fill this gap, combining them with evergreen ivy, periwinkle or euonymus, for all-over coverage. Bulbs need never look untidy—once they are past their best, simply lift them and heel them in in an out-of-the-way spot in the garden, or even another container. When the foliage has died away completely, the bulbs can be dried off and stored in a box until next year.

Plant bulbs in outdoor containers quite close together. This will give you the best display, and provided the bulbs do not actually touch each other or the container, the bulbs will be none the worse for the experience. Keep them well watered, too. Lastly, if a heavy frost threatens, cover and wrap the containers in heavy sacking, plastic or even weighed-down newspapers, to provide a little protection.

These bulbs are suitable for outdoor containers:

Crocus
Cyclamen (*C. coum, C. alpinum*)
Daffodil (*Narcissus*)
Dog's tooth violet (*Erythronium dens-canis*)

Bulbs in containers add charm to the display of flowers in a small garden without taking up flowerbed space

Glory of the snow (*Chionodoxa*)
Grape hyacinth (*Muscari*)
Iris (*I. reticulata, I. danfordiae*)
Lily (*Lilium candidum, L. regale, L. speciosum*)
Snowdrop (*Galanthus*)
Squill (*Scilla*)
Tulip (*Tulipa*)
Winter aconite (*Eranthis*)

Layered planting of bulbs
If you want a really massed effect with your bulbs, indoors or out, double up on your planting by putting them in tiers in the container. Plant one set of bulbs deeper than you normally would, making sure you leave at least a bulb's

height available above them. Cover the bulbs with soil or mixture, so only their tips are visible, then place another layer of bulbs on top, in the spaces between, making sure that none touches another, in any direction. Finally, cover the top layer of bulbs with soil or the mix in the usual way.

Color for a cold greenhouse
Many unheated greenhouses, conservatories and sun rooms can be used for bulbs, as long as they are frost-free. The potted-up bulbs will still need their normal period in cold, dark surroundings, to form roots. The pots can then be put on the greenhouse benches or shelves to get the full benefit of the sunlight. For the plants, the transition from the cold and dark to a sunny, unheated or gently heated environment is much easier and safer than moving directly to a centrally heated room. They can remain in the greenhouse to flower, or be transferred, when the buds are showing color, to their final destination in the house.

Plant two layers of bulbs, evenly spaced, in a well-crocked pot

Choosing bulbs for shade
There are a large number of bulbs that can thrive happily in a shady spot, though if the shade is light, rather than deep, and dappled with bits of sunlight now and again, the choice of plants is wider.

Many of the squill genus (*Scilla*) actually prefer a position under deciduous trees. They flower before the trees are in leaf, getting the full benefit of the sunlight, and protection from wind at the same time. Try *Scilla tubergeniana* or *S. peruviana*.

The winter aconite (*Eranthis hyemalis*), planted this fall, (see page 131) is ideal for shade, even deep tree shade.

Taking your cues from nature is always a good idea. Bluebells (*Endymion non-scriptus*, sometimes listed as *Scilla non-scripta* or *S. nutans*) thrive in light woodland. Likewise, the dog's tooth violet (*Erythronium dens-canis*) and the sweet little wood anemone (*A. nemorosa*) are suitable. Wood anemones are also happy in fairly heavy shade.

Try snowdrops in light shade, perhaps a double snowdrop (*Galanthus nivalis* 'Flore Pleno') or a giant snowdrop (*G. elwesii*). The star of Bethlehem (*Ornithogalum nutans*) is a suitable candidate for shade, and there is even a shade-loving tulip, *Tulipa sylvestris*. Its nodding, yellow flowers are fragrant and appear in May. It spreads freely by means of underground divisions and seed.

LAWNS

New lawns can be made this month from seed, in the same way as for March (see pages 40–1). If you want instant results, and are prepared to pay for them, then you can make a new lawn from turf (see pages 136–7).

You are much more likely, though, to have an existing lawn in need of attention, and it is a good time to repair any threadbare patches and ragged edges. In the case of bumps, slice off the top layer of turf—it does not matter if the piece is oddly shaped—and dig away the soil underneath to reduce the bump. Use a special half-moon turfing iron, if you have one, to cut through the bump. Otherwise, use a spade. Either replace the turf or, if you have some good turf to spare in an out-of-the-way spot, use the sliced-off turf as a template to cut out a piece of turf in better condition. The worn-out turf is placed in the out-of-the-way spot, and the good turf is placed where the bump was.

The same procedure holds for hollows, though instead of slicing away excess soil, you will be adding soil to fill the hollow once the turf has been temporarily removed. With any newly laid turf, make sure it is in firm contact with the soil, and keep it watered. Use fine soil to fill in any cracks between the pieces of turf.

Ragged edges on an otherwise healthy lawn can be repaired by simply cutting out a square of turf that includes the offending edge and reversing it. The ragged edge will be much less noticeable, and should quickly send out new growth. If it doesn't, you can always sow it with grass seed.

Balding patches on a lawn are best dealt with by re-seeding. Break up the surface of the soil with a fork, as the soil is likely to be compacted. Work the surface to a fine tilth, sow the seed and protect it with plastic mesh raised on twigs, or crumpled chicken wire. Treat the newly emerged grass gently, particularly when mowing or using weedkillers, for the first season. If the same patch of lawn becomes bald regularly, it may well be that the foot traffic in your garden is such that no lawn could survive there. Lawn near a door or gate is particularly vulnerable, and should eventually be replaced by paving stones, gravel or another hard surface which can stand up to wear and tear.

SMOOTHING BUMPS IN THE LAWN

1 *Cut into the turf around the bump and lift it in sections*

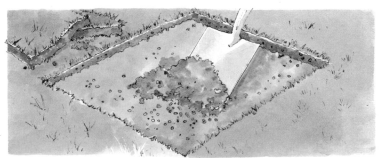

2 *Remove enough soil to level the ground across the bared area*

3 *Replace the original turf, or fit new turfs if necessary*

1 *To repair a broken lawn edge, cut squares of turf using a straight edge*

2 *Lift the sections of turf with a spade, supporting the broken edge*

3 *Turn the turf and relay it, with the clean-cut side edging the lawn*

4 *In the rough patch now inside the lawn area, apply soil and grass seed*

LAYING A LAWN FROM TURF

September is one of the traditional months for making a new lawn from turf. April is the other month, and both share the growing conditions necessary for success. The soil is warm, the air is warm without being hot, and there tends to be enough moisture in the soil and the air to keep the turfs from drying out until their own roots begin to function.

Laying a new lawn from turf is one of the quickest and most satisfying garden tasks. A day's hard work and a patch of bare soil is magically transformed into a carpet of emerald green. But to get the best results, and a good many years' wear from your turf, then a certain amount of before- and after-care is necessary. Though it may look like a carpet, you are working with thousands of small, growing plants and you want to give them the best possible start.

Carefully dig over the site first—it may pay you to hire a cultivator for the day if you are turfing a large area. If you have some well-rotted compost, farmyard manure, peat or even spent mushroom compost available, dig this in as you go. Incorporating organic matter is especially important if you are gardening on free-draining sandy or gravelly soil, both of which tend to dry out in summer. The opposite problem, poor drainage, should be seen to as well, and in the case of clay soils, dig in organic matter, as before, and sharp sand or grit, to improve drainage. Really waterlogged clay soils may even need to have a drainage system installed—a herringbone system of narrow trenches, sloping towards a covered dry well. The trenches are filled first with rubble or stones, then topped with gravel and a layer of topsoil.

Once you have sorted out whatever shortcomings your soil may have, leave the soil for a few weeks to settle. Towards the end of this time, you can level it (see page 40), because any unevenness in the finished surface will show up once the turf is laid, and you will have difficulty in joining up the turfs satisfactorily.

When you are happy with the levels and the soil has been broken down to a fine tilth and firmed, systematically sprinkle a good, all-purpose fertilizer over the area to be turved, to get the grass off to a flying start.

Buying turf

Turf can now be bought ready-grown, often on a mesh backing in rolls, like carpeting. The turf is usually of the finest quality, and laying it is easy, but its cost is considerably more than that of the conventional turf, so you need to weigh up the cost and the time and money involved.

Like other plants, the quality of turf can vary considerably, from meadow turf—meadow grass pre-treated with a selective weed-killer – to more expensive, specially-grown turf or turf stripped from parkland or downland. If you are already paying extra for specially-grown turf, you may well decide that it is worthwhile investing in the sort grown on mesh, and save time in laying it.

Make sure you see a sample of the turf you are going to buy before committing yourself. The turfs should be of the same quality and thickness throughout, and weed-free, or you will have problems both in laying and caring for

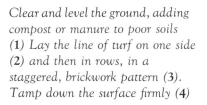

Clear and level the ground, adding compost or manure to poor soils (1) Lay the line of turf on one side (2) and then in rows, in a staggered, brickwork pattern (3). Tamp down the surface firmly (4)

your lawn afterwards. Check also that the turfs are free from coarse grasses.

If you are not buying rolls of turf 1 × 3 ft (30cm × 1m), the other alternative is to buy turf in small pieces, or 'tiles', usually 1 ft (30cm) square.

Have the turf delivered as close as possible to the day you intend laying it. If you have to postpone the operation for a few days after it has been delivered, keep it stacked in rolls, preferably out of direct sunlight. If conditions are very dry, water the turf well, using the finest possible spray–almost a mist–or you may well wash the soil out of the roots, and in any case, soaked turfs are very hard to handle and can break under their own weight. Small turfs that have to be left for some time should be stacked flat, or the soil backing is liable to crack. Again, keep them out of direct sunlight, and water as necessary. If left in rolls or stacked for longer than 5–7 days, turf will quickly deteriorate and soon becomes useless.

Laying turf

Choose a day when the prepared area to be turfed is reasonably dry, or the soil may stick to your shoes, making working conditions more difficult than they need be and a smooth finished level impossible. As with any other planting operation, laying turf should not take place when the soil is frozen or waterlogged.

To get the best results, you will need some sort of tamping tool, to press the turfs down firmly into the soil. You can make one by nailing together two 1 ft (30cm) square wooden boards, then fixing a broom handle into a block on top. For turfing a small area, use the head of a rake to press the turfs into place.

Start at one side, slightly overlapping the final edge of the lawn with the first row of turfs, to allow for any shifting and readjusting. If the turf is being laid to butt onto an existing hard surface—path or patio—it is very important that the turf is laid so that it is above the level of the hard surface, rather than flush with it, or even below. There are several reasons for this. Firstly, it allows for the inevitable settlement that will take place in the next year or so. Secondly, mowing turf that is lower than the adjacent hard surface can wreak havoc on a lawn mower and lastly, there is an unsatisfactory look to turf sitting below its neighboring hard surface. Make sure the turf is laid right up against the hard surface and wedged firmly. Press the first row of turfs down with a tamper, making sure they are as straight as possible, then lay the second row. Stagger the joints, as you would with a row of bricks. Make the joints of the second row come mid-way between the joints of the first row. This usually means cutting some of the end turfs in half, but these can usually be put to good use. If there is a small gap between turfs, fill it with a sliver of turf, but never use these small pieces for edging, as they will inevitably crumble away. If the gap is on an edge, move the turf out to the edge, and fill the inner gap with small pieces of turf.

As you lay each piece of turf, check it quickly for obvious weeds and remove any you find. If the piece of turf looks distinctly substandard, put it to one side, and use it for cutting and filling.

Work your way across the lawn, always standing on a plank of wood on the laid turf, and not on the soil. Butting the turfs tightly against each other is important to the finished look of the job. If you are doing a large area, leave a gap, slightly smaller than the length of one piece of turf, in each row. When you have finished laying a row, go back and fill in the gap by tightly ramming the turf in. This has a knock-on effect which helps to close up tiny gaps in the row.

If you have a curve of any kind to negotiate, use an edging tool to cut the turf into the correct shape—bending the turf into a curve in the hope that it will remain curved is wishful thinking.

When all the turfs are laid, fill in any cracks still remaining with sieved soil. Next, give the area a going-over with a light garden roller, or with the roller of a reel mower, first making sure that the blades are high enough to clear the grass. You can also walk over the newly laid lawn on the plank, moving it along as you do so. Each of these methods ensures that the roots of the turf come into firm contact with the soil.

Trim the edges to a good, straight finish, using an edging tool and a plank to cut against. If you are cutting a curved edge, use a hose to mark out the edge. As with flowerbeds, loose curves are much better than tight ones, which tend to look contrived.

Finally, give the turf a top dressing made of a mixture of sieved soil, coarse sand and peat, or topsoil alone. Brush it into the grass with a brush or broom.

Keep the lawn well watered—if you allow the turfs to dry out, they will shrink and leave unsightly gaps which take a long time to mend. If the weather is fine and dry, use a sprinkler, if you have one, and leave it in position for an hour before moving it on.

5

6

7

8

Butt the turfs to fill the area (5) and make sure they are lying level or with the ground slope (6). Make clean cuts as necessary with an edging iron (7). After laying, sprinkle on a top dressing and spread it with a brush or broom (8)

CHOOSING AND CARING FOR ROSES

The roses in our gardens today are the result of at least seventy million years of history – fossils of this popular plant have been found dating from that time. Roses come in many forms – from climbers reaching the tops of small trees to miniatures only 4 in (10cm) high – so choosing the right ones for you and your garden can be tricky. Though there are many ways to classify roses, the following is a simple guide to the main types of roses available.

Wild roses

These are the original species roses, found in nature. They tend to have five-petalled, single flowers, in white, pink, crimson or yellow. Wild roses make tough, medium-sized or large bushes or climbers, and are mostly deciduous. They are more resistant to pests and diseases than modern roses, and many have attractive, large red hips in fall. Wild roses bloom briefly, in early summer, with no recurrence of flowers. Well-known examples of wild rose include the pale-pink dog rose (*Rosa canina*), the scented, deeper-pink sweet briar (*R. rubiginosa*), the white field rose (*R. arvensis*), the yellow incense rose (*R. primula*), the orange-red Austrian copper briar (*R. foetida bicolor*) and the ramanas or Japanese rose, *R. rugosa* with large rose-purple flowers and big globose red hips.

Old garden roses

This group comprises good-sized shrubs. They are hybrid roses which have been developed from the species roses, and are mostly 100 years old, often considerably older. Some of them are repeat-flowering, and continue to produce fresh blooms throughout the summer. China roses (*R. chinensis*) are an example, and flower from late spring through to the end of fall. Many others, though, including the Alba, Gallica and Centifolia roses, flower only once a year, with a display lasting weeks rather than months. They are renowned for their strong fragrance, and many have huge, loose, cabbage-like blooms.

Modern shrub roses

These are also hybrid, medium-sized to large shrubs, but they have been developed in the last hundred years or so. Some, such as the Rugosa roses, flower from early summer through fall. Named Rugosa cultivars include the double, deep-red 'Roseraie de l'Hay', the semi-double white 'Blanc Double de Coubert' and the double pink 'Sarah van Fleet'. Others, such as the yellow, single or semi-double *Rosa* 'Fruhlingsgold' and the rose-pink 'Constance Spry' flower for a relatively short period of time. *Rosa* 'Ballerina' is a small modern shrub rose, growing only 3 ft (1m) high and as much across, and has masses of small, single pink flowers. *R.* 'Nevada' reaches a height of 8 ft (2.4m), and has a similar spread. Its arching branches are covered in June with huge, creamy white, single flowers.

Large-flowered (Hybrid tea) roses

These are the largest and by far the most popular group of roses. Large-flowered roses form small or medium-sized bushes, though they can be trained to form standards. They flower continuously over many months and come in a wide color range. The flowers are big and showy, and if you have limited space and want color value for money, these are the ones to go for. They are excellent for cutting, too.

The breeding is quite complex, but their popular group name, Hybrid tea, comes from the fact that one of the main influences in their development was the old Tea rose. These are hardly ever seen nowadays, being unreliably hardy and needing greenhouse treatment in cold areas. Their exquisite flowers were said to smell like freshly picked tea, and were produced one to three per stem. The other major parent was the hybrid perpetual, another class of old garden rose. It gave to the Hybrid tea the vigor needed to make it popular.

One of the most famous roses in the world – the pink-tinged, yellow 'Peace' – is a Hybrid tea, and there are hundreds and hundreds of cultivars, with new ones brought out every year – rather like new car models.

Rosa rubiginosa – sweet briar rose

R. chinensis 'Minima' – *miniature rose*

R. 'Nevada' – *modern shrub rose*

R. 'Peace' – *large flowered bush rose*

R. 'Elizabeth of Glamis' – cluster-flowered bush rose

R. 'Mermaid' – climbing rose

R. 'Albertine' – rambling rose

R. 'Spice Drop' – miniature rose

Cluster-flowered (Floribunda) roses

Another group of hybrid roses with complicated parentage, cluster-flowered roses produce masses of small blooms, for several months of the year. Usually small bushes, they can also be hand-trained as standards. What their flowers lack in size, fragrance and quality, compared to the large-flowered roses, cluster-flowered roses make up for in sheer quantity of bloom. The semi-double or double flowers cover the bush in color, month after month. They have the added advantage of being generally hardier than large-flowered roses, and more resistant to disease, especially mildew and black spot. Again, there are innumerable named cultivars, which include such popular forms as the white 'Iceberg' and the scarlet-orange 'Impatient'.

Climbing roses

Contained in this group is a huge range of roses, some of which are true climbers, descended from wild roses, while others are climbing versions of modern large-flowered or cluster-flowered roses.

Though the edges are a bit blurred because of the complex parentage, there are certain characteristics that all climbers share. Their tough, woody stems help them to support themselves, and they use their thorns to hook onto other shrubs for additional support. Their flowers are usually large,

double, semi-double or single and many of them are repeat flowering, giving one display in early summer and another in the fall.

You can train climbing roses against walls, fences, screens, pillars and poles. The shorter-growing climbers are used for pillars and poles and are sometimes called pillar roses. 'Old American Pillar' is one of the best-known of these roses, with double, scarlet flowers in early summer.

Climbing sports of modern roses are relatively recent additions to the rose scene. They produce the flowers of their large-flowered or cluster-flowered parent, but have a climbing habit. The prefix Cl, or 'Climbing', in catalogs or on labels indicates a climbing sport. 'Cl. Queen Elizabeth' and 'Cl. White Dawn' are two examples.

Rambling roses

This category encompasses many roses, but they differ from climbing roses in several respects. Rambling roses have much more supple wood, and always need support. If left to their own devices, ramblers will scramble through other shrubs or loosely over the ground. In fact, some ramblers make good ground cover, given a bit of pegging down. They also make very good weeping standards, grafted onto a strong, woody stock. The flowers of ramblers tend to be smaller than those of climbers, and are carried in bigger clusters. Some ramblers

have single flowers, and the majority bloom just once a year, in midsummer. With climbers, the flowers are produced on laterals growing from the woody main framework, while ramblers produce much more new wood from the base of the plant, and it is this new wood that carries the flowers.

Ramblers are eminently suitable for growing over pergolas or up into large trees.

Popular ramblers include 'Albertine', with double, coppery-pink flowers, 'Max Graf' with bright-pink flowers and 'Blaze'.

Miniature roses

These tiny roses are becoming increasingly popular, probably because of the small-sized gardens most of us now have. Miniature roses are hybrids, again developed through complex breeding, and range from a mere 4 in (10cm) to 1 ft (30cm) in height. They are also house plants, and may be brought into a cool, light room for a day or two when in flower. Miniatures can be grown in tubs or pots, window boxes or hanging baskets. In the open ground, grow them as part of dwarf bedding schemes or as edgings to paths or borders.

The flowers are usually double, and appear over a long period in summer. Popular forms include the salmon-pink 'Spice Drop', the mauve 'Lavender Jewel', the white 'Snow Bride' and the bright yellow 'Center Gold'.

Buying roses

Roses are sold in shops, garden centers and nurseries in three ways: pre-packed in plastic bags or boxes, bare-rooted, or containerized. Bare-rooted roses are usually sent out by specialist growers to keep down the weight, and thus the cost of transport, though they are occasionally sold in garden centers as well. The danger is that the plants may have dried out waiting for a customer or, indeed, travelling in the mail. If the stems look shrivelled and the roots dry, you need to take remedial action. Prune stems back hard, removing any shoots with leaves, buds or flowers on them. Cut out any decayed or dead shoots and plunge the entire plant in a bucket of water for several hours, or overnight. After this initial soaking, keep the roots moist, by wrapping them in damp sacking, until you are ready to plant. Before planting, check the roots carefully and prune back any that appear to be damaged or very long and straggly.

With roses that arrive from specialist nurseries, you have only two options: attempting to resuscitate them, if necessary, or, *in extremis*, sending them back. With roses you buy over the counter, you have a chance to examine them carefully before buying, so make the most of this opportunity. The branches should be plump, a good green, reasonably hard and unwrinkled. Ideally, the buds should still be dormant. It is

less good if they have broken into growth, but avoid at all costs plants which have produced pale-green—almost white—shoots. These indicate that the plant has been stored for too long or in excessively warm conditions, or possibly both.

Containerized roses tend to be expensive but, if properly grown, are easy to transplant. Watch out, though, for roses that have been recently dug up and jammed into the containers. These poor plants have to suffer the consequences of moving twice—once to the container and a second time to the garden—in a short space of time, and won't take kindly to it. If possible, check by easing the plant out of its container,

though this is not recommended if the plant is in a sleeve 'pot'. There should be fine roots showing round the outer edge of the soil. Reject plants with roots which have grown through the bottom of the container and into the ground beneath.

It is very tempting to flick through the heavily illustrated catalogs sent out by specialist rose growers, and choose your roses on the basis of close-up color photographs of single flowers. While the photographs may not be wrong, they can be misleading as to the actual scale and size of the flowers. More importantly, they give no indication of the size or growth habit of the plant which produces these flowers, or the

length of the flowering season. It is truthful to say that many roses have awkward, if not downright ugly, habits of growth. The angular, upward-growing branches of the large-flowered and cluster-flowered rose bushes look unnatural, and if you can get a variety with a more natural, open habit of growth, it is certainly worth doing so, even at the expense of flower size. Some roses have attractive, shiny semi-evergreen leaves, or leaves tinged gray or coppery-purple when young. Others have attractive, orange or red hips in the fall. It really does pay to read the small print in catalogs to get as full a picture of the plant as possible, before you make a decision you might regret.

R. 'Paddy McGredy'—*cluster-flowered bush rose*

R. 'Cécile Brunner'—*dwarf polyantha rose*

R. × *paulii* – *species rose*

R. 'Mme Hardy' – *old shrub rose*

R. 'Dorothy Perkins' – *old rambler*

Siting roses

Until relatively recently, it was traditional to grow roses in beds by themselves, with no underplanting to relieve the monotony of the bare earth. Not only did the plants look unattractive for at least half the year, but growing large numbers of one type of plant together is a virtual invitation to pests and diseases affecting that plant. Lastly, though bare soil is not a pretty sight, you may, if you are not prepared to weed regularly, have the roses smothered in a healthy growth of weeds, encouraged by the rich soil and extra food that you have provided.

Modern-day attitudes to growing roses allow for more flexibility. Rose beds are often underplanted with complementary ground cover, such as pansies and violas, lesser periwinkle (*Vinca minor*), and campanula (*C. portenschlagiana*). You could make use of the ground beneath the roses for an early display of dwarf bulbs, too. Winter-flowering iris (*I. reticulata*), snowdrops (*Galanthus nivalis*) and crocus are good choices where winter banking is not needed. Biennials such as forget-me-not (*Myosotis sylvatica*) or double daisies (*Bellis perennis*) will happily share a bed with roses.

Another solution is to grow roses in mixed borders or shrub borders. That way, their visual weaknesses become less glaring. Roses trained as standards and half-standards look lovely in amongst mixed flowers, and form instant focal points in the border.

At the other end of the scale, some roses make admirable ground cover for large areas. Besides the evergreen, pink-flowered 'Max Graf', *Rosa × paulii* 'Rosea', with its pale-pink, single flowers, is another possibility. The latter grows 3 ft (1m) high, making an impenetrable, very spiny thicket, and is suitable only for the larger garden.

Good roses for hedging include many of the Rugosa roses. 'Roseraie de l'Hay', 'Blanc Double de Coubert' and 'Sarah van Fleet' are good choices, but be prepared to give them plenty of room. Allowing for a 5 ft (1.5m) spread is not at all excessive for these roses.

R. 'Königin von Dänemark' – *old shrub rose*

Caring for roses

As with many garden plants, the more attention you can give roses, the better the results in terms of general health and flowering.

Feeding Roses are notoriously greedy feeders. They take a great deal out of the soil in which they are growing, so you have to replace the nourishment in the form of organic or inorganic fertilizers. Even before planting, incorporating well-rotted manure, garden compost, or peat and bone meal into the soil where the rose is to grow is necessary to provide a long-term source of food.

Roses need nitrates, phosphates and potash, and there are several rose fertilizers on the market that provide these in exactly the right balance. A spring feed, before the leaves open fully, gets the plant off to a good start. Regular feeds through June and July are a good practice, but feeding later in the season encourages sappy growth, and will render the rose vulnerable to damage by the first hard frost which comes along.

If you are worried about whether your roses are getting enough food, there are certain symptoms to look for. A rose that needs feeding has smaller flowers than it should. They may be deformed, and may shed their petals prematurely. Growth will be stunted, and the foliage may be pale or discolored, with blackened edges. The plant will certainly be more vulnerable to any disease going.

Watering Because roses are deep rooted once they are established, they are far less susceptible to drought than many other shrubs. Newly planted roses, though, will need plenty of water if there is a dry spell. Other roses needing special consideration in this department are those trained against walls and those growing in containers.

Deadheading and disbudding Unless you are intending the roses to form hips, either for seed or for fall color, you should remove the dead flowers whenever practicable. Obviously, a rambling rose making its way to the top of a large tree is out of the question, but smaller, repeat-flowering roses, such as large-flowered and cluster-flowered bushes, should be regularly gone over. Otherwise, the plant will waste vital energy producing unnecessary fruits, and flowering suffers accordingly.

Disbudding is done for two reasons. With large-flowered roses, the side buds are pinched out as soon as they appear, to allow the single remaining bud to grow without competition. With cluster-flowered roses, the 'crown', or central, bud is removed, to allow all the side buds to develop evenly. If left on, the crown bud would produce a larger, and earlier flower, and be well past its best when the side buds opened.

Pests and diseases Well-cultivated roses are much less prone to infection than poorly grown ones. That having been said, you can still take preventive action by applying systemic insecticides and fungicides in spring (see page 50). There are now available 'cocktails', which combine both chemicals in one solution. These are usually applied once every ten days or so. Choose a windless day, preferably overcast. Spray the dry leaves, making sure that the undersides have been sprayed, as well as the upper sides.

Roses are vulnerable to all manner of pests—thrips and frog-hoppers, sawflies and capsids, red spider mites and aphids. The last-named are the ones most often encountered, and are easily spotted as colonies on the soft stems and buds. Of the diseases—virus and mildew, rust and black spot, among others—black spot is the most troublesome. Warm, clammy weather seems to encourage it. Interestingly, industrial pollution seems to discourage black spot, which is virtually absent from industrial areas. In any case, it is highly infectious, and should be tackled the moment the first black spots appear. It spreads rapidly and causes premature leaf fall. Good garden hygiene—removing and burning any infected leaves, and also fallen leaves from the nearby ground, has some effect in keeping black spot under control (see page 184).

A powdery gray coating is the sign of mildew, here on flower stems

Orange blisters characteristic of rust are found on undersides of leaves

Black spot is a common rose disease, appearing first in older leaves

Pruning Newly planted large-flowered (Hybrid tea) and cluster-flowered (Floribunda) roses need hard pruning during their first year. This allows them to develop a strong root system and encourages them to produce sturdy shoots near the base. Normally, this is done when the bush is planted, but pruning can be done any time the plant is dormant, or when the new growth is just beginning. At that stage, the buds will be swollen, but no leaves will have appeared. Prune the stems back to three or four outward-pointing buds from the base. Cut out completely dead, diseased, weak and crossing wood. For maintenance-pruning, after the first year, see page 22.

Newly planted standards should have their branches cut back to within 8 in (20cm) of the main trunk, cutting just above a healthy bud. Once established, annual maintenance-pruning consists of shortening these branches by half their length. Weeping standards are slightly different, and should have their branches pruned to within 6 in (15cm) of the trunk initially. Thereafter, every spring, prune completely the old flowering branches, to encourage the growth of new wood. Every spring, also lightly tip new wood, to encourage the formation of side shoots.

True climbing roses need relatively little pruning. In the dormant season, cut back the laterals to four or five buds from the base—it is the laterals

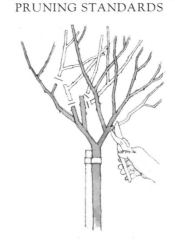
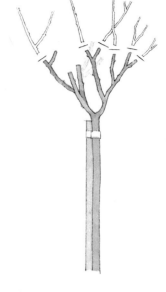

On planting, cut back stems above buds. Thereafter, remove dead and crossed wood and cut half the length of established branches

that produce the flowers. Ramblers are pruned rather like blackberries; old, flowered wood is cut to the ground to encourage the growth of new, flowering wood. Keep the young, new season's growth and tie it in as necessary.

Miniature roses benefit from pruning, too, though their small size makes the thought of removing even a few

inches of growth disastrous. Nonetheless, prune them back to four or five buds from the base, and remove completely any weak, crossing, diseased or dead growth. You may find that miniature roses send up 'water' shoots—over-vigorous growths that seem very much out of scale with the rest of the plant. Cut these out entirely.

With all grafted or budded

roses, keep an eye out for suckers, growing from the ground or from the join below the stem. Trace the sucker back to where it joins the root, and pull it away. In all the cold parts of North America, where the stems are killed in winter, banking the plants with soil at least 8 in (20cm) high or protecting them with plastic cones is necessary.

PRUNING TRUE RAMBLERS

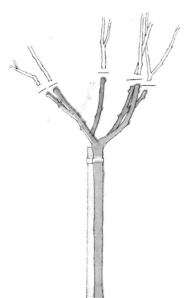

Prune a young plant hard, just above ground level. In an older plant, cut out old wood each year and tie in new growth

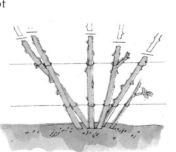

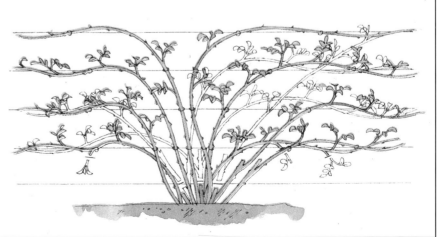

TREES & SHRUBS

FRUIT

Conditions at this time of year are likely to mimic those of April– warm soil, warm air, cool evenings, and hopefully a bit of rain. If so, plant nursery-grown evergreen shrubs now, to give them time to settle in before winter. If it turns windy, protect them from drying out by putting up screening on the windward side.

Continue deadheading flowering shrubs as they finish, and watering if the weather is dry.

Semi-ripe cuttings root quickly if taken now, and inserted in sandy mixtures or soil in a propagating frame. The method is the same as earlier in the summer (see page 119). Remember to keep the sun off them for the first few weeks, and to keep them watered.

If you have time, you can put it to good use by weeding round the bases of shrubs, much as you did for cane fruits and soft fruit bushes when they finished cropping, earlier in the summer (see page124).

Towards the end of the month, if you live as far north as New England, you would be well advised to take in any tender shrubs that have done duty as bedding– fuchsias, for example–or house plants out for the summer. Indian azaleas, abutilons, and Cape leadworts (*Plumbago capensis*) come into the latter category. Before bringing them in, give them a check for self-seeded weeds in the pot, or any sign of infestation. One thing you don't want to do is bring outdoor problems inside, and if you are in the least worried, you might want to give your plants a precautionary spray.

Fruit trees and vines are still vulnerable to mildew, so continue spraying, if necessary (see page 184). Gooseberry bushes are worth checking for mildew, too.

A quick chore is fitting grease bands round the trunks of fruit trees, apple trees in particular. Various moths and other insects crawling up the trunk, to lay their eggs on the twigs, get caught as they come into contact with the sticky substance on the bands. Fix them about 2½ ft (75cm) from the ground.

If you haven't already done so, finish planting new strawberry beds from rooted runners (see page 124), as early as possible this month. Fall-fruiting strawberries should be producing their fruit now. You must continue to keep the fruit protected from birds and from mud and slugs.

Fall-fruiting raspberries, such as 'Heritage', will be cropping now, too, as will other varieties, so check the canes every day.

Fruit trees trained against walls need pruning and tying in, a grad- ual and ongoing job that, ideally, should have been begun early in summer (see page 110). Once your fan-trained peaches, apricots, nectarines and cherries have cropped prune all the fruited shoots back to replacement shoots, which will provide next year's peaches. As they grow, the new shoots should be tied in, spaced evenly apart.

If you are planning on putting in new fruit trees or bushes during the next few months, you should prepare their planting sites well in advance. Though it is very tempting to leave the digging until later, it is far better if any manure, compost or fertilizer you incorporate has a chance to work its way into the soil. If the weather is hot and sunny, put this particular task off until things cool down.

HARVESTING FRUIT

With all these soft fruits, you should try to harvest them in dry weather, because they are so prone to mildew.

Depending on the size of your

Fall-fruiting raspberries provide an extension to summer pleasures – check canes daily for ripened fruits

fruit garden, you could be harvesting apples, pears, plums, figs, peaches and grapes this month. With the exception of grapes, ripe fruit should come away easily from the tree. If you have to pull and pull, the fruit is not ready. Some pears, though, are deliberately picked before they are fully ripe. 'Kieffer Pear' is one, and 'Beurre Borc' another. Pick them when they are full-sized and the skin is just starting to change color. Put the nearly ripe pears in a warm, dry spot to finish ripening.

A good way to tell if a melon is ready for picking is to press the end opposite the stalk with your thumb. If it gives slightly, then it is ripe. A fully ripe melon should be filling the air with its delicious aroma.

THINNING FIGS

Figs need thinning this month because in Mediterranean climates, fruit can ripen in the course of one growing season, but in cooler, temperate climates, those fruit that form at the beginning of the growing season will never ripen by the time the cold weather comes. They will also be big enough to be ruined by winter frost, and will not be able to continue the ripening process the following summer. But tiny, embryonic figs that form, from now onwards, may overwinter successfully; providing there is no severe winter weather they continue ripening next summer and provide you with luscious fruit. Removing the larger fruitlets now, sad though it is, will encourage the production of the tiny, late-season fruit that will eventually reach maturity.

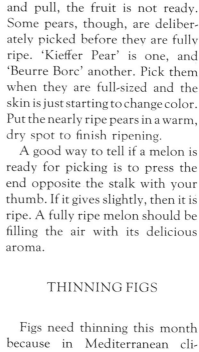

VEGETABLES

There is still some sowing to be done in the vegetable garden. How much depends on the climate and on the protection you give the young seedlings, in the form of cloches, cold frames, or a sunny, sheltered garden. You can make a fresh sowing of lettuce. Try 'Winter Density' if you want a cos-type lettuce, or 'Arctic King', for a cabbage lettuce. Be prepared to give them cloche protection, and you will have crops next spring.

Summer radish, spring cabbage and onion are other vegetables to sow where possible. It is late for Japanese onions, though, so choose an old-fashioned fall type, such as 'Autumn Triumph'.

Of the herbs, parsley and borage can be sown now. The latter has flowers of the clearest blue, and the plant is equally at home in the flower or vegetable garden.

PROTECTING YOUNG PLANTS

If you have room in the cold-frame, dig up a few young parsley plants, and move them under cover. Chives can be treated in this manner, too, and they can also be potted up and brought indoors to a sunny windowsill. All of these methods will extend the season for fresh herbs well into the fall.

Continue checking seedlings sown in nursery beds in the last few weeks, and thin them as necessary. Weed the seedlings as you thin them, paying particular attention to thin-leaved seedlings, such as onions, which can easily be swamped. Transplant slightly tender seedlings to cloches or frames, if there is room, and others, such as spring cabbage, may now be moved to their final destination in the milder areas.

Pitting your wits against the weather is always a challenge, especially in September, when frosts may start without any warning at all. Cloche crops–peas and shell beans, for example–that will be killed outright by drops in temperature. In the North, tomatoes should be harvested by the end of this month. It is also worthwhile covering them with cloches if cool weather starts early in the month. This can prolong ripening into early October if no frost occurs. If you put the unripe tomatoes somewhere warm and dry, they may continue ripening. Some people advocate putting the tomatoes on a sunny windowsill; others prefer wrapping them in paper and putting them in a dark place to ripen. Whichever method you choose, there are bound to be a few small, green tomatoes that resolutely refuse to change color. They are perfect for chutneys, though, so don't throw them away.

HARVESTING VEGETABLES

Start lifting maincrop potatoes by the end of September for storage through the winter. Traditionally, the foliage turning yellow was taken as a sign that the tubers were ready, but you can sensibly lift them before that. If the plants are badly infected with potato blight, there is little point in delaying harvesting, as the potatoes are unlikely to swell further. You can get special forks with blunt tines for lifting potatoes, but any fork will do. Dig up one plant to check

Let lifted potatoes dry out slightly before dusting off the earth

the size of the tubers and, if they are sufficiently large, continue harvesting.

It pays to make a thorough search for tubers still in the soil, once the main lot has been lifted. Besides increasing your harvest, it is important for the sake of good garden management to remove them. If left in the ground, the potatoes will sprout next year, making nonsense of your carefully planned crop rotation.

Badly diseased or damaged potatoes should be discarded. Keep a look-out, too, for wireworm infestation, which makes storage impossible. Slightly imperfect potatoes should be put on one pile, for eating immediately. Those being stored should have the soil brushed off. Store them in a dark, dry and frost-free place, but make sure it is mouse-proof.

Continue harvesting salad crops (see page 125) and blanching endive, a few at a time. Give celery its final earthing-up, until only the tips of the leaves show. Leeks, too, can be earthed up, but with leeks and celery postpone earthing-up if the soil is drenched, or the vegetables encased in the soggy soil may possibly rot away.

Since many of the vegetables in the garden now are nearing the end of their natural lives, the fight against pests and diseases becomes slightly less important than when the plants were young. Still, it pays to be on the look-out for the eggs of cabbage white butterflies, or you will find that your brassica crops, and the seedlings you were raising for next year's crops, have been reduced to skeletons by the voracious caterpillars. If the weather has been at all wet, slugs and snails will become active again, to the detriment of flowers and fruit as well as vegetables.

October

The dying leaves of trees and shrubs
and the flowers of late perennials make October the
most colorful month of the year in the North. The
colors span the spectrum from palest gold to deepest
copper, purple and red. But the sun's rays grow
weaker and the days shorten, both clear signs that
winter is not far away. Less work in the garden
means more time to plan your garden, and order
shrubs and trees to brighten up the spring.

*The handsome foliage
of a variety of maples (left)
puts on a show of color to
brighten even the dullest day*

Jobs for the month

General
Sweep up leaves
Apply slow-acting fertilizers
Provide frost protection to tender
plants outdoors
Clean out the greenhouse
Put up greenhouse insulation

Flowers
Lift and store dahlias, gladioli,
montbretia, tuberous begonias
and cannas
Lift and store pelargoniums, if
necessary
Protect still-flowering
chrysanthemums from frost
Finish bringing in late-flowering
chrysanthemums
Revive frosted chrysanthemums
in pots, if necessary
Clear out summer annuals
Plant bought-in perennials and lift
and divide existing perennials
Continue planting out biennials
and spring-flowering bulbs
Plant lily-of-the-valley
Sow sweet peas
Thin annual seedlings
Pot on butterfly flowers indoors

Pot calceolaria, cineraria and fairy
primrose into final containers
Rest greenhouse flowers

Lawns
Sweep up leaves and worm casts
Treat fusarium patch disease
Finish sowing seed or laying turf
Aerate the lawn

Roses
Prepare new beds for planting
Finish pruning rambler roses
Deadhead roses
Sweep up leaves
Spray with fungicide or
insecticide, if necessary
Take hardwood cuttings

Trees and shrubs
Sweep up leaves
Plant evergreens
Prepare ground for planting
deciduous trees and shrubs and
hedges
Trim young hedges
Take hardwood cuttings
Add new deciduous trees and
shrubs to your garden

Fruit
Finish harvesting figs, grapes,
pears and apples
Mulch trees and bushes
Take hardwood cuttings of
currants and gooseberries
Cut back old fruited blackberry
canes and tie in new growth
Spray against peach leaf curl and
bacterial canker
Plant new apple and pear trees

Vegetables
Cut down asparagus foliage and
mulch beds
Cut down Jerusalem artichokes
Cut down globe artichokes and
detach suckers for re-planting
Finish lifting root crops
Plant out spring cabbage and
lettuce in the warm states
Thin seedlings
Finish earthing up celery and leeks
Continue blanching endive
Finish harvesting summer crops
Lift chicory roots for forcing
Begin blanching Batavian endive
Lift herbs for winter use
Plant mint root for forcing

Tidying up the garden continues, with clearing fallen leaves from lawns, paths, patios and rock gardens a priority. In the case of rock gardens, the leaves would otherwise smother and rot the plants, and for that reason it is also a good idea to clear them from beds with young biennials or seedlings of any sort. With herbaceous and mixed borders, you will have to weigh up the pluses and minuses. On the plus side, the leaves slowly release nutrients and act as a form of frost protection. On the minus side, dead leaves offer splendid winter accommodation for snails, slugs and mice.

While spring and early summer called for frequent applications of quick-acting, nitrogenous fertilizer, now is the time to apply slow-acting fertilizers. Fruit trees and bushes, beds that have perennial plants, shrubs or bulbs in them, and any part of the garden lying fallow, will benefit from a dose of bonemeal, which supplies valuable phosphates for next spring's growing season. Mulching with well-rotted organic matter also releases nutrients slowly into the soil and acts as winter protection at one and the same time.

Towards the end of October will be a time of increasing your garden stock—either buying in new plants from specialist nurseries or garden centers, or making more of your own from hardwood cuttings. This almost certainly means that the beginning of the month will be devoted to preparing new ground for planting, so the newly arrived plants can be quickly accommodated.

The arrival of frosts, too, can be counted on, so the sooner any remaining tender plants are lifted and brought indoors or covered with cloches the better. Turning your back on this job, or procrastinating, may cost you your tender plants, so be sure to do it.

If you are overwintering them in a greenhouse, take the opportunity to clean it out. Choose a mild day, as you should really remove any plants in the greenhouse while you complete the task. Sweep up all the dead flowers, fallen leaves, and other vegetable matter, from the floors and shelving or benches. Wash everything down with diluted mild disinfectant, too.

Cold nights will become more frequent, so it pays to tack up temporary insulation, as a form of 'double glazing'. Rolls of special insulation material, which lets in the light but not the cold, are available at garden centers. Even with insulation, you may need to heat the greenhouse on the nights when frost is predicted.

Clearing leaves is a continual chore from the fall into winter, but it saves work later if the garden is kept as clear as possible now

FLOWERS

Lifting and storing tender plants will take up a lot of your time in the flower garden. Dahlias, for example, may already have had their above-ground growth blackened by frost, and their flowers are a sad, dishevelled ghost of their former glory. Cut off the dead stems just above the tubers—be careful not to nick the tubers themselves—and leave them to dry for a few days. Dust off any earth still clinging to the tubers, then pack them away for the winter. Check each tuber first, for any sign of disease, then store them in shallow boxes filled with slightly moist peat. Too wet and the tubers will rot; too dry and they shrivel, but erring on the side of dryness is safer. Keep the box in a cold, but frost-free place. Some people leave dahlias in the ground year after year, and get away with it in mild areas. One bad winter, though, will surely end your display so it's wise to take precautions.

STORING TUBERS

1 *As foliage dies and shrivels, cut stems just above the tubers, without damage to the tubers themselves*

2 *Lift the tubers and let them dry for a few days. Dust off earth and check there are no signs of disease*

3 *Lay the tubers on a cushioning layer of peat in the bottom of a box and pack in more peat around them*

4 *Store the box in a cool place, but protect from frost until time for replanting*

In the North, summer bulbs, as gladioli, need lifting too. Wait till their foliage has yellowed, then dig the bulbs up carefully, as they are likely to have produced a clutch of tiny new corms. These cormlets can be detached, stored over the winter and planted in a nursery bed next spring. Some may even flower late next summer; the next will bloom the following year. When lifting gladioli, you may also find a shrivelled corm at the base of the large one. This should be discarded, as it has been replaced by the vigorous, new corm above. Cut off the foliage, dry off rapidly in a warm room for three to four days, then store in trays at about 50°F (10°C).

Montbretia (*Crocosmia*) is likewise lifted and the corms overwintered in a frost-free place. With the old, cottage-garden sorts (C. × *crocosmiiflora* and its cultivars, also the more recent C. *masonorum*) this is somewhat less necessary, but there are other, more tender – and more expensive – forms of this South African genus, which deserve special treatment, at least in cold areas. Treat them as for gladioli, or, alternatively, plant the corms in a cold frame and move them back to their flowering positions next spring.

The tuberous begonias should be dug up now, any foliage cut back, earth cleaned off, and boxed for winter storage.

If you have any cannas—those old-fashioned dot plants seen more in public parks than private gardens—take these in as well, and treat the rhizomes as for begonias (above).

You know your garden and its winter climate better than anyone else does, and the list of plants to take in very much depends on your assessment. In the South and on the West Coast, some people leave their pelargoniums out over the winter months with no ill effects. Elsewhere it is best to pot them up and bring them indoors. You can still combine cutting them back, to compensate for any root loss during the move, with propagation, by using the severed shoots as cuttings. In overwintering pelargoniums, you can be less generous in their accommodation than at other times of the year. Because they will be dormant, if kept cool and almost dry, and because the arrangement is a temporary one, you can pack them quite closely together in boxes or pots. Make sure that the air can circulate freely round the plants, or they may fall prey to fungal infections.

Still flowering chrysanthemums that are to remain outdoors will need some protection from sharp frosts. Rig up a framework of bamboo canes or stakes and cover them with sacking or fine mesh if night frosts are forecast. If you haven't moved late-flowering chrysanthemums indoors, do so at the earliest possible moment, or you risk losing them.

There is no point in leaving any straggly annuals in the ground after this month, so clear them out to make way for re-planting, if you haven't already done so. You may wish to plant the newly vacant ground with perennials, either bought in from a garden center or propagated by division from your own existing stock. The method for dividing perennials is the same as for spring (see page 30).

All manner of biennials—wallflowers (*Chieranthus*), Canterbury bells (*Campanula medium*), sweet William (*Dianthus barbatus*), foxglove (*Digitalis*) and forget-me-not (*Myosotis*)—can be planted out now, for next spring's display. Many spring-flowering bulbs can still be put in this month. The sooner they are planted the better, though; the method is the same as for last month (see page 131). Tulips can be delayed until November if need be.

Lily-of-the-valley is traditionally planted this month. Select a lightly shaded spot, where the soil is free-draining and has plenty of leaf-mold or other organic matter incorporated. Plant the rhizomes

Young shrubs will benefit from the protection of a simple windbreak

Container-grown plants should now be back indoors or in the greenhouse, protected from cold and frost at night

quite shallowly, so the crown is barely visible, just breaking the surface of the soil.

This is a good time to sow sweet peas outdoors in warm areas, to get an early start for next summer's display. Space them as for spring plantings (see page 49) and remember to plant a few spare ones at the ends of the rows to cover any losses that may occur. Mice, in particular, are fond of the seed. Give cloche protection, if you can, to the young plants. You can also sow sweet peas in pots or boxes, which are then placed in a cold frame. Once the young seedlings appear, give them plenty of ventilation, covering them only if very wet or frosty weather threatens. They can either remain in their containers until being planted out next spring, or be brought into the greenhouse, if it is heated, and brought on to flower in late spring.

Any hardy annuals you may have have sown last month (see page 128) will need thinning out and a last going-over for weeds.

In the greenhouse, butterfly flower (*Schizanthus*) and stock (*Matthiola*) seedlings can be potted up into small pots, and the calceolaria, cineraria and fairy primrose plants moved on into their final, 5 in (12.5cm) pots for flowering. You will have to strike a balance between keeping them well ventilated but not exposed to frost.

There will be greenhouse flowers in need of a rest period, too. These include the lovely hot-water plant (*Achimenes*) and the later-flowering batch of gloxinia (*Sinningia*), also the tuberous-rooted begonias that you began resting in late summer (see page 117). With all of these plants, the withholding of water should be a gradual process, and the dormancy spent in frost-free conditions.

If, by accident, pot-grown chrysanthemums have been frosted, try this shock treatment: saturate the soil and the foliage with ice-cold water and move the plants to a frost-free place—a garage or shed is ideal. If they show signs of recovering after an hour or two, bring them into the warmth. Cut out all damaged growth and dust the cut ends with fungicide against graymold attack.

Flowers for the month

Flowers in the garden this month will be all but overshadowed by the color of leaves. Beech trees and hedges add their bronzy brown, while cherries, both ornamental and fruiting, add yellow, fiery orange, deep pink and red to the colors already provided by the maples, birch and Virginia creeper from late September.

Flowering dogwood (*Cornus kousa*), sumach (*Rhus typhina*) and the smoke bush (*Cotinus coggygria*) add to the dazzling leaf display, cooled and contrasted by the– hopefully– blue sky and the blue of various garden flowers. The blues and mauves of the Michaelmas daisy (*Aster*) are joined by the intense clear blue of the fall-flowering gentian (*Gentiana sino-ornata*) and the aconite (*Aconitum carmichaelii*). Annual asters (*Callistephus*) add last-minute touches of white, blue, purple and pink, if the weather has been kind.

In warm, sheltered gardens, the strawberry bush (*Arbutus unedo*) will be doing double duty now, its branches hung with lily-of-the-valley flowers and red fruit from last year's flowers. The fruit hasn't the slightest taste of strawberry, or any taste at all, for that matter, but it is lovely to look at, nonetheless. Another unusual ornamental that produces edible fruit now is the Chinese lantern (*Physalis alkekengi*). A rather scruffy-looking plant, and often invasive, it still earns its keep in many gardens because of its attractive lantern-shaped, bright-orange, papery calyces covering the round, orange-red fruit.

Stonecrops (*Sedum*) brighten up the rockery and herbaceous border this month, from the low-growing *S. sieboldii* to the taller-growing 'Autumn Joy' and purple-leaved 'Atropurpureum'. Both the Chinese lanterns and the stonecrops will continue their service indoors, in dried flower arrangements.

Of the climbers, late-flowering clematis (C. 'Ernest Markham', C. 'Ville de Lyon') continue to bloom, together with the foamy white flowers of the Russian vine (*Polygonum baldschuanicum*) and, in very sheltered gardens, the globular crimson flowers of the evergreen berberidopsis (*B. corallina*) will continue until the first frosts.

1 *Cornus kousa* 2 *Rhus typhina (fall foliage)* 3 *Aconitum carmichaelii* 'Arendsii' 4 *Gentiana sino-ornata* 5 *Callistephus* 'Starry Sky' 6 *Physalis alkekengi*

LAWNS

Trees in the garden will start shedding their leaves this month and these will need sweeping up regularly. Not only do the leaves look unsightly, but they can discolor the lawn beneath and cause a rotting of the turf, itself harmful. Leaves do, though, make valuable compost, so sweep them with a broom or a rake into a heap. Collect the gathered-up leaves by clapping the heap together with two boards, and move them to an out-of-the-way corner. Don't put leaves on the compost heap, but keep a special leaf-mold pile, covered with netting to keep the leaves from being blown about. In a year's time, you should have lovely leaf-mold to feed your plants. Evergreen leaves are not really worth putting on the leaf pile, nor are plane tree leaves, as both take a longer time to break down.

As you are sweeping, keep an eye open for worm casts, and sweep these up, too. Worm casts spoil the look of the lawn and, if in

Problems with the lawn: (left to right) worm casts, a profusion of moss, and a patch of fusarium fungus disease

quantity, can cause small bald patches when flattened and compacted by the mower roller. Any moss that declares itself should be raked up now, and fusarium patch disease treated. The latter is a fungal infection which is encouraged by the falling temperatures at this time of year, and tends to attack lawns that have been heavily treated with quick-acting fertilizer. Small, circular brown patches on the lawn are the main symptoms, so spray with a suitable fungicide (see page 184).

Much of the activity of September—laying turf, sowing seed, and repairing existing turf—can continue safely into October. With sowing lawn seed, though, be careful of the weather. If it has turned cold, or threatens to turn cold, you are likely to be wasting your time as germination will be nil or the grass seedlings vulnerable to harsh weather.

The need for regular mowing will decrease dramatically this month, but at least one last mowing will be necessary. It is also the time to aerate the lawn (see page 12) with a hollow-tined fork if you have one, or a garden fork if you don't. This task is especially important if the lawn has been compacted by children playing on it during the past few months.

ROSES

As next month marks the start of the rose-planting season in the warm states, start preparing any new rose beds (see page 12). Remember that roses stay for many years where they are planted, and every bit of extra care you take now will result in healthy, long-lived plants.

If you have not yet finished pruning rambler roses (see page 143), do so early in the month.

Continue deadheading as long as there are still blooms on the roses, keeping bushes and ground clear of fallen leaves and petals

Deadheading will still need doing, though production of flowers will slacken naturally with the onset of cold weather. Cold weather is also related to the shedding of leaves. Some roses—termed semi-evergreen—will keep most of their leaves in mild winters, but the vast majority are deciduous. Sweep or rake the leaves as they fall, to keep any lurking pests or diseases at bay. Any end-of-the-season takeover bids by black spot and mildew should be looked out for, and thwarted with proprietary fungicides (see page 184).

Many roses—species and shrub roses, climbers and ramblers—can be propagated this month from hardwood cuttings (see page 153). It is a simple operation, well worth doing if you want more roses.

In the North, give roses some protection.

TREES & SHRUBS

Gathering fallen leaves will be a major job by the end of the month. As with lawns, suitable leaves should be put on a leaf pile, and all others – diseased, infested, or leathery, tough leaves – burnt.

Planting of evergreens can be done in October, while the last traces of summer warmth remain, but don't leave it too late. Those that were planted last month should be watered at the first sign of dry soil. You should also be getting ready to plant deciduous shrubs, from the end of the month onwards. Prepare the planting sites now, making sure they are free of perennial weeds.

New hedges that were planted last spring can be given a trim now, to keep them from ending up straggly and open at the base. If you ordered hedging plants to put in this fall, prepare the site as soon as possible, so there is no frantic, last-minute rush. Often, hedging plants arrive bare-rooted, and should be planted before the roots have a chance to dry out. *In extremis*, you can heel them in (see page 20) until the site is prepared, but why make extra work for yourself?

Besides removing weeds, site preparation involves breaking up any compacted soil and correcting problems in drainage, fertility and acidity. Incorporating well-rotted organic matter helps correct all three problem areas. When added to heavy soils, it helps 'open them up' and improve drainage, while the same organic matter added to excessively free-draining soils helps them to retain more moisture. It also improves soil fertility

1 *Dig a trench to the depth of the spade, with even, straight sides all around. Remove all the earth*

2 *Fork over the base soil in the trench, turning it another spit's depth to loosen the texture*

3 *Dig manure or compost into the loosened earth; gradually fill in the trench, adding organic matter*

and helps correct extremes in acidity or alkalinity. Digging two spits deep–that is, two spades' depth–is the traditional planting preparation, but this is very hard work indeed, and digging one spit deep, with the second spit broken up with a garden fork, is just as good.

TAKING HARDWOOD CUTTINGS

Having increased your stock of plants by taking soft cuttings in spring and semi-ripe cuttings in summer, now is the time to propagate shrubs and trees from hardwood cuttings. The method is much the same–a severed piece of stem is partially buried, vertically, in soil or compost and left to get on with the process of forming roots. There are minor differences, though. Much longer, and firmer, shoots are used for hardwood cuttings, 8–12 in (20–30cm) or more. They may be green at the tip, but it doesn't matter. They are sometimes detached with a heel–a bit of the old wood–which is then neatly trimmed. Otherwise, hard-

wood cuttings are cut back to just below a pair of leaves or buds. Unlike soft and semi-ripe cuttings, which do better with bottom heat, a moist atmosphere and cossetting generally, hardwood cuttings are buried by a third to half their length directly in the garden soil or cold frame. They are also slow to form roots. In the northern states do this in March.

In the fall, shrubs and trees enrich the background to late-flowering plants, as their foliage gradually turns through a variety of colors

You can use a hormone rooting powder, but this is generally felt to be unnecessary with hardwood cuttings. What you should do is remove any leaves that would be buried by the soil, as they would otherwise rot. The butterfly bush (*Buddleia*), weigela, privet (*Ligustrum*) and mock orange (*Philadelphus*), forsythia and willow are easy to propagate from hardwood cuttings, but try experimenting with any woody shrub that takes your fancy. Taking cuttings is free, and if they don't succeed, no harm will have been done.

DECIDUOUS TREES AND SHRUBS

Azalea (*Rhododendron* hybrids) These deciduous members of the rhododendron genus enjoy free-draining, acid soil, sun or light shade and shelter. The species azaleas are not much grown nowadays, though their trumpet-shaped flowers, produced in spring and summer, and vivid fall leaf color are quite attractive. They have largely been replaced by hybrids as Ghent, Exbury, Mollis and Knap Hill. The Mollis hybrids are the first to bloom, in May, and their flowers, though scentless, are extremely beautiful. The colors range from salmon pink to orange and deep red, and the shrubs can eventually reach 8 ft (2.4m) in height and as much across. Good forms include 'Spek's Orange', 'Koster's Brilliant Red' and the pink 'F. de Konick'.

The Knap Hill and Exbury hybrids bloom next, and are scented as well as highly colored. Their young leaves are often an attractive russet-bronze. Exbury hybrids include the rose-pink 'Berryrose', the orange-red 'Hotspur' and the salmon-orange 'Cecile'. Good Knap Hill forms include the pale-yellow, pink-flushed 'Lapwing' and the orange, pink and red 'Sunset'.

Ghent azaleas tend to be taller than the above, and can reach up to 12 ft (4m) in time.

Their flowers are honeysuckle-shaped and relatively small, though some are very fragrant. Good cultivars include the pink- and cream-striped 'Bouquet de Flore', the yellow 'Nancy Waterer' and the red and orange 'Pallas'.

Broom (*Genista*) The broom family encompasses *Cytisus*, *Genista* and *Spartium*, all with pea-like flowers, usually creamy white or yellow. Poor, well-drained soil and lots of sun are what brooms need to thrive. For a small garden, try *Genista lydia*: it grows in a very attractive, arching way, and reaches a height of 1–1½ ft (30–45cm), though its spread can be twice or three times this. Its bright-yellow flowers appear in May and June.

Butterfly bush (*Buddleia*) The leaves and growth habit of the butterfly bush are coarse, but not unattractive. It is tolerant of an amazing range of sites and soils, and quickly reaches a height of 6 ft (2m) or more, and as much across. It flowers in July and August. Of the *Buddleia davidii* cultivars, good cultivars include 'White Cloud', 'Royal Red', the violet-blue 'Empire Blue' and 'Harlequin', which has deep-red flowers and creamy white variegated leaves. A more unusual, graceful, and earlier flowering species is *Buddleia alternifolia*. Its clusters of pale-lilac flowers appear along the length of the arching stems and the leaves are slender and willow-like.

Rhododendron 'Spek's Orange'

Cytisus scoparius – common broom

Buddleia davidii – white form

Buddleia davidii – lilac form

Cherry (*Prunus*) The flowering cherries, almonds and plums are the most popular trees for small gardens, though their flowering period in spring is a relatively short one. They are tolerant of most well-drained soils and flower best in a sunny spot. Bush forms are available. The dwarf Russian almond (*Prunus tenella*) makes a 3–4 ft (90–120cm) high suckering shrub, with deep pink flowers. When choosing a tree-sized cultivar, check on the ultimate height, as some can reach 40 ft (12m) or more. Try, too, to choose a cultivar that has particularly attractive bark or leaf color. *Prunus serrula* has glossy, peeling bark, while Sargent's cherry (*P. sargentii*) has bronzed leaves in spring and bright red and orange leaf color in the fall.

Daphne (*D. mezereum*) A winter-flowering shrub, daphne produces clusters of purplish red flowers along its bare branches. The flowers are followed by poisonous red berries, so it is not a shrub to choose if children use your garden. There is a white-flowered form available, *D.m.*

Prunus serrula (bark)

Daphne mezereum alba

Deutzia 'Magician'

'Alba', which has yellow berries. Both forms have an upright habit of growth, and eventually reach a height of 4 ft (1.2m).

Deutzia A good shrub for the small garden, deutzia grows to a height and spread of 5 ft (1.5m). Happy in sun or light shade and any well-drained soil, deutzia can be had with white or pink, single or double flowers, which appear in June. The cultivar 'Magician' has white-edged, pink flowers with deep pink on the reverse. *Deutzia × rosea* hybrids are

Fuchsia magellanica molinae

Ribes sanguineum 'Brocklebankii'

compact forms; try the white-flowered 'Multiflora' or the rose-carmine 'Carminea'.

Flowering currant (*Ribes sanguineum*) Extremely tough shrubs, tolerant of both shade and poor soil, flowering currants grow 7 ft (2.1m) or more high and produce their pink flowers in April and May. Some people find the scent of the flowers mildly unpleasant. 'Pulborough Scarlet' has deep-red flowers. 'Brocklebankii' has bright-yellow leaves.

Forsythia (*Spring bell*) Showers of bright-gold flowers on bare branches in spring make this shrub a must in most gardens. Sizes range from the 10 ft (3m) high weeping forsythia (*F. suspensa sieboldii*) to the 3 ft (1m) high, ground-covering 'Arnold Dwarf'. Sun or light shade and reasonable soil will give good results.

Fuchsia There are semi-hardy fuchsias, as well as tender ones, that can survive the winter if it is mild. Most common is *F. magellanica* which grows to a height of 6 ft (1.8m) and produces small scarlet and purple flowers. It is the parent of some lovely cultivars. These include the white-flowered 'Alba', the dwarf 'Pumila', and the cream, pink and gray-variegated 'Versicolor'. Other hardy fuchsias to try are 'Alice Hoffman', a small shrub with scarlet and white flowers, and 'Tom Thumb', a dwarf form with scarlet- and violet-colored flowers.

Hardy plumbago (*Ceratostigma wilmottianum*) The bright-blue flowers of hardy plumbago come in the late summer and continue well into the fall. Slightly dry soil and full sun suit this small shrub best. Its leaves turn red in late fall, as an added bonus.

Hazel (*Corylus*) There are various cultivars of common hazel (*C. avellana*), all of which make large shrubs. The yellow catkins in late winter and early spring are a cheerful sight. Try the cultivar 'Aurea', which has pale-yellow leaves, or the corkscrew hazel (*C.a.* 'Contorta'), which has spiralled and contorted twigs and branches. A close relative of hazel is filbert (*C. maxima*), and the best garden form is 'Purpurea', with purple leaves.

Hibiscus (*H. syriacus*) Sometimes called the tree hollyhock, or the flowering mallow, hibiscus is an exotic-looking shrub, and needs a sunny, sheltered spot to do well. It also prefers a long, hot summer, and flowering, to a large extent, depends on it. The flowers, which are large and trumpet-shaped, appear from late summer onwards, and continue into the fall. It is fairly slow growing, but can reach a height of 8 ft (2.5m). Good cultivars include the violet-blue, single-flowered 'Blue Bird', the white, double-flowered 'Admiral Dewey' and the double-flowered, pink and white 'Lady Stanley', with crimson-maroon markings.

Japonica (*Chaenomeles*) Often grown as a wall shrub, japonica can take almost any aspect and a wide range of soils. It is also called cydonia, Japanese quince and flowering quince. The flowers produced in early spring are saucer-shaped, and range in color from white through pink, salmon, orange, red and crimson. They are followed in the fall by bright-yellow fruit. Try the white-flowered *C. speciosa* 'Nivalis', the red-flowered 'Simonii', or *C. × superba* 'Crimson and Gold', with crimson flowers and conspicuous yellow anthers. Heights range from 4 ft (1.2m) to 8 ft (2.4m).

Kerria The bright-green, arching stems and golden-yellow, pompon-shaped flowers make kerria a popular cottage-garden shrub. 'Pleniflora' ('Flore Pleno') is a double-flowered form, and grows 8 ft (2.4m) high; 'Variegata' has leaves edged in creamy white and is half the size of 'Pleniflora'. Kerrias are happy in sun or light shade and any well-drained soil.

Corylus maxima 'Purpurea'

Corylus avellana–hazelnuts

Chaenomeles speciosa 'Simonii'

Ceratostigma wilmottianum

Hibiscus syriacus 'Blue Bird'

Kerria japonica 'Pleniflora'

Laburnum × *watereri* 'Vossii'

Weigela 'Variegata'

Philadelphus coronarius 'Aureus'

Chimonanthus praecox

Hamamelis japonica 'Zuccariniana'

Laburnum This small tree produces racemes of golden-yellow flowers in late May or early June. Despite its awkward growth habit and its highly poisonous seeds, it is a cheerful sight in spring and unfussy as to soil and light shade. The most graceful form is *L. anagyroides* 'Pendulum', which has a weeping growth habit.

Mock orange (*Philadelphus*) Mock orange is sometimes called syringa—the botanical name for lilac—but the two are unrelated. The scented, pure-white flowers of mock orange appear in June and July. Heights range from 3 ft (1m) for the double-flowered 'Manteau d'Hermine', to 10 ft (3m) for *P. delavayi*. *P. coronarius* 'Aureus' has bright-yellow leaves, though the flowers are rather small. Mock oranges are happy in town gardens and any well-drained soil.

Tree peony (*Paeonia*) The tree peony has a brief flowering in May or June. The flowers, which are yellow in *Paeonia lutea ludlowii* and white, pink or red in *Paeonia suffruticosa* cultivars, are huge and exquisite. The tree peony needs a fairly humus-rich soil, partial shade and shelter. Though the plants are perfectly hardy, they start into growth early in spring, and the young shoots are vulnerable to frost.

Weigela This spring- and summer-flowering shrub is sometimes called diervilla. It reaches a height and spread of 6 ft (1.8m), and is happy in well-drained soils, and sun or light shade. The flowers are shaped like foxgloves and range in color from white to deep rose-pink. Particularly striking and compact forms are *W. florida* 'Foliis purpureis', with mallow-pink flowers, and *W.f.* 'Variegata', with cream-edged leaves and pink blooms.

Wintersweet (*Chimonanthus praecox*) The sweetly scented, pale yellow, purple-centered flowers of wintersweet appear on the bare branches in winter and early spring. It is not much seen in small gardens because for most of the year, when in leaf, it can be rather dull-looking. The form 'Luteus' has larger, pure-yellow flowers.

Witch hazel (*Hamamelis*) The bare branches of witch hazel are covered with spidery blooms from December until March. Chinese witch hazel (*H. mollis*) is a popular species; good named forms include 'Brevipetala', with red-centered, yellow flowers, and 'Pallida', with pure yellow flowers. There is also a Japanese witch hazel (*H. japonica*); *H.j.* 'Zuccariniana' is a lovely, late-flowering form with green-centered, yellow flowers. Witch hazels make large shrubs or small, multi-stemmed trees, and their leaves provide fall color. A sheltered, sunny or lightly shaded spot is best, and a humus-rich, lime-free soil.

FRUIT

Collect the last of the summer's fruit now—the figs and grapes, pears and apples. Though figs are sun-dried in their native land, here, sadly, there is often neither sun nor abundance of figs to make it worth while. Some pears and apples can be stored, though, for use through the winter. Make sure they are blemish-free—and pest-free, too—as one rotten apple in storage can infect the rest. Store them in a frost-free, rodent-free place. Apples can be stacked, three or four deep, but pears should be spread out in a single layer, and not touching one another.

Use your compost to good effect this month, by mulching fruit trees and shrubs. Keep the mulch from touching the stem, or rot may set in.

Hardwood cuttings (see page 153) can be taken from gooseberries and currants now. There are slight variations in the method, though, because of their different habits of growth. Blackcurrants should send out lots of stems from below the ground, so when planting the cuttings, leave all the buds intact, and make sure that three-quarters of them are actually below ground. Gooseberries, red currants and white currants are grown on 'legs', or short single stems, so they should have all the buds that would be buried in soil rubbed off. Bury the cuttings by half their length, instead of three-quarters.

Blackberry canes that have fruited should be cut back to their base, and the new shoots, which will provide next year's crop, tied into place. Once you have cleared

away the old growth, you can quickly check that the support system is in order, and do any repairs or replacements necessary.

Now is the time to spray peach trees against the fungal infection, peach leaf curl (see page 184). Cherry trees that have suffered in the past from bacterial canker should be sprayed now as well (see page 184).

This is a good time to plant apple and pear trees. They will have a bit of time to settle in before the coldest weather comes, and still be spared the shock of being moved in full leaf.

BLACKCURRANTS

1 Cut strong stems from the bush. Strip leaves and cut the top above a bud and the bottom below a bud

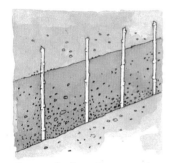

2 Leaving buds on the stems, plant in a trench with three-quarters of their length below ground

GROWING APPLE AND PEAR TREES

Choose a frost-free, sunny spot for planting apples and pears, as their flowers are vulnerable to late-spring frosts, and damaged flowers mean ruined crops. The soil need not be extremely rich—in fact, too much of a good thing can lead to excessive leafy growth at the expense of fruit. The soil must be well drained, as fruit trees dislike waterlogged conditions.

Apples and pears are available in several sizes and trained forms. Standards, half standards and dwarf trees are basically the same shape—a clear, main trunk topped by several branches. Standards have the longest trunks, and hence make the largest trees; dwarfs make the smallest and are most suitable for small gardens. Dwarf pyramids are shaped like Christmas trees, with the branches growing from a tall, central trunk. Even more compact is a cordon-trained tree; basically, it is a single main stem with branches which are heavily pruned to keep them almost stubby. Cordons are

usually grown at an angle, rather than upright, to get the maximum length of main stem, and heavy crops. There are double and triple cordons, with two and three main stems respectively, but these are not often seen nowadays. Because of the way the branches are trained and pruned, cordons look rather like two-dimensional trees. They take up very little space, and can be grown as a fence, trained on wires, or against a wall.

Another ingenious space-saving form is the 'family' tree. In this case, three different cultivars are grafted onto one main trunk. With apples, it is usually two kinds of eating apple and one cooking apple. Since most kinds of apple tree need cross-pollinating, and therefore at least one more apple tree nearby to exchange pollen with, the family fruit tree gets over this problem nicely, and is ideal for the one-tree garden, where space is short.

Besides being able to buy fruit

When apples are fully ripe, the base of each stalk will detach easily from the main spur

trees trained in different ways, you can buy trees of different ages. Maiden trees are the least expensive, as they are only one year old and consist of a single stem. The branches, which appear later in the growing season, will need your attention in the form of pruning and training. Two-year-old trees, partly trained, are available, but for the ordinary gardener a three- or four-year-old tree, with a well-established crown, is the best bet. It does cost more, but unless you are buying vast quantities, the extra money cuts out two or three years' wait and is well worth it.

If your fruit trees arrive before you have fully prepared the ground, heel them in (see page 20) if they are bare-rooted, or store them wrapped, in a sheltered bit of the garden if the trees are containerized. Don't forget to water them as they can dry out.

Inspect trees before planting, and cut off cleanly any damaged or diseased roots or branches. Be careful not to plant the tree too deeply; you can use the soil mark round the stem as a guide. Because fruit trees are grafted—the roots of one tree are joined to the above-ground portion of the desired cultivar—it is vital not to cover the scar where the rootstock joins the stem. Rootstocks are sometimes used to give strength to a weak cultivar, but in the case of fruit trees, rootstocks are often chosen for their dwarfing qualities, which keep the cultivar to a more easily manageable size.

The planting hole should be large enough to take the spread-out roots—never jam a tree into a too-small hole. Fork over the bottom of the hole to break it up, and incorporate peat and bone meal or well-rotted manure or compost

into the bottom of the planting hole. If you are staking the tree—and it is a good idea with all newly planted trees—fix the stake securely in the hole before planting the tree. This eliminates the possibility of damaging the tree's roots.

Once you have positioned the tree, fill the planting hole in stages, shaking the tree from time to time, so the soil fills the spaces between the roots.

Cordons and espaliers need support in the form of wires and posts. Espaliers are not often seen in garden centers nowadays, though there are lovely old specimens to be found in the kitchen gardens of some big country homes. Espaliers are trained so that the branches grow horizontally, in two or three tiers, giving, again, a two-dimensional effect. Like cordons, their traditional home is against walls or in the open, against posts and wires. With cordons, start the wires 2 ft (60cm) from the ground, with 2 ft (60cm) intervals thereafter. Espaliers need wires spaced at 16 in (40cm) intervals. If you are wiring up a wall, use vine eyes at

regular intervals to give good support. Free-standing support systems will need strong posts.

Traditionally, cordons were planted with their stems pointing north, to give the trees the maximum exposure to sunlight, but the layout of your garden may make this impossible.

Dwarf apple trees are sufficiently compact to be grown in close company with other crops

Heavy pruning at appropriate times keeps the shape of sturdy cordon-trained branches (below left). An espalier-grown pear tree (below) shows a heavy crop

PRUNING AN OLD APPLE TREE

You may find that you have inherited, with your garden, an overgrown, non-productive apple tree. Now is the time to devote an afternoon, or even a whole day, to pruning it. While it is still in leaf, you can easily identify dead wood. Make a note of it, so that, when the leaves have fallen, you can prune out all the dead wood back to healthy growth. You will need to be fully armed for the task—a sharp knife or heavy-duty pruning shears, probably a fine-toothed, sharp saw, and a proprietary compound to seal the larger cuts afterwards.

After the dead wood has been removed, prune out wood that appears diseased or weak. You will want to let as much light and air as possible into the center of the tree, to ripen the wood—and thus promote fruiting—and also keep diseases at bay. Work from the center outwards, and from large to small, ideally ending up with four or five thick, main branches. If you have to remove any main branches, select them so that the remaining branches are evenly spaced out, one from another and also evenly distributed around the crown. Once you've got the main framework in order, go back again over the branches, removing any crossing wood and cutting some of the very twiggy wood back to base. If, in the end, the tree looks well balanced, chances are that you've done a good job.

A further encouragement—and a good idea in any case—is to give the tree a thick mulch of well-rotted manure or garden compost. If it is a very old tree, it is likely to have used up all the minerals in the soil, especially potash. The mulch will help replace the minerals, and sulphate of potash can be given as an additional help.

If the tree is in a lawn, apply a granular general fertilizer. To prevent scorching of the grass, spike the lawn first and brush in the fertilizer. Water in if the weather has been at all dry.

The purpose of pruning is to open up the center of the tree and to remove old wood that is no longer fruitful. In an old or neglected tree, cut out weak, diseased or dead wood, along with any crowded and convoluted branches. Work towards an evenly-spaced arrangement of strong, healthy branches radiating from the crown. Some of the large central branches should be cut out to let in air and light. The tallest branches on tall trees should be cut back to a lateral. Thin out any complicated spur systems, but do it gradually over several seasons. Clear the tree base of weeds and grass and lightly fork over the soil. If growth is slow, do all the pruning at once; if vigorous, spread it over several years.

1 *To remove a branch, saw upwards from below, flush with the trunk*

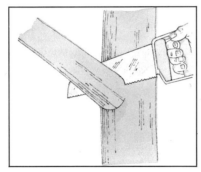

2 *Make a second cut downwards from above the branch, to meet the first*

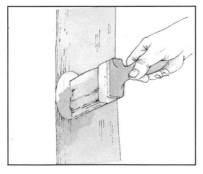

3 *Cut away ragged edges with a knife and paint the wound with tree paint*

VEGETABLES

If you have an asparagus bed, then cut down the stems once the foliage turns yellow. Give the bed a good raking, too, to clear up any debris. Follow this with a mulch of well-rotted organic matter—compost or manure—as asparagus is a greedy feeder. Because it grows wild by the sea, asparagus was traditionally mulched with rotted seaweed, but fortunately this is not essential.

Artichokes—both globe and Jerusalem—need attention now. Cut down the old stems of the latter, but leave a little stump so you known where to dig when you want tubers. Globe artichokes should also have their stems and yellowed leaves removed, and their crowns given frost protection in the form of dry leaves, straw or old hay, held down with wire netting. If you need more globe artichoke plants, now is a good time to remove the new season's suckers and plant them out. Choose suckers 6–8 in (15–20cm) tall and try to detach them with some roots and a bit of the parent plant still attached.

Finish lifting and storing root crops still left in the ground—turnips, rutabagas, parsnips, beets as well as carrots, for example. With many root crops, getting them out of the ground now is more a matter of convenience than necessity. Though they can stay in the ground until you need them, if there is a long period of frost, digging them out becomes impossible. With today's smaller gardens, you are likely to want the space available for something else.

In warm areas set out spring

Spring cabbages transplanted from a nursery bed are firmed in position in a straight, well-spaced row

cabbage sown in a nursery bed, but do it as early in October as possible. Winter and spring lettuce can also be planted out now. All the seeds sown last month (see page 145) should be thinned, again, as early in October as possible.

Blanching of endive can continue, and if you haven't finished earthing up celery and leeks (see page 113), do that immediately.

If the weather has been kind, then you may still have harvesting of summer crops to do, especially if you have been able to provide cloche protection. By the end of October, virtually all of the summer crops will have finished and the ground will need clearing up. Pick the last of the peas and beans, spinach, eggplants, tomatoes and peppers. If you are lucky enough to have a surplus, then the freezer should come in handy. Old-fashioned alternatives include drying, bottling, preserving in salt, and pickling. Last but not least, there are sure to be friends and neighbors with whom you can share your bounty.

Storing pumpkins and squashes presents no problem at all. Simply hang them, one per net, in a cool, dry, place, where they will often keep for the whole winter and into the early spring.

Towards the end of the month, you can lift chicory roots for forcing during the long winter months. Some people lift the lot, and store the roots in a cold but frost-free place, until needed for forcing. Other gardeners leave the roots in the ground, lifting a few at a time, as needed. With the latter method, it will be impossible to dig the roots up if the ground freezes hard in very cold weather.

Whichever method you choose, select healthy-looking roots, 1–2 in (2.5–5cm) across at the top. Trim off any straggly roots, so that you end up with a main root 6–8 in (15–20cm) long. Trim the foliage back, too, so that ¾ in (2cm) is left. Then pack them in peat, stacked horizontally, and store in a cold, dark place, or pot some up for forcing (see page 13).

Batavian endive, grown especially for cold-weather salading, can be blanched now. It will take at least a month for the blanching process to be completed, so make

a start by the end of the month. One way of doing it is tying the large, outer leaves up, to enfold the inner heart of the plant. You can also cover it with a cloche, and drape black plastic over the cloche, which also protects the plant from sudden frosts.

LIFTING HERBS FOR WINTER

Now is a good time to bring in some pieces of rooted herbs to ensure a continuing supply through the winter. Continue lifting and protecting or bringing in chives and parsley (see page 145), and try potting up other herbs as well. Sage, lemon balm, marjoram, basil, thyme and tarragon can become winter residents of a windowsill, too. When you lift them, try to keep as much of the roots attached as possible. Cut the plants back a bit, to compensate for any roots that may have been lost, and water in well. Thereafter, water sparingly, as these plants grow naturally in dry places, and soggy potting soil can be fatal.

FORCING MINT

If you are likely to want a supply of mint for winter use, then dig up a handful of the 'roots' (actually underground stems or rhizomes). Cut them into 4–6 in (10–15cm) pieces and lay them horizontally on the surface of a soil mix, in boxes or pots. Cover the 'roots' with a thin layer of the mix (about ¾ in (2cm)), and put the containers in a warm spot—in the greenhouse or on a sunny windowsill. Water lightly and once the fresh shoots appear—in two or three weeks' time—water the mint more frequently.

November

Late fall is a quiet time in the garden,
with short, cold days and long, perhaps even frosty,
nights. Most plants are more or less resting now,
though the occasional bright flower and sunny
afternoon may tempt you outdoors, to clear up the
garden and to put in new plants for next spring.

*Helping to provide year-round color
in the garden, Cotoneaster horizontalis (left)
displays its dark, bottle-green foliage and
bright red berries against a background
of bergenia leaves*

Jobs for the month

General
Continue raking up leaves
Dig over vacant ground
Check stakes, ties and supports
Plant trees and shrubs, heeling
them in if conditions are
unsuitable
Provide greenhouse heating and
decrease ventilation
Clean greenhouse windows and
clear leaves from the roof
Finish preparing ponds for winter

Flowers
Finish planting tulips
Check bulbs for forcing
Cut back early-flowering
chrysanthemums, and bring into
the greenhouse, if necessary
Cut back late-flowering
chrysanthemums that have
finished flowering
Protect alpine plants from damp
Cloche Christmas roses
Protect tender plants from frost
Cut back herbaceous plants
Stop fall-sown sweet peas
Plant carnations and pinks on free-
draining soils

Lawns
Rake up leaves
Prepare the site for a new lawn
Mow, if necessary
Clean mower and arrange for
repairs or servicing, if necessary

Roses
Start planting

Pot up roses for forcing
Continue pruning
Continue taking hardwood
cuttings

Trees and shrubs
Plant deciduous trees and shrubs
Rake up leaves
Protect tender shrubs from frost
Stratify seeds to encourage
germination
Finish taking hardwood cuttings
Layer clematis
Pot up shrubs for forcing
Trim deciduous hedges

Fruit
Plant hardy trees and bushes
Plant grape vines and prune
established ones
Begin pruning bush fruit
Finish taking hardwood cuttings
Protect buds from birds
Check fruit in storage

Vegetables
Sow peas for spring growth
Lift runner bean roots for
overwintering
Protect cauliflower curds from
frost
Dig up rhubarb crowns for forcing
Continue forcing chicory
Continue blanching Batavian
endive
Force seakale
Harvest Jerusalem artichokes and
Brussels sprouts
Finish lifting herbs for forcing

Because of the dipping temperatures and light levels—November tends to be a foggy month, as well as a wet and cold one—most plants in your garden will be dormant now, and their immediate requirements, in terms of your time and energy, will be minimal. There are still jobs to be done—leaves to be raked up and stacked in piles or put on the bonfire; ground to be dug over for next spring's planting; stakes, ties and supports to be checked. On the whole, these are tasks that can be done whenever you have the opportunity, and whenever the weather is suitable, between now and early spring.

One long-term job that begins in earnest this month is planting deciduous trees and shrubs, both ornamental and fruiting. Timing depends very much on when they are delivered and what condition the ground is in—it could be frozen hard, waterlogged, or in perfect tilth, depending on the climate or weather. If necessary, heel in bare-rooted subjects (see page 20) and store containerized ones (see page 159), until things improve.

Though plants in the greenhouse will still need occasional watering, the greenhouse air is likely to be damp and cold, a combination favorable to various unpleasant fungal infections. Ventilation is still necessary, to get fresh air in the greenhouse, but it must be balanced against draughts and sudden frosts. If your greenhouse is a heated one, you will find daytime heating more and more necessary as the month passes. Artifical lighting is much more the province of the commercial grower, but you can take steps to ensure that whatever sunlight is around reaches your plants. Remove dust and dirt from the glass or plastic, and clear leaves from the roof.

Garden pools may well need a final clear-out (see page 128). If your pond has a pump, remove it for the winter, and clean it thoroughly, or have it serviced, if necessary.

Though leaves and other garden debris decomposing in the pond can foul the water, plants immediately surrounding the pond create a beneficial microclimate, which helps delay the surface freezing in winter. Even though it might be unsightly, leave the dead foliage of waterside plants intact, to act as a shelter through the winter.

A pane of glass supported horizontally protects alpines from excessive moisture settling in the leaves and rotting them

FLOWERS

Mid-November is the latest you should plant tulips in the North. Later than this they will still grow, but the flowers may not be as good.

The bulbs that you prepared for forcing earlier in the fall (see page 133) may be showing signs of life. Look over them regularly, and if there is 1 in (2.5cm) or more of leaf and bud growth, move them to a slightly warmer, slightly lighter spot. Don't worry about the pale-looking leaves, because once they are exposed to light, they will turn green. If there are bulbs showing no signs of growth, check that their bulb fiber or soil mix is moist and then return them to the plunge bed, cold frame or wherever they are being stored for rooting. Don't be tempted to bring them on with extra warmth and light at this stage, or their roots will never develop properly.

Outdoors, the early-flowering chrysanthemums which had their flower buds protected from frost last month (see page 150) will now have finished flowering. Cut them back to nearly ground level, and either leave them outdoors or pot them up, to overwinter in a greenhouse or cold frame, depending on the hardiness of your particular chrysanthemums and how sheltered or exposed your garden is. Keep in mind, too, that chrysanthemums are very prone to rotting, and if your soil is a sticky, heavy, waterlogged clay, you should really lift the plants for the winter and put them out in the garden next spring. Overwintering, dormant chrysanthemums can be given quite crowded accommodation in pots, boxes or

a cold frame. Make sure, though, that they have plenty of ventilation and just enough water to keep them from wilting.

Some of the tender, late-flowering chrysanthemums, already in the greenhouse, may have finished their display. Cut these back, too, and cut down on watering. Store under the greenhouse benches or shelving.

If you have a rock garden or alpine plant collection, some of the more delicate subjects will need winter protection. In most cases, it is not frost which kills them, but cold, soggy soil and cold, wet air. This is particularly true of plants with hairy or woolly leaves, and those with gray leaves, all of which may rot away. The traditional method of protection is to fix a pane of glass over the plant. Use wire or wood supports, so the air can circulate freely. You could use a cloche, as long as you leave the ends open. An additional precaution is to put a layer of gravel under sprawling or trailing alpines, so the leaves and stems rest on the gravel rather than on wet soil.

If you are growing Christmas roses (*Helleborus niger*), cloche these as well. This isn't essential to keep them alive, as it is with alpines, but it does bring the flowers on a bit, so you may even have them in time for Christmas.

Old hay, leaves or straw held down with wire mesh will suffice to protect such tender plants as red-hot poker (*Kniphofia*) and Dutch or Spanish iris. With the red-hot poker, loosely tie up the foliage first, as it must not be buried under the protective mulch. Give plants which might be killed in a severe winter *in-situ* protection or dig them up to

WINTERING CHRYSANTHEMUMS

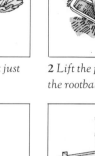

1 *Cut back the stem of the plant just above ground level*

2 *Lift the plant with a fork, easing up the rootball*

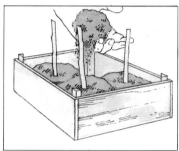

3 *Strip leaves and pot up individual plants to overwinter under glass*

4 *Alternatively, place several plants in a box and pack them with soil*

overwinter under glass. A third option is to take a tiny rooted piece of the plant, or even an unrooted cutting, to bring on under glass. That way, if the parent plant succumbs you're covered.

By now, most of the beauty provided by a herbaceous border will have been replaced by dead and dying foliage. Cut back all the withered, above-ground growth of hardy deciduous plants. Some gardeners allow the dead leaves of tender plants to remain attached to the plant over winter, and clear them up in spring. This way, the leafy debris acts as protection to the living crown, in much the same way as old hay or straw does.

The sweet peas you sowed last month in the open ground in warm areas will need stopping, using the same method as for spring-sown

ones (see page 86).

Fall planting is sometimes advocated for carnations and pinks but this very much depends on the nature of your climate. Light, sandy soils, which never get waterlogged, or 'cold' will encourage fall-planted carnations and pinks to form good strong root systems. The plants can then more easily withstand drought next spring. Wet, heavy, 'cold' soils are just as likely to rot them, and fall planting is best avoided. If you are determined to put your plants in now, then do it as early in November as possible. Make sure that the bottom leaves are clear of the soil and that the stem has not been buried. Firm well, stake if necessary (see page 86) and check regularly to see if they have been lifted by heavy frosts.

Flowers for the month

There is still color to be seen in the garden, but mostly from newcomers, and on a modest scale. The fall-flowering cherry (*Prunus subhirtella* 'Autumnalis') starts displaying its white or pale pink, semi-double flowers now, and will continue, on leafless branches, in mild areas through the winter months.

One of the most cheerful late-fall plants is *Jasminum nudiflorum* with its tubular bright yellow flowers which may open in succession from now to next spring. Towards the end of the month, scent will be provided by that cottage-garden favorite, *Viburnum farreri*, still seen in catalogs and nurseries under its former name, *V. fragrans*. Try also its more vigorous hybrid *V. × bodnantense*, or *V. opulus* 'Compactum', with red berries.

Among the evergreens, the exotic-looking *Fatsia japonica* is graced with starry heads of small white flowers, and the much-loved laurustinus (*Viburnum tinus*) shows its tight, pink-tinged buds, ready to open flat and purest white. *Mahonia japonica* and *M.j. bealei* will also be garlanding their handsome foliage with sprays of fragrant, yellow flowers.

In mild climates the winter-flowering heathers (*Erica carnea*) will be starting to open their white, pink, rose or reddy-purple bell flowers, set off to perfection by the blue gentians in bloom now (*Gentiana sino-ornata*, *G. farreri*). The lovely Algerian iris (*I. unguiculosa*, formerly named *I. stylosa*) will be sending up its short-stemmed flower buds. These can be picked in bud, and brought indoors, where they will reveal their pale violet petals, marked with white and yellow, as they open in the warmth.

Another good plant for cutting for the house is the kaffir lily (*Schizostylis coccinea*). Its tall spikes of starry flowers—crimson in the species, rose-pink in 'Mrs Hegarty' and palest pink in 'Viscountess Byng'—are a welcome sight in the garden or house.

Of the bulbs, some of the true autumn crocuses still flower—*C. laemigatus* (lilac), *C. ochroleucus* (white) and *C. longiflorus* (lilac-purple)—and the first of the snowdrops (*Galanthus nivalis reginae-olgae*) may even put on a cheerful display before its leaves have appeared.

1 *Viburnum opulus* 'Compactum' **2** *Fatsia japonica* **3** *Mahonia japonica* (*young leaves*) **4** *Iris unguiculosa* **5** *Schizostylis coccinea* 'Mrs Hegarty' **6** *Galanthus nivalis* 'Plena'

LAWNS

Leaf raking will continue well into November, with perhaps a late storm or windy spell bringing the last of the leaves down.

If you are planning on sowing or turfing a new lawn or making a vegetable or flower garden next spring, now is the time to dig over the ground in the warmest regions. Remove every trace of perennial weed as you dig, and put on one side all the stones and bits of garden debris that you find. Dispose of them properly, once and for all, or they will turn up, unwanted, again and again in various bits of your garden. If weeds are a real problem, use a proprietary weedkiller. When you have finished digging, roughly level the soil, for there are no hard frosts to 'lift' the surface. (The action of the frost actually breaks down the rough clods of soil, and makes achieving a smooth, even-surface tilth that much easier.)

Depending on the weather, an end-of-season cut may be necessary. Set the mower blade high, and choose a day when the ground is reasonably dry, as wheels and rollers will skid over a wet surface, and drag the grass with it. Where frosty weather sets in, walk on the lawn as little as possible to avoid compacting the soil.

Before you put your mower away, give it a good clean and thorough going-over so that it will be ready and in working order the next time you want to use it.

If your mower is an electric one, unplug it and move it onto a pathway or other convenient hard surface. Hose down the cylinder or cutters, the rollers and wheels.

Fallen leaves must continuously be cleared from the lawn. They are useful as a base for compost, kept trapped inside wire netting

If mud is still caked on the surface, you'll have to resort to a stiff hand brush and elbow grease. Dry the machinery thoroughly, then wipe all moving parts with a lightly oiled rag. Check that the blades or cutters have not become nicked or distorted. Check the electric power cable for holes or cracks, and check that the plug and/or circuit breaker is properly and safely wired up.

In the case of a battery mower, top the battery up with distilled water, give it a charge, then store in a dry place.

Power mowers should have their tanks drained of gas and oil, the spark plugs cleaned and, if necessary, adjusted. Fill the tank with clean oil before storing the mower for the winter.

Never store a mower on a damp surface, or in a damp place, or it will almost certainly be difficult to start it next spring. Stand it on cardboard or a block of wood, if necessary, and keep the area well ventilated, to avoid condensation.

Any new parts needed or repairs should be sorted out now, rather than postponing booking in the mower until you need it in the spring. You are likely to find that most other mower owners have similarly waited until spring, and the waiting line for repairs will most probably be a long one.

To prepare ground for sowing a lawn, clear weeds, dig over and rake for a fine, even texture

ROSES

Start planting roses (see page 12) where the weather and soil conditions are favorable. Where not, and you have already bought the roses and either heeled them in or settled containerized ones in a sheltered spot, check that they are in good condition. Water sparingly, if necessary, adjust any knocked over by wind, and keep your fingers crossed that the weather changes for the better so that you can plant them properly.

Roses can be potted up now and brought into the greenhouse next month to provide early blooms to brighten next spring. Choose small bushes—even miniatures—and those with scented flowers, if possible. The cooler the conditions are, the better, until you are ready to bring them into bloom. Remember to prune them back as for a newly planted rose outdoors (see page 12).

Established bush roses in your garden can be pruned in the South, according to variety and habit of growth (see page 22). There is one school of thought which advocates pruning roses towards the end of winter, rather than at the beginning. The reasoning behind it is this: should a bush be pruned hard and then exposed to a severe winter, the chances of its survival are lessened. If your garden is an exposed one, or a hard winter is forecast, this is worth considering. In the cold parts of the U.S. and Canada lightly prune the roses now, and then finish off the job in spring.

In the propagation department, hardwood cuttings can still be taken (see page 153).

THE CITY GARDEN

In towns and cities garden space is very precious. A peaceful spot in which to relax and unwind can be a welcome refuge from the pressures of modern urban living.

City gardens are usually small and are inevitably overlooked by neighbors or passers-by. Careful planning is vital to squeeze the best out of every inch of space. The initial costs of setting up this particular garden are high, but it has been designed for a busy working couple who have no wish to spend their free time mowing lawns or grubbing out weeds. Everything has been chosen for maximum effect and minimum maintenance – the plants need very little in the way of pruning, training and so on, yet give color throughout the year.

The garden is attached to an older terraced house with a basement kitchen and dining room. The style of the garden and the materials used to construct it have been carefully chosen to be compatible with the house. Straight lines echo the rather severe, linear style of the architecture. Two contrasting paving materials have been used – brick and paving stone.

Immediately adjacent to the house, an area has been excavated to provide an outside eating and entertaining space within easy reach of the kitchen. It is spot-lit for evenings and has a built-in

barbecue with a convenient herb bed nearby. The fact that this area is on a lower level helps to screen it, and the bank of plants behind the benching increases the feeling of privacy. Underneath the benching is storage space for garden tools and the like.

Pots of flowering plants have been used to decorate the area during the summer. They can easily be shifted to other areas of the garden which are temporarily lacking in color. The angled steps lead into a tiny private haven. This part of the garden catches most sun and is therefore the best place for spring or fall relaxation. The pond is in fact a shallow circular stream. Water trickles slowly over large stones covering the plastic pond lining and is pumped back along a narrow channel running under the flower bed to re-emerge at the top of the small waterfall. The tiny bridge provides easy access to the stepping stones within the flower bed.

Some of these plants are on the tender side. In colder areas substitute hardier specimens as necessary.

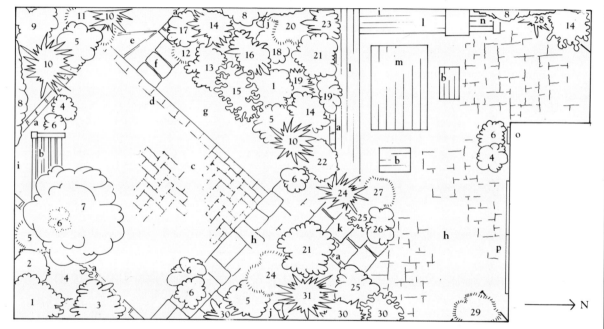

1	Rosa foetida	19	Ajuga reptans	c herringbone old brick
2	Clematis × 'Jackmanii Superba'	20	Berberis darwinii	d edging bricks
3	Euphorbia griffithii	21	Arundinaria nitida	e stepped waterfall
4	Geranium pratense	22	Rosmarinus officinalis	f paving stone bridge
5	Alchemilla mollis	23	Hebe albicans	g 2 in (5cm) deep pond with pebbles in bottom
6	Pelargonium	24	Yucca filamentosa	h paving stone
7	Catalpa bignonioides	25	Juniperis communis	i brick wall
8	Hedera helix	26	Hebe pinguifolia	j spotlights trained on beds for evenings
9	Rosa rubrifolia	27	Convolvulus cneorum	k steps
10	Iris kaempferi	28	Herb plot: sage (Salvia officinalis), parsley (Petroselinum crispum), chives (Allium schoenoprasum)	l winged bench with tool storage underneath
11	Buddleia alternifolia			m wooden table
12	Arundinaria variegata			n barbecue
13	Kniphofia galpinii	29	Ceanothus × 'Autumnal Blue'	o lighting
14	Aucuba japonica	30	Fatshedera lizei	p sliding door to living room of house
15	Hosta sieboldiana elegans	31	Yucca gloriosa	
16	Choisya ternata			
17	Cotoneaster conspicuus	a	retaining wall	
18	Cotinus coggygria	b	wooden bench	

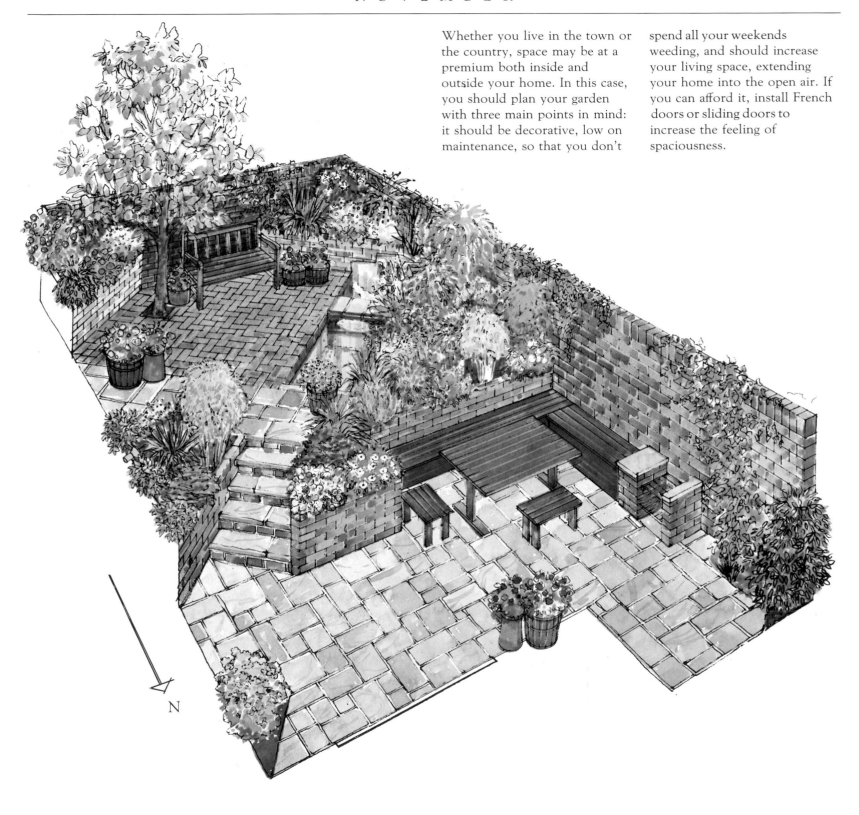

Whether you live in the town or the country, space may be at a premium both inside and outside your home. In this case, you should plan your garden with three main points in mind: it should be decorative, low on maintenance, so that you don't spend all your weekends weeding, and should increase your living space, extending your home into the open air. If you can afford it, install French doors or sliding doors to increase the feeling of spaciousness.

N

TREES & SHRUBS

This month is prime time for planting deciduous trees and shrubs. The method is the same as for spring (see page 36) and you may have already prepared the soil last month (see page 153) to receive the new plants. It is also a good time to transplant reasonably young shrubs and trees from one part of your garden to another, or, perhaps, from a friend's or neighbor's garden to your own. The normal planting rules apply, but in addition you must try to keep as much of the root system as possible intact, with plenty of soil attached, when you lift the plant. Any large-scale root loss must be balanced by equally large-scale pruning of above-ground growth. On the whole, transplanting is best confined to well-rooted cuttings, being moved from a nursery bed to their final position, and young plants which have been in one position for no more than three to four years.

Large and long-established specimens can be moved, it is true, but advanced preparation in the form of root pruning is usually necessary and the risk is a high one. Unlike furniture, which can be moved whenever you feel like a change, established trees and shrubs resent being moved. This is why you must plant them with their ultimate size and spread in mind and give them plenty of room to grow.

Continue raking up fallen leaves, and adding them to your leaf pile or bonfire as appropriate (see page 153).

Though tender fuchsias, Cape leadwort (*Plumbago capensis*) and other frost-vulnerable shrubs should be safely under glass by now (see page 144), there will be other tender shrubs which are either too big to move, or you simply haven't got room for in a greenhouse. Also, there are some

Shrubs need protection from frost at the roots and this can be given by surrounding the base of the plant with a layer of dried hay or straw

semi-hardy shrubs–rosemary and *Abelia × grandiflora* for example– which are safe nine winters out of ten south of New York.

Mulching is one form of protection–a 4 in (10cm) thick layer of dry leaves or straw around the base of vulnerable shrubs, such as Chilean glory flower (*Eccremocarpus scaber*) or *Solanum jasminoides* (sometimes called potato vine), will keep the frost off the roots. Then, even if all the top growth is cut by frost, new growth will spring from the base.

Screening around a tender shrub also gives protection. Stakes and wire mesh, interwoven with straw or hung with plastic or sacking, will do the job nicely. Newly planted shrubs, especially evergreens, are likely to benefit from this treatment during their first winter.

This vertical protection serves a definite purpose, and must not be left on for months on end. While it is protecting the plant from frost, it is also shielding it from any sunlight available and cutting down on the air circulation, both of which the plant needs. Lastly, a garden dotted about with shrouded plants is not especially attractive to look at, so be ready to remove the screening whenever the temperature rises and the wind drops, and your plants are safe.

Though it is often easier to grow new shrubs from cuttings, or by division if the shrubs are multistemmed, it is fun to grow new shrubs from seed. In the case of hard stones–cherries, apricots, plums and peaches, for example– and fleshy seeds, such as rose hips, stratification is necessary for a good germination rate. The seed, complete with outer flesh in the case of rose hips, is stored in

SCREENING SHRUBS

Mesh stuffed with straw or hay protects tender shrubs from frost

Alternatively, tie sacking or plastic around four stout canes

layers, in a box or pot filled with soil or a mixture of sand and soil. Place the container outdoors, in an out-of-the-way spot, but one that is fully exposed to the weather. The winter cold, wet and frosts help to break down the hard, protective coating of the seed. The seed may prove very tempting to mice or birds, so cover the top of the container with wire mesh. The seeds will be ready for sowing in seed mixture early next spring. If only a few seedlings are required, try extracting seed from the fruits and sowing directly. Cover very thinly with soil and then with fine gravel. Plunge outside until early spring, then bring into a cool greenhouse or frame.

You can continue to take hardwood cuttings this month (see page 153), and check that any taken last month have not been lifted by frost. It is also a good month for layering clematis (see page 52), but remember to mark its position clearly, so you don't undo all your good work with a well-meant raking or forking over later in the season.

One way of bringing spring forward, in the greenhouse, is to buy shrubs, such as lilac, hydrangea and broom, this month and pot them up. Hydrangeas, being slightly less hardy than the others, should be given the protection of a cold frame, but the lilac and broom can be left in a sunny, sheltered spot outdoors. In a month or two, when winter is at its most depressing, bring the pots into a cool greenhouse. The protection and extra heat given are enough to have the plants in flower several weeks ahead of their outdoor cousins. As with forced bulbs, you do the plant no kindness at all by giving too much warmth and, in extreme cases, make it difficult for the plant to survive, let alone flower well. Once flowering is over, harden off the shrub before planting out.

Any of the Indian azaleas bought now can also be put in a cool, frost-free spot to keep their buds tightly closed, until you are ready to bring them indoors to flower.

Give a final trim to deciduous hedges now, and cut back hard in the case of those that have gone bare and leggy at the base.

FRUIT

The planting of new hardy fruit trees and bushes starts in earnest this month, and will compete with the planting of ornamentals as the major task of November. Hopefully, the soil will have been prepared and enriched well in advance, and all the weeds cleared, so you can enjoy the quick and easy job of planting (see page 158).

Be careful not to get the spacing wrong, especially with fruit trees, which can look deceptively small compared to their ultimate size. Space semi-dwarfs at least 15 ft (5m) apart, and double the spacing for standards. They do look lonely to start with, but quickly fill out the space allotted them. In the long run, generous spacing results in healthier, longer-lived trees and heavier crops. Obviously, the spacing for cane and bush fruit is much tighter (see page 37), but even a single fruit tree is worth having as much for its ornamental appeal as its edible harvest.

If you are faced with the problem of accommodating fruit trees in a tiny garden, don't forget espaliers and cordons (see pages 110–11). Give the former a good 12 ft (4m) of growing space, with cordons needing only 2 ft (60cm) between trees.

Grape vines can be planted and cut back this month now that they are dormant. Towards the end of the month, prune established vines (see page 172).

PRUNING BUSH FRUIT

Any bush fruit newly planted this month should be cut back hard (see page 37), each according to

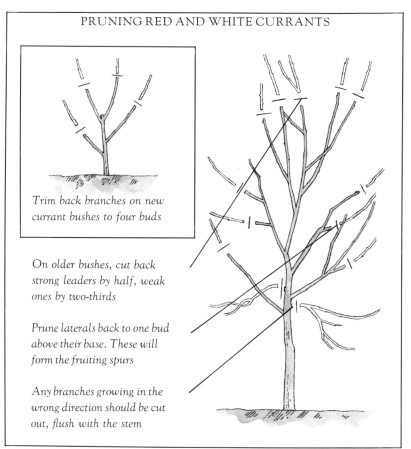

PRUNING RED AND WHITE CURRANTS

Trim back branches on new currant bushes to four buds

On older bushes, cut back strong leaders by half, weak ones by two-thirds

Prune laterals back to one bud above their base. These will form the fruiting spurs

Any branches growing in the wrong direction should be cut out, flush with the stem

its kind and growth habit. The purpose is the same for all: to prevent an immature plant fruiting before it is ready, and thus suffering permanent damage.

How much pruning of established bush fruit depends on how much summer and early-fall pruning you've already done (see page 94). Here is a quick checklist: all blackberry, loganberry and raspberry canes that have finished fruiting should be cut back to ground level, and new canes tied in to their supports. Inspect any canes already tied in, and their supports, as strong fall gales can be very damaging to both. Blackcurrant bushes should have a good proportion–about half–of the old fruited wood cut back to

ground level, again to make way for the new fruiting growth. Red currants, white currants and gooseberries should have the fruiting side shoots–or spurs–cut back to about 1 in (2.5cm) of the stems, and the main stems should be lightly cut back, to leave about 4 in (10cm) of the last season's growth (see above).

If you have summer-pruned your tree fruit (see page 110), then the winter-pruning should not be a daunting task. Cordon and espalier-trained trees should have their side shoots cut back to three dormant buds from the main stem, and any sub-laterals–side shoots growing from the main side shoots–cut back to one dormant bud. Open-grown bushes and

PRUNING A VINE

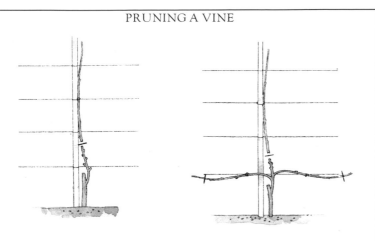

First year *Cut back the stem to 18 in (45cm) above ground, leaving only three buds to start new growth*

Second year *Lower the side shoots and train them horizontally. Cut back the leading shoot again to three buds*

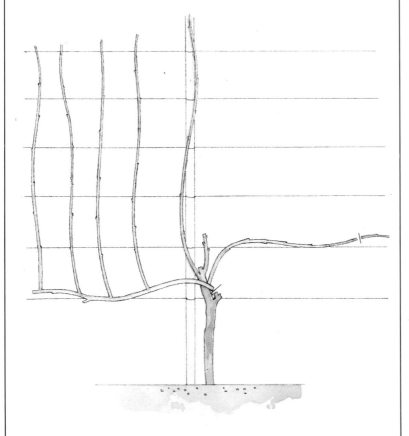

Third year *Cut off the branches that have borne fruit on lateral growths and prune back the main stem. Lower the two branches on the next tier and train them horizontally. Prune the tips, especially if weak*

trees should also have their side shoots pruned back to about 4 in (10cm) from the main branches. The new growth, made last summer, on the ends of the main branches, should be cut back by a quarter or a third of its length. As you prune, keep an eye open for any weak, diseased or crossing wood, and remove that too.

Fan-trained apricots, peaches, nectarines and Morello cherries should need very little in the way of pruning now, as their pruning normally takes place after fruiting (see page 144). If you missed summer pruning, simply cut out each old fruiting side shoot back to a new replacement shoot at its base and tie it in.

As far as propagation goes, you can still take hardwood cuttings (see page 153), but don't leave it too late in the month, as totally dormant cuttings do not readily form roots.

SAFEGUARDING FRUIT

Sadly, some birds may already be active, pecking at the buds of fruit trees and bushes, so check any netting or cages.

You should be making good use of the apples and pears in storage, but remember to check them over regularly for any signs of rotting, and remove any suspect fruit.

PRUNING A GRAPE VINE

Vines need heavy pruning, especially during their first years, if they are to crop well. Because vine sap starts to rise earlier in the season than that of other fruits, get your pruning done now, if you haven't already done so. Leave it much longer, and the vines will 'bleed' when pruned.

When planting an apple tree, allow plenty of room for its eventual spread

Newly planted vines should be cut back to about 18 in (45cm). When the buds break in spring, rub out all but three with your thumb; these three buds will form the laterals, or side shoots which are trained horizontally along wires as they grow.

If you are using the double guyot system of training (see page 95) cut the two side rods that have finished fruiting back to the main stem. Replace them, to the right and left, with two of the new shoots that grew last season. Carefully tie the replacement shoots to the wires, and cut back to six buds. Cut back the central, third replacement shoot to three or four buds. The shred-like, peeling bark of the main stem makes perfect winter accommodation for mealybugs and scale insects, so gently pull away any loose bark and spray with an appropriate pesticide (see page 184).

VEGETABLES

Fall-sown crops in the North are risky, but if you live in a warm, sheltered area, and your soil is not too heavy, it is worth trying. In such cases, you need to select particularly hardy cultivars, bred especially for fall sowing. For broad beans, 'Aquadulce' is a good bet, or the dwarf cultivar, 'The Sutton'. For peas, try 'Meteor' or the dwarf 'Little Marvel'.

Sow the broad beans in the same way as for a spring sowing (see page 13), but peas should be sown rather more thickly than for a spring sowing, to allow for some mortality. Both vegetables will crop two or three weeks earlier than their spring-sown counterparts, given a mild winter, and fall-sown broad beans have the additional advantage of being tougher and thus less vulnerable to aphid infestation. Against this, a bad winter can kill the young plants and you'll have to start again in spring. If you have the cloches to spare, protect the young plants in severe weather. Remember that too much protection is as bad as none at all, and leaving the cloches on when the weather is warm and sunny will result in soft, very vulnerable, young growth.

Though runner beans are treated as half-hardy annuals, they are, in fact, perennial plants which come up year after year in their native South America. To get an earlier crop of runner beans next spring, try digging up a few of the tuberous roots of the plants to overwinter in a frost-free place, rather like dahlia tubers. Carefully dig up the roots, and leave them in

PROTECTING CAULIFLOWER CURDS

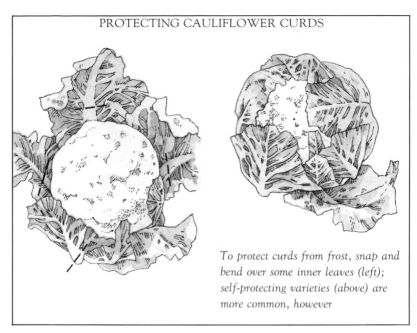

To protect curds from frost, snap and bend over some inner leaves (left); self-protecting varieties (above) are more common, however

a warm, dry and well ventilated spot to dry out for a few days. Scrape the soil away, and store the tuberous roots in a box filled with slightly moist peat. Next spring, pot them up, start them growing again and plant out once all danger of frost is over.

Cauliflowers will have formed their creamy white curds, and it is a good idea to protect them from frost by half snapping some of the inner leaves over the curds, if they are not the self-protecting type.

If you intend forcing rhubarb, dig up a few of the crowns towards the end of the month. Leave them on the ground for a week or so, or until they have experienced frost. This fairly brutal treatment encourages them to send out succulent shoots more rapidly once they are brought into the warmth.

Continue bringing in chicory roots for forcing (see page 161) and outdoors, blanching Batavian endive. If there is a possibility of heavy frost, though, cloche the endive, or lift them with as much

of the roots intact as possible, and move them to a cold frame.

Seakale is forced in much the same way as chicory. Now is the time to dig up a couple of plants— leave the rest in the ground for successional forcing, or dig the whole lot up, and store those not needed at once in a sheltered, frost-free spot. Plant the thick roots, several to a large pot, in compost or free-draining garden soil. Exclude every bit of light, with an upturned pot over the

crowns, a piece of foil covering the drainage hole, or with black plastic. Keep the compost slightly moist and the temperature around 55°F (13°C), and you will soon have succulent shoots.

Don't forget your Jerusalem artichokes—the stumps you left last month (see page 161) should show you exactly where to dig for the nutty-flavored tubers. Those dug fresh from the garden now just need a good scrub. Older tubers, and those that have spent some time out of the ground, will need to be peeled, a time-consuming task because of their oddly intricate shapes.

Brussels sprouts will be reaching maturity this month. Always pick the sprouts from the bottom of the stalk upwards, the order in which they mature naturally. This encourages the production of further sprouts towards the top.

Herbs can still be lifted to bring indoors or into a greenhouse or frame (see page 161) for winter use, but do so fairly early in the month, before a hard frost withers the above-ground growth.

Brussels sprouts mature from the bottom of the cluster first, so pick in that order – from bottom to top

December

At the end of the year,
most gardening takes place by the fireside, as
catalogs arrive, gardening books are read and
plans made. Take advantage of any mild spells,
especially during the holidays, to continue outdoor
garden tasks, and to add more winter color to
brighten up your garden.

*Frost covers the lawn
and sparkles on the foliage of
evergreen trees and shrubs in the
tranquility of a winter garden*

Jobs for the month

General
Order seed catalogs and make plans for next year
Check drains for fallen leaves
Break the ice on garden ponds
Ventilate the greenhouse according to the weather
Improve difficult soil

Flowers
Continue digging and tidying up of herbaceous beds where possible
Bring forced bulbs indoors
Take root cuttings
Cut back late-flowering chrysanthemums and take cuttings
Take pipings from perpetual-flowering carnations
Check bulbs, corms and tubers in storage
Water overwintering plants in the greenhouse
Remove flowering house plants to the greenhouse after Christmas

Lawns
Mow, if necessary
Treat lawns infested with beetle grubs or earthworms

Roses
Continue pruning roses
Spray against black spot where necessary
Continue planting roses in mild areas
Check newly planted roses and hardwood cuttings after frosts and re-firm if necessary

Trees and shrubs
Check defences against drying
Continue planting deciduous trees, shrubs and hedges
Protect plants from damage by animals
Water containerized plants and check for wind rock
Start pruning clematis (C. 'Jackmanii')
Take root cuttings
Choose plants for winter color

Fruit
Continue pruning fruit trees and bushes
Spray with miscible oil wash, if necessary
Continue pruning grape vines and use the prunings for hardwood cuttings
Continue checking supports and ties of cane fruit, grape vines and fruit trees trained against walls, and netting against birds
Continue planting or heeling in trees and bushes as necessary

Vegetables
Continue digging over ground for spring sowing or planting
Continue protecing cauliflower curds from frost
Earth up or stake brassicas
Force rhubarb
Continue blanching endive and forcing chicory and seakale
Protect bay trees from frost
Plan a vegetable garden

Write off for seed catalogs so you can browse through them during the Christmas vacation.

Check that the drains are not blocked by fallen leaves and gently break any ice on garden ponds – it can deprive the fish of oxygen.

Garden tools can be put in order this month. Shears, saws and pruning knives can be repaired, oiled and sharpened. Spades and hoes need sharpening and cleaning, as will forks and rakes. Straighten any bent tines.

In the greenhouse, stagnant, cold air quickly leads to a build-up of fungal diseases, and it is better for the plants to have fresh air, as long as it is not frosty.

IMPROVING YOUR SOIL

Garden soil that is not all that it should be can be tackled in some places. Soil is a complicated mixture of inert and organic material, together with water, air and nutrients. The major types are gravelly, peaty, sandy, clay or loam. To find out which type of soil you have, make enquiries locally. Find out also whether it is acid or alkaline.

Alkaline, or basic, soil is limy. The iron and other trace elements become 'locked' in the soil. Digging in peat, and applying flowers of sulphur or sequestrene (chelate of iron) will help. Alternatively, make a raised bed and fill it with peat, or grow acid-loving plants in pots filled with a special, lime-free soil mix.

Acid soil can be made more alkaline by giving it a dressing of hydrated lime, old plaster or limestone. For sandy soils, use 8 oz per sq yd/225g per sq m, double for heavier soils.

Clay soil is tough to dig over, can be waterlogged in wet weather, and rock-hard in drought. Because it holds water, it tends to be cold, and slow to warm up in early spring. Dig it over if possible, so frosts break down the clods and dig in as much organic matter as possible. Aim for two bucketsful per sq yd/sq m and leave at least a month before adding lime.

Sand does not retain water, and vital nutrients get washed through to the subsoil. It is much improved by the addition of organic matter. Besides providing nutrients to the plants, it helps retain moisture. Sandy soil is often acid, and benefits from the addition of lime, as well as organic matter.

Gravel-based soils are often light and shallow, don't hold water well and are extremely poor. You can increase the acidity by regular applications of flowers of sulphur or sequestrene. Alternatively, grow some of the many lime-loving plants. By regular applications of organic matter, a wide range of plants can be grown.

Winter is the best time to put tools in order, while they are infrequently used. Keep them clean and oiled

FLOWERS

Digging new beds, digging over established beds and planting herbaceous perennials can all be done this month, in warm areas. Tidying of herbaceous beds can continue (see page 165), with raked-up leaves being put on the leaf pile, soft material going on the compost heap, and any woody or diseased material on the bonfire.

Bulbs that have been prepared for forcing should have made enough growth by now to be brought into the light and slight warmth. Bulbs growing on a windowsill will grow towards the direction of the light source. Turn the bowl or pot in which they are growing once each day to keep the plants straight.

Taking root cuttings from herbaceous perennials may be easy and quick to do, and will give you masses of new plants for stocking your garden in late spring or early summer. Suitable candidates include oriental poppies (*Papaver orientale*), perennial mullein (*Verbascum phoeniceum* cultivars), alkanet (*Anchusa azurea*), phlox (*Phlox paniculata*) and blanket flower (*Gaillardia*). Cut large, fleshy roots into 2 in (5 cm) sections, and bury them vertically in a free-draining mixture in boxes or shallow pots. It is important that they are pushed into the soil the right way up. With roots that taper visibly, the thicker end should be planted uppermost. A foolproof method is to angle the bottom end of each root cutting, as you prepare them, leaving the top end cut straight across. The upper surface of the cuttings should just be visible in the surface of the

medium. Finer, more delicate roots can be separated into single strands, and placed, horizontally, on the surface of the mixture. Cover the roots with no more than ⅖ in (1 cm) of mixture. To complete the exercise, lightly water the pots or boxes and put them in a cold frame or greenhouse. Sometimes in spring, new shoots will appear, and after being hardened off, they can be planted out.

In the greenhouse, late-flowering chrysanthemums will need attention as they finish their display. Cut them back and place the stools under the benches (see page 165). Those prepared last month will be sending up shoots which are ideal material for cuttings now (see page 21). Cut off 2–3 in (5–7.5 cm) shoots, from the base of the stool if possible, or as low down the stem as possible, if no basal shoots have been produced. Carefully remove the lower leaves, making sure that you don't tear the soft stem. Using a sharp knife or razor, cut the bottom of the shoot just below a leaf joint, or node, dip it in hormone rooting powder, and push it into a pot of firm soil mix. Water lightly. If you can give them a little bit of bottom heat, from an electric propagator, rooting will take place more quickly. But heat is not essential, and too much heat can be harmful. Once rooted, the cuttings can be removed from the propagator to the greenhouse benches or a sunny windowsill.

Pipings can be taken from perpetual-flowering carnations this month. Take 3 in (7.5 cm) long side-shoots from part-way up the stems. Those at the base of the plant are likely to be too tough; those at the top, too soft. Pull each shoot slightly upwards, till it sepa-

ROOT CUTTINGS FROM HERBACEOUS PERENNIALS

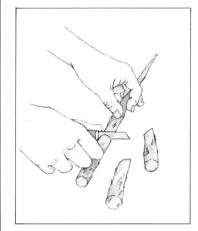

1 *Cut large roots into 5cm (2 in) sections, angling the bottom end to avoid planting the wrong way up*

2 *Bury them in soil mix, with the angled end down. Finer roots are placed horizontally on the surface*

rates from the main stem, and place it in a sandy soil mix, to half its length. More warmth is needed for cuttings of carnation than those of chrysanthemum, and a bottom heat temperature of at least 50°F (10°C) should be provided for them to grow well.

If you have time, check all the bulbs, corms and tubers in storage now for any signs of rot or disease. These include dahlia, gladioli, tuberous-rooted begonias and the more special forms of montbretia (*Crocosmia*). Any rot should be cut back to healthy flesh and the cut treated with a fungicide. Badly rotted bulbs should be discarded.

Overwintering geraniums and fuchsias will need an occasional light watering, to keep them from drying up . Too much water, especially in a cold greenhouse or cold frame, will mean attacks by gray-mold and probably death.

Christmas is a time for house plants–taking them indoors from the greenhouse, and giving or re-

ceiving them as gifts. To keep them healthy, you should try to provide a reasonably kind environment. For most house plants, especially cineraria, azalea, cyclamen and primulas, centrally heated houses are too hot. Combined with the heat, dry air, droughts and low light levels conspire to do many a plant in, often quite quickly. During Christmas week, put flowering plants in a light, airy spot, but remove them thereafter to a cool greenhouse or a cool – 60°F (16°C) – airy and light room in the house. Avoid over-watering, the most common cause of death to house plants, though azalea and cyclamen need a moister atmosphere than is found in centrally heated houses. This can be solved by frequently misting the plants with water at room temperature, or standing the pots in a pebble-filled bowl which contains water below the base of the pot. As the water evaporates, it creates a moist microclimate for the plant.

Flowers for the month

Berries, as much as flowers, provide color this month. The bright-red holly berries, or yellow in the form 'Lutea' are putting on their Christmas display, though the birds may have already taken their toll. The milky-white mistletoe berries and the black berries of ivy complete the traditional yuletide trio, as likely to be found in the wild as in the garden. Firethorn (*Pyracantha*), neatly trained around doors and windows of suburban houses, cotoneasters and skimmias are in berry now, orange, red or yellow according to species and cultivar.

Early camellias may be in flower where the weather is mild. These include the named forms of *C. sasanqua*: the bright-red 'Crimson King', the deep-red, peony-flowered 'Sparkling Burgundy' and the single pink 'Hugh Evans'. A few rhododendrons also bloom now if weather permits. Try the evergreen *R. × nobleanum* 'Venustum' with pink flowers and the deciduous *R. mucronulatum* with rose-purple blooms.

The Glastonbury thorn (*Crataegus monogyna* 'Praecox') and the fall-flowering cherry (*Prunus subhirtella* 'Autumnalis') will brighten the garden in mild weather, with their creamy white and pale-pink flowers, respectively.

The shrubby honeysuckles—*Lonicera fragrantissima* and *L. standishii*—are less popular than their climbing cousins, perhaps because their flowers are less showy and, when not in flower, are quite dull-looking bushes. What their flowers lack in size they make up for in scent. A single bush can fill a garden—and a single branchlet can fill a room—with rich fragrance.

The crocuses mentioned last month (see page 166) should still be performing and will be joined by the lovely satiny, lilac-purple and buff *C. imperati* at the end of the month, mild weather permitting.

The clump-forming snowdrop (*Galanthus nivalis*) will start to put in an appearance towards the end of this month and, if the weather has been mild, the graceful hardy cyclamen (*C. coum*).

In the greenhouse, Christmas cactus (*Schlumbergera × buckleyi*) will be in flower, from now until February—usually brilliant fuchsia-pink, but there are pale cultivars and a white one is also available.

1 *Ilex aquifolium* 'Lutea' **2** *Ilex aquifolium* **3** *Viscum album, better known as mistletoe* **4** *Skimmia japonica* 'Rubella' **5** *Cyclamen coum*

LAWNS

It is not too late to give your mower a going-over (see page 167), if you didn't have time to do so last month. You may even want to use it, if December has been mild and not too wet. A very light mowing will leave the garden looking tidier and perhaps bring back memories of the summer. New lawns, sown from seed in the fall, can be lightly mown too on a sunny, dry day.

Japanese and various other beetle grubs can be a real problem on lawns, especially in the warm months of the year, and now is a good time to deal with them. They feed on grass roots and basal stems just beneath the surface of the soil. The main indications that these subterranean pests are at work are brown patches of dying turf as soon as the weather turns dry, and increased bird activity on the lawn, as they search out the beetle grubs. If your lawn is badly infested, then huge tufts of grass will come away in your hand. Treat the lawn with a proprietary pesticide, according to the manufacturer's instructions (see page 184). You can get lawn treatments that deal with worms as well as with beetle grubs.

Though earthworms are generally held to be good for the garden, improving the soil drainage and aeration by burrowing, the casts they turn up on the surface of the lawn are not in the least beneficial. Besides looking unattractive, they make the surface of the lawn uneven, and muddy and sticky in wet weather. Once the casts are flattened out into a patch of bare earth, colonization by moss,

weeds or coarse grasses can take place. Worms are most often associated with heavy, moisture-retentive soils, with a high organic content, and their presence is a traditional sign of good soil. Still, if your lawn standards are high, try to get rid of them at this time of year, or confine them to beds, borders and compost heaps.

ROSES

Continue last month's pruning of roses (see page 167), whenever the weather is pleasant enough to work outdoors. There is no great hurry, except that very straggly, long branches can get blown about and damaged in a strong wind, and the sooner they are removed the better. In mild winters and warm areas, you may even find the odd flower bud on recurrent roses— 'New Dawn', for example–to pick and take indoors.

Roses that suffered from black spot in the past can be sprayed with a suitable fungicide this month (see page 184). Prevention

A dusting of frost on winter foliage can have an attractive visual effect, but make sure plants that are not completely hardy have protection

is often the best cure, and keeping the ground beneath roses free of all dead leaves or other debris is as important as spraying, as fungal spores tend to collect and overwinter there.

Planting of new roses can continue through December, where the soil is workable. Check any roses planted last month, to see that they haven't been lifted by frost. Firm them back into the soil, if necessary. Any hardwood cuttings of roses taken last month should also be checked, and firmed in again, if lifted by frost.

TREES & SHRUBS

Check your defences against winter, adjusting screening or protective coverings if they have come adrift. Though you sometimes get mild spells in December, you also get hard, sharp frosts that can

easily destroy next spring's display of ceanothus or next summer's display of passion flower (*Passiflora caerulea*), so be on the alert.

If there is a stretch of mild weather, and the ground is not waterlogged, you can continue planting deciduous trees, hedges and shrubs (see pages 23 and 36).

One indirect problem caused by harsh weather is that of rodents, rabbits and deer eating the bark of young shrubs, because their usual source of food is unavailable. Small-mesh wire netting wrapped securely round the stem is one solution; purpose-made, perforated plastic tree guards is another. The height of protection needed depends on the animal involved— and there is very little you can do if deer take a fancy to your shrubs and low tree branches–but young standards, half standards and bush trees can have their entire trunk protected.

A plastic sheath protects bark of a standard or young tree; a sturdy stake provides it with a firm, upright support

Mahonia × media 'Charity'

Acer palmatum 'Atropurpureum'

Cornus mas

Cornus alba 'Sibirica'

Pyracantha coccinea lalandii

Look over any ornamental trees and shrubs grown in pots. Unlikely as it may seem, they could be in need of watering, if the weather has been warm and sunny. If it has been wet and windy–far more likely–check for wind rock. The latter occurs when a plant takes the full force of the wind, and a hollow is formed in the soil mixture round the base of the stem or stems. When it rains a pool of water can collect in the hollow, and eventually rot the stem or stems at soil level. Newly planted trees and shrubs are particularly vulnerable, as their roots have not yet had time to become established.

You can start pruning *Clematis* 'Jackmanii' and other late-flowering clematis now (see page 25), or leave it until later in winter, depending on the weather and your workload in the garden.

Root cuttings can be taken from the California tree poppy (*Romneya coulteri*) this month; the method is the same as for root cuttings of herbaceous plants (see page 177).

TREES AND SHRUBS FOR WINTER COLOR

Because there is a general lack of color at this time of year, anything in flower or berry now, or with particularly attractive bark, is doubly valuable.

White winter flowers
Camellia (*C. japonica* 'Alba Simplex')
Ornamental peach (*Prunus davidiana* 'Alba')
Glastonbury thorn (*Crataegus monogyna* 'Praecox')
Shrubby honeysuckle (*Lonicera fragrantissima*)
Sarcococca (*S. humilis* and *S. ruscifolia*)
Viburnum (*V. farreri* 'Candidissimum', *V. tinus*)
Winter-flowering heather (*Erica carnea* 'Springwood White')

Yellow or orange winter flowers
Clematis (*C. cirrhosa balearica*)
Cornelian cherry (*Cornus mas*)
Mahonia (*M. japonica* and *M. ×* 'Charity')
Wintersweet (*Chimonanthus praecox* 'Luteus')
Witch hazel (*Hamamelis mollis*)

Pink or red winter flowers
Camellia (*C. sasanqua* 'Hugh Evans')
Daphne (*D. mezereum*)
Rhododendron (*R.* 'Rosamundi', *R.* 'Lee's Scarlet')
Viburnum (*V. farreri* and *V. × bodnantense* 'Dawn')

Colored bark or twigs
Birch (*Betula albo-sinensis* and others)
Ash (*Fraxinus excelsior* 'Jaspidea')
Dogwood (*Cornus alba* 'Sibirica', *C. stolonifera* 'Flaviramea')
Mahogany cherry (*Prunus serrula*)
Ornamental bramble (*Rubus cockburnianus*)
Kerria (*K. japonica*)
Scarlet willow (*Salix alba*) selections
Snake-bark maple (*Acer pensylvanicum*)
Strawberry tree (*Arbutus andrachne* and *A. × andrachnoides*)

Berries
Cotoneaster (*C.* 'Cornubia')
Firethorn (*Pyracantha atalantioides*)
Holly (*Ilex aquifolium*)
Skimmia (*S. japonica*)
Thorn (*Crataegus crus-galli*)
Viburnum (*V. davidii*)

FRUIT

The pruning of fruit trees and bushes can continue through December (see page 171). Always collect up the prunings immediately and burn them—leaving them lying around on the ground is an open invitation to disease. The bonfire ash can then be used to top-dress the trees and bushes, giving them a useful feed of potash. The ash must be used while it is still fresh and dry, as wet ash has lost most of its value.

Winter spraying of fruit trees and bushes can start this month. An oil is the traditional spray, and is available under several brand names. Always follow the manufacturer's instructions, as with any garden chemicals, and don't spray in windy, wet or frosty weather. The oil spray kills any scale insects overwintering on the plants, as well as eggs of aphids and various caterpillars. It also kills any moss or lichen growing on the bark, and weeds growing beneath the tree.

GRAPE VINE CUTTINGS

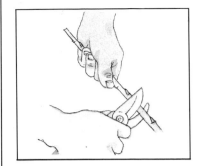

1 *Trim any soft wood from prunings and cut into 10 in (25cm) lengths*

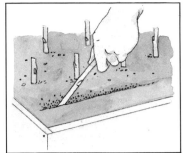

2 *Plant them in a sheltered spot, leaving one-third above ground*

Whether spraying with the oil every winter is necessary or not depends on several factors. If your trees are healthy, well fed and pruned and cropping well, then annual spraying isn't really necessary, and every alternate, or every third, winter will suffice. You should also consider its effect on the garden as a whole. The oil spray will kill beneficial insects as well as harmful ones, and can lead, indirectly, to a build-up of red spider mite. Lastly, it isn't the home grower but the commercial grower who has to worry about picture-perfect, unblemished fruit. They also have a lot more to worry about, because monocultures—growing hundreds, or even thousands, of one type of plant to the exclusion of all others—are vulnerable to pests and diseases on an epidemic scale. In short, if you have a fruit tree, or even a few fruit trees, in your garden, and the fruit they produce is generally unblemished, treat oil sprays as an occasional, rather than a regular, exercise.

Continue pruning grape vines (see page 172). You use the prunings of one-year-old shoots to make more. Cut them to 10 in (25cm) lengths, and bury the shoots in the ground by two-thirds of their length. If you have room for the cuttings in a cold frame, so much the better, but any sheltered spot outside will do.

Continue checking cane fruit—raspberries, blackberries and loganberries—grape vines and fruit trees trained against walls, to make sure that they have not come away from their wires and supports. Other routine checks include netting against birds and examining apples and pears in store.

Planting of fruit trees and bushes is another open-ended winter task, to be done as soon as the plants arrive, providing climatic conditions are suitable. If planting has to be postponed, heel in the trees and shrubs or otherwise protect them (see page 20).

While snow covers the garden, use the time to study its shape and layout and to make plans

NETTING PRUNED FRUIT BUSHES

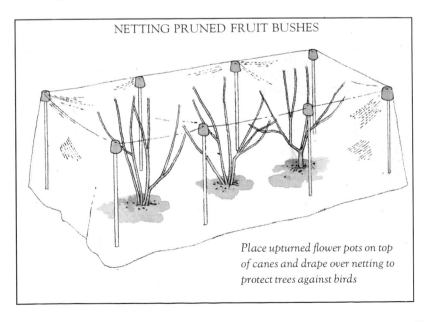

Place upturned flower pots on top of canes and drape over netting to protect trees against birds

VEGETABLES

If the ground is workable, dig over the vegetable patch, incorporating well-rotted garden compost or manure for crops that need rich soil. Runner beans are particularly fond of plenty of organic matter, and so are peas, leeks and squashes. Other crops—carrots and potatoes, for example—resent rich growing conditions, so it is important to have a good idea of what is being planted where next spring, before you begin working.

Cauliflower curds will still need protecting from frost (see page 173). If the weather has been stormy, brassicas as a whole may need earthing up in areas where they are still growing.

Rhubarb crowns that were left on the surface of the soil and exposed to frost last month can be brought into the relative warmth of the greenhouse now. To get pale, succulent, less acid stalks, pack the crowns—right-way up—close together in large boxes, filling the boxes with moist soil or peat. The tops of the crowns should just be showing at the surface. Total darkness is necessary, so fix a screen of black plastic sheeting or sacking to go around and over the boxes. If the boxes are under greenhouse benches, simply hang black plastic sheeting down from the benches. A temperature of 50°F (10°C) is necessary to start with, and once the shoots have started growing, raise the temperature to 60°F (16°C), or even a bit higher.

Rhubarb can also be forced outdoors (see page 13), but the process is a much slower one.

Continue blanching endive (see page 125) and forcing chicory and seakale. Chicory, seakale and rhubarb roots, once forcing is finished, should be discarded, as they are totally worn out and won't crop well again.

Bay (*Laurus nobilis*) is a Mediterranean tree and vulnerable in our country to strong, cold winds and prolonged, hard frosts. If you have a bay growing in a pot or small tub which is easily moved, it is a good idea to put the plant in a greenhouse or otherwise out of the weather for the next couple of months, until the worst of the winter weather is over. If a tubbed plant is to stay outside, cover the tub to prevent the root ball from freezing solid. If the bay is growing in the open ground, or too heavy to move, you can protect it with screening or sacking as for tender ornamental shrubs (see page 170). In a severe winter, the leaves may turn brown at the edges, but it is more than likely that new leaves will grow in spring.

PLANNING A VEGETABLE GARDEN

Now is the time to plan your vegetable garden for next spring, while you have long evenings to devote to it and plenty of time to order seeds. If you are starting a vegetable garden for the first time, try to choose a spot that is sunny and open, though sheltered from prevailing winds. If it is overhung by trees or surrounded by high walls, fences or hedges, the area within is likely to be shaded and humid, and any vegetables growing there vulnerable to disease. Trees and hedges have the additional disadvantage of competing with your vegetables for nutrients and water in the soil. Try not to site your vegetable garden on low-lying land, which is likely to be a frost pocket in winter, or badly drained land.

On a more practical level, make sure there is a source of water nearby. Salad vegetables, especially, need regular supplies of water and if you have to carry it, can by can, over long distances in hot weather, chances are the vegetables will eventually go without.

A good concrete or stone path from which to work is another vital requirement. It will keep your feet from becoming muddy whenever you go to collect vegetables in wet weather. The hard path will also greatly facilitate using a wheelbarrow in wet weather, when it would otherwise form ruts or sink into the mud.

Traditionally, rows of vegetables are set out running north to south, so each plant gets the full advantage of the sun. Though a rectangular plot is ideal for straight rows, an irregularly shaped one can still be useful.

Different vegetables take different nutrients from the soil, and if grown in the same spot year after year will eventually deplete the soil of those particular nutrients. Additionally, crops grown in the same soil every year tend to encourage a build up of certain pests and diseases in the soil. For this reason, when planning your vegetable garden, it is a good idea to group the crops that require the same type of treatment together. You can then rotate the crops every year to get the best results and keep the soil healthy. There are three main groups, which means that, with normal crop rotation, the soil will carry a particular crop one year in three.

Legumes and salad crops include peas, beans, squashes, spinach, sweetcorn, lettuce, peppers, tomatoes, celery, leeks and onions. These vegetables prefer a rich, freshly manured soil.

FORCING RHUBARB

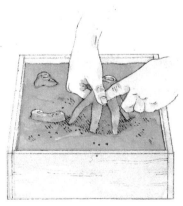

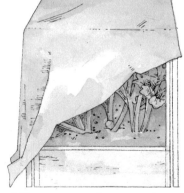

1 *Expose the crowns to frost, then pack them in a wooden box and almost cover with moist soil or peat, leaving the tops just showing*

2 *Place an inverted crate over the top and drape with sacking or black plastic to exclude the light. Provide a temperature of 50°F (10°C)*

PLANNING A VEGETABLE GARDEN

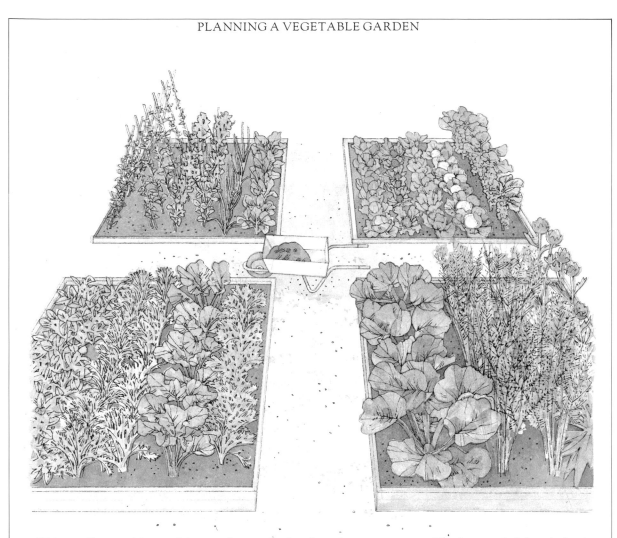

Brassicas include cabbage, kale, Brussels sprouts, cauliflower, rutabagas, turnip, kohlrabi and sprouting broccoli. These crops do best on land that was manured for a previous crop, and so it is sensible to grow them on land previously used for the first group of vegetables, legumes and salad crops. Brassicas gain additional benefit from following peas and beans in the rotation plan, because the roots of the latter add nitrogen to the soil.

Root vegetables include potatoes, chicory, carrot, beets, Jerusalem artichoke and parsnip, and should not be grown on heavily manured soil, or the roots may fork or become otherwise distorted. These vegetables do need an application of fertilizer before sowing, for best results, and they follow brassicas in the traditional crop rotation plan.

Crop yields from a 5 ft (1.5m) row

Beans, broad	12 lb (5.5kg)
Beans, shell	8 lb (3.6kg)
Beans, runner	12 lb (5.5kg)
Beets	6 lb (2.7kg)
Broccoli	4 lb (1.8kg)
Brussels sprouts	8 lb (3.6kg)
Cabbage, spring	5 lb (2.2kg)
Cabbage, summer	6 lb (2.7kg)
Cabbage, winter	7 lb (3.1kg)
Carrots	7 lb (3.1kg)
Cauliflower	5 lb (2.2kg)
Celery	11 lb (5kg)
Leeks	5 lb (2.2kg)
Lettuce	5
Onions	6 lb (2.7kg)
Peas	2 lb (1kg)
Shallots	3 lb (1.3kg)
Spinach	3 lb (1.3kg)
Rutabagas	7 lb (3.1kg)
Turnips	6 lb (2.7kg)

This small vegetable patch is divided into four equal-sized plots. One plot is given over to perennial vegetables (bottom right) – rhubarb, asparagus and globe artichokes. The same plants will crop year after year, so manure very thoroughly before planting.

The other three plots are given over to a simple crop rotation system. The top left-hand plot, legumes and salad crops, should be well manured before sowing. A tall double row of runner beans shades the other crops as little as possible. A double row of dwarf peas runs next to the maincrop onions, followed by a row of summer spinach.

The top right-hand plot is planted with brassicas. The ground should be limed in the winter to deter club root disease. A handful of fertilizer per square yard (square meter) is added before sowing. Brassicas are rather slow-maturing, so faster-growing crops can be grown in between.

The bottom left-hand plot is for root crops. These do badly on recently manured soil, but add a handful of fertilizer per square yard (square meter) at sowing time.

The following year at sowing time rotate your crops. The peas and beans will be grown where the root crops are now. The brassicas will change place with the peas and beans, as they do best on land manured for a previous crop. The root crops will move to the cabbage patch.

SYMPTOMS	TREATMENT

FRUIT GARDEN

Aphids
Aphids are visible on leaves and shoots. Curling, sometimes yellow leaves. Sticky honeydew, perhaps covered in sooty molds. Gall-like swellings on leaves.

Spray accessible colonies with malathion, rotenone or nicotine. Otherwise spray with a pyrethrum insecticide. On houseplants, spray or dip in warm, soapy water.

Apple sawfly
White grubs inside fruit. Fruits fall very small.

Bacterial canker
Pale-edged spots on leaves. At an advanced stage, gum seeps from the bark and infected branches die off.

Spray with derris or other approved material one week after main petal fall.
Spray the foliage thoroughly with Bordeaux mixture in mid-August, mid-September and mid-October.

Blackcurrant gall mite or
Big bud mite
Swollen buds, which fail to open, then shrivel up.

Codling moth
Pale pink grubs in fruit. Sawdust-like frass inside apples and pears.

Spray with lime sulphur or a miticide 2–3 times during May–June.
Spray with malathion 4 weeks after petal fall, and again 3 weeks later.

Gooseberry mildew
White, powdery deposit on leaves, young fruit and shoots.

Spray when first noticed with lime sulphur (if available), or washing soda on sulphur-shy cultivars: 1 oz (30g) soda to 1¾ pt (1 liter) water, plus a wetting agent, just before blossoming and when fruit has set.

Gooseberry sawfly
Leaves are skeletonized.

Spray with derris or malathion.

Graymold
Furry, gray mold on stems, leaves, fruits and flowers.

Dust with captan or spray with thiram or zineb. Remove all diseased tissue.

Mealy bugs
Clusters of white, waxy fluff on stems and the underside of leaves. Honeydew deposits. Only occurs under glass.

Spray with malathion or Sevin. Brush severe attacks with spray-strength insecticide.

Peach leaf curl
Large reddish blisters on leaves. Early leaf fall.

Spray with lime sulphur, liquid copper or Bordeaux mixture just before leaf fall and in late winter or early spring.

Powdery mildew
White, powdery deposit on leaves and shoots. Growth is stunted, flowers do not set and leaves fall.

Spray with any mildewstop. Burn any severely infected leaves and shoots before spraying.

Red spider mite
Leaves become mottled, turn bronze and fall prematurely. Very fine white webbing on leaves and stems, with tiny spidery mites on the underside of leaves.

Spray with malathion, derris, pyrethrum or Sevin as soon as symptoms are seen; repeat at 10–14 day intervals. Spray houseplants with derris or malathion.

Scab
Dark green or brown spots on leaves, blistered twigs, disfigured fruit, distorted and cracked surfaces.

Spray with captan or any approved material available. Mulch with organic matter and cut out damaged shoots.

Scale insects
Sticky, sooty leaf surfaces. Tiny, immobile, shell-like insects on stems and underside of leaves.

Spray with malathion, nicotine or diazanon during late spring and early summer. Prune heavily infested parts.

Woolly aphids
Waxy white wool on stems. Woody gall on affected areas.

Spray with malathion or Sevin.

FLOWER GARDEN

Black spot
Black, rapidly-spreading spots which cause premature leaf fall in roses.

Spray at two-week intervals from spring to fall with captan or maneb or systemic Benomyl.

Caterpillars
Irregular holes in leaves, buds and young shoots.

Spray with Sevin or systemic. Pick off the caterpillars by hand.

Flea beetle
Numerous small round holes in leaves.

Dust or spray with derris or pyrethrum.

Leaf miner
Tunnels and flattened blisters within leaf tissue.

Spray with systemic insecticide. Pick off and burn badly infected leaves.

Powdery mildew – see Fruit garden.

VEGETABLE GARDEN

Carrot fly
Leaves turn reddish, then yellow, and wilt. Roots are riddled with tunnels.

Dust or spray with malathion or Sevin at seed sowing and in late summer.

Celery fly
Brown blotches on leaves.

Spray with malathion or Sevin.

Potato and tomato blight
Brown spreading patches on leaves, with white fungus on the underside in damp weather.

Spray with an insecticide approved in your area at 10–14 day intervals during summer.

LAWNS

Fusarium patch disease
Patches of brownish, waterlogged dead grass.

Treat with any approved material for your area.

Japanese and beetle grubs
Irregular brown patches.

Treat with milky spore disease to prevent recurrence in future years.

GLOSSARY

Acid (soil) Lacking in lime. Most peaty soils and some very sandy soils fall into this category.

Alkaline (soil) Having a high lime content.

Alpine Strictly, a plant native to a zone between the upper limit of tree growth and the permanent snow line. Loosely, any small plant suitable for a rockery.

Annual A plant that grows from seed and completes its life cycle within one growing season.

Anther The part of the stamen that contains pollen.

Axil The angle between leaf or lateral (*q.v.*) and stem.

Bark-ringing Cutting out a thin ($\frac{3}{16}$ $\frac{1}{4}$ in/4–6mm wide) strip of bark half-way round the trunk of a tree. This reduces the flow of sap, and hence growth, and should encourage flower production.

Bedding plant A plant used for short-term garden display.

Bent Short for 'bent grass'. Any grass of the genus *Agrostis*.

Biennial A plant with a life cycle spanning two growing seasons, flowers and seeds being formed in the second.

Blanching Excluding light from the stems and/or leaves of certain vegetable crops, e.g. chicory, leeks and seakale.

Block-sowing Sowing a small area entirely, rather than sowing in drills.

Bolting Applied to a vegetable prematurely running to seed.

Bottom heat Heat applied from below to ensure that cuttings take root more efficiently.

Brassicas Plants of the genus *Brassica*, including cabbage, Brussels sprouts, kale and kohlrabi.

Budding Grafting a single growth bud from one plant onto the system of another.

Bulbil A small bulb formed on stems above ground.

Catch crop Any fast-maturing crop that can be grown between rows of a slower-maturing one or between the maturing of one crop and the planting of the next.

Chicon A young, white chicory shoot.

Chitting (seed potatoes) Putting them in a cool, but not cold light place so that they will sprout.

Cloche Panes of glass or plastic sheeting, held together by shaped wires or canes, or plastic tents, used for forcing outdoor plants.

Clone One of several identical plants obtained from a parent plant by vegetative propagation (*q.v.*).

Cold frame An unheated four-sided wooden structure with a glass top, used to protect young plants from rough or cold weather.

Compost Manure substitute made from rotted vegetable matter, such as leaves, weeds and most general garden waste often fortified with some chemical fertilizer and with lime.

Cordon A plant restricted to a single stem by pruning.

Corm A food-storage organ found in some plants, consisting of a thick, fleshy stem with a papery sheath around it.

Crown (1) Part of a herbaceous perennial from which the roots and shoots grow. (2) The main branch system or head of a tree.

Cultivar Short for 'cultivated variety'. A variant of a species, arising in the wild or in gardens, maintained in cultivation.

Curd Part of the edible head of cauliflower or broccoli.

Damping off A fungal disease that attacks the stems of seedlings in excessively damp conditions.

Deadheading Removing faded blossom from a plant to prevent seeds from forming and to prolong the flowering season.

Deciduous Applied to a plant (particularly a tree or shrub) that sheds its leaves each year at the end of the growing season.

Dibber A stick for making holes for seedlings to be transplanted.

Disbudding Removing surplus buds or shoots so that those remaining grow larger or stronger.

Dot plant A plant grown singly or well spaced in a bed to emphasize a feature such as color, height or texture.

Double Applied to a flower with more than the usual number of petals.

Drawn Applied to a plant grown too warm or kept without sufficient light so that it is spindly and pale.

Drill A shallow furrow in which seeds are scattered or sown.

Earthing-up Drawing soil up around a plant's stem to blanch it, to cover tubers and prevent greening, or to support it.

Espalier A tree with branches trained to grow horizontally in tiers about 15 in (37cm) apart.

Eye (1) A dormant growth bud, e.g. on a potato tuber. (2) A center of a flower-head. (3) A single budded cutting, e.g. vine.

F₁hybrid (= first-generation hybrid) The result of crossing two related, pure-bred plants with certain desirable characteristics.

Fan-trained Applied to a shrub or tree with its main branches trained like the ribs of a fan.

Filler plants Plants used to infill a planting scheme while the main species are growing up.

Firming Pressing down the soil around the base of a plant's stem.

Force To cause a plant to grow more quickly and to produce early flowers or an early crop, usually with the aid of artificial heat.

Genus (pl. genera) A group of plants with common characteristics that are different from those of all other such groups. A genus comprises one or more species.

Germination The first stage in the development of a plant, indicated by the appearance of a root (radicle) growing from a seed.

Greenwood cutting A tip or section cut from a current season's stem after growth has slowed down.

Half-hardy (1) Applied to a plant that can withstand mild winters outdoors but which needs protection from severe cold. (2) A plant which is so susceptible to frost damage that it can only be grown outside during the summer.

Half-standard (1) A tree or shrub with 3–4 ft (1–1.25m) of stem beneath the branches. (2) A semi-dwarf.

Harden off To acclimatize plants grown in warmth to outside conditions.

Hardwood (or ripe) cutting A cutting taken once the growth has ceased and become woody.

Hardy Applied to an outdoor plant capable of surviving frost anywhere in U.S., and Canada in some cases.

Heeling-in Temporarily covering with soil the roots of new trees.

Herbaceous Applied to a non-woody perennial plant that dies back to ground level at the end of the growing season and reappears the following spring.

Herbaceous border A flower bed containing perennials.

Hybrid A plant derived from crossing any two distinct parents.

In situ In the permanent or growing position.

Infill planting See Filler plants.

Intercropping Sowing fast-growing vegetables and slow-growing ones near to one another.

Lateral A side growth branching away from a main stem.

Layering A method of propagation in which a shoot is induced to send out roots while still attached to the parent plant (see page 52).

Leader The leading shoot at the end of a stem or main branch of a tree or shrub.

Leguminous Concerning the *Leguminosae* family, most of which have pea-shaped flowers and bear seeds in pods, e.g. sweet pea and broad bean.

Loam An ideal, fertile soil type consisting of a mixture of sand, clay and decayed vegetable matter.

Mulch A layer, often of organic material, spread on top of soil around plants to conserve moisture, condition the soil, feed the plants and inhibit the growth of weeds.

Node The point where a leaf and bud join a stem.

Offset (1) A young plant borne at the end of a short runner, e.g. house-leek (*Sempervivum*). (2) A small bulb formed at the base of a larger one.

Perennial In a garden sense, a non-woody plant that lives for several years.

Pinching out Removing the growing tip of a shoot by pinching with the nails of the thumb and forefinger.

Pipings Tip cuttings taken from carnations and pinks.

Plunge bed A special bed in which a pot containing a young plant or cutting can be buried up to the rim to guard against unwanted fluctuations of moisture content and temperature in the potting medium.

Pot-bound Applied to a container-grown plant with no more space available for the roots to extend.

Potting on Repotting a plant in a larger pot to allow further growth.

Pricking out Transplanting and spacing out seedlings or small rooted cuttings in small holes in soil or other medium.

Propagation All means of increasing a desired plant, e.g. by seeds, cuttings, layers, grafting.

Propagator A container that protects planted seeds and cuttings and promotes growth by providing a moist, warm environment.

Raceme A flower cluster with each flower borne on a short stalk from an unbranched stem.

Rhizome A thick, horizontal, underground or soil surface stem sending out roots and shoots.

Ring culture Growing plants in bottomless containers which stand on a bed of free-draining aggregate.

Ripe cutting See Hardwood cutting.

Root ball A plant's roots and the soil or mixture surrounding them.

Rootstock A root system and stem onto which another plant is grafted.

Runner A prostrate stem of certain plants (e.g. strawberry and blackberry) that forms new plants and roots easily.

Scarifying Using a spring-tooth rake to pull out moss and dead vegetation from a lawn.

Seedling (1) A young plant newly emerged from seed. (2) A seed raised until it reaches the flowering plant stage, particularly used of fruit trees and orchids.

Semi-double Applied to a flower with only some stamens converted to petals.

Semi-hardy See Half-hardy.

Semi-ripe (or semi-hardwood) cutting A cutting taken when new growth from spring has started to 'ripen', or become woody.

Set The successful fertilization of flowers, resulting in young fruit formation.

Shrub A perennial plant with a number of persistent woody stems.

Single Applied to a flower with usually one row of petals.

Soakaway A pit filled with stones and rubble that assists in draining an area, such as a lawn, and prevents it becoming waterlogged, a dry well.

Soft (or softwood) cutting A tip or side shoot cut from a vigorously growing non-woody stem.

Species A plant, or a group of closely related plants, within a genus. Species have distinctive characteristics and always breed true to type from seed.

Spit The depth of the blade of a garden spade or fork.

Sport (mutation) A plant that markedly differs from normal.

Spring-tooth rake A rake with a fan-shaped set of slender metal ribs bent down at the open end.

Spur (1) A short branch bearing flower buds. (2) A tubular or horn-shaped prolongation of a petal.

Stamen The male reproductive organ of a flower, comprising a stalk (the filament) bearing a pair of anther (*q.v.*) lobes, which contain pollen.

Standard (1) A tree or shrub with 5–6 ft (1.5–2m) of bare trunk beneath branches or a full-sized tree. (2) Upper petals of pea-flower or iris.

Stem-rooting Applied to a plant, such as types of lily, which puts out roots directly from the lower stem.

Stool The crown of a dormant or cut-back plant.

Stopping Removing the growing tip of a shoot by cutting or pinching.

Strap-like Applied to narrow, non-tapering leaves that are several times longer than they are wide.

Sub-lateral A side shoot growing from a main lateral (*q.v.*).

Sucker A stem growing from below ground level.

Tender Applied to any plant that would be damaged by low temperatures when growing outdoors.

Tendril A slender leaf or stem that twines around a support, enabling certain plants to climb.

Terminal bud The topmost bud on a stem.

Tilth The soil surface well broken down to a fine crumbly consistency by raking and ready for sowing.

Tine A slender prong of a fork or similar tool.

Tipping Removing the growing tip of a shoot to encourage growth.

Top dressing A surface application of compost, fertilizer or fresh soil (see also Mulching).

Topiary The art of trimming trees and bushes into ornamental shapes.

Transpiration Emitting water vapor.

Truss A cluster of bud, blossoms or fruit.

Tuber A thickened, fleshy root or underground stem providing food storage, e.g. dahlia and potato.

Umbel A cluster of flowers with stalks arising from the same point.

Vegetative propagation Growing a new plant from a part taken from another plant.

Wind rock The loosening of the base of the main stem and sometimes also the root system of a plant by the action of strong winds.

ACKNOWLEDGMENTS

The publishers are grateful to Judy Martin and Eric Smith for their help in preparing this book for publication, and to Roger Brierley for drawing the keys to the garden plans.

The publishers would also like to thank the following for their permission to reproduce the photographs in this book:

Bernard Alfieri: 145, 157 l, 158 br, 161; *Heather Angel:* 55 b, 57 center r, 118 center br, 138 center b; *A–Z Collection:* 11 center b, 32 br, 43 t, 43 center, 53 bl, 54 t, 55 center, 56 center r, 74 t, 88 bl, 102 center br, 106 tr, 118 bl, 119 b, 152 t, 152 bl, 156 center l, 180 tl; *K.A. & G. Beckett:* 122 bl, 155 tr, 157 br; *Pat Brindley:* 21 tl, 31 bl, 31 r, 32 tl, 32 tr, 32 center r, 33 center r, 33 b, 51 center tl, 67 bl, 75 center, 76 bl, 77 bl, 77 center b, 87 center tr, 87 center r, 89 bl, 106 br, 118 tl, 118 center tr, 122 tl, 122 center r, 122 br, 130 center tl, 130 center bl, 130 center tr, 138 center t, 139 t, 139 center b, 151 bl, 151 center br, 154 t, 155 tl, 155 br, 157 tr, 166 center tr; *B. Burbidge:* 154 br; *Anne Conway:* 126/127, 149 b; *R.J. Corbin:* 53 tr, 53 center r, 57 br, 104 r, 112 t, 113 b, 117 t, 121 t, 125 bl, 135, 136, 137, 142 b, 150 b, 164, 167, 170 l, 172 r, 176, 179 b; *E. Crichton:* 157 tl; *Brian Furner:* 76 center r, 173 b; *Bob Gibbons:* 106 l; *John Glover:* 125 t, 153 b; *Derek Gould:* 114/115, 150 t; *Iris Hardwick:* 54 b, 60 t, 156 bl, 166 center tl; *Jerry Harpur:* 101 br, 119 t, 121 b, 174/175, 179 t; *Jacqui Hurst:* 131 t, 134, 140 r; *G.E. Hyde:* 130 center br; *ICI:* 142 center; *Impact/Pamla Toler:* 18/19, 46/47, 50 bl, 65 b, 79 b, 138 t, 162/163, 180 tr; *Leslie Johns:* 166 center bl; *Susanna Longley:* 8/9; *Tania Midgley:* 23 tr, 28/29, 52 br, 62/63, 78 t, 81 b, 85 t, 92 center b, 94 t, 96 t, 103 tr, 112 b, 122 center l, 139 b, 146/147, 151 tl, 159 t, 159 bl, 159 br; *Murphy Chemical Ltd:* 152 center b; *C.K. Mylne:* 178 bl; *National Fruit Trials – Crown Copyright:* 144; *Nature Photographers/A. Cleave:* 105 t; *PBI Ltd:* 152 br; *Richard Revels:* 154 center; *Harry Smith:* 13 t, 13 center, 21 bl, 24 tl, 24 center l, 25 tl, 25 center l, 31 tl, 31 center l, 31 center r, 32 center l, 32 bl, 33 center l, 44 b, 51 bl, 51 center tr, 51 r, 55 t, 56 center l, 56 r, 58 tr, 64, 67 tl, 67 center tr, 67 center br, 67 r, 74 center, 74 b, 76 center l, 76 br, 87 bl, 87 center l, 89 center b, 93 l, 102 bl, 102 center tl, 102 center bl, 102 center tr, 105 center l, 105 center r, 107 far l, 107 l, 107 r, 107 far r, 117 b, 118 center tl, 118 center bl, 122 tr, 129 tl, 130 tl, 130 bl, 133 r, 140 l, 141, 142 t, 151 center tr, 151 r, 154 bl, 155 center, 156 t, 156 center r, 156 bl, 157 center r, 166 center br, 166 r, 178 tl, 178 center l, 178 r, 180 bl, 180 center r, 180 br, 181 b; *Tessa Traeger:* 69 t, 98/99, 108 t; *Nicolas Viane/La Maison de Marie Claire:* 4/5; *Michael Warren:* 11 br, 21 r, 33 tr, 51 center bl, 51 center br, 54 center, 56 bl, 67 center l, 75 t, 84, 88 center l, 93 r, 102 tl, 118 tr, 130 tr, 151 center l, 156 br, 166 l, 178 center r.

INDEX